Icarus in the Boardroom

LAW AND CURRENT EVENTS Masters

DAVID KAIRYS, SERIES EDITOR

David Skeel

Icarus in the Boardroom

The Fundamental Flaws

in Corporate America and

Where They Came From

OXFORD
UNIVERSITY PRESS

2005

OXFORD
UNIVERSITY PRESS

Oxford   New York
Auckland   Bangkok   Buenos Aires   Cape Town   Chennai
Dar es Salaam   Delhi   Hong Kong   Istanbul   Karachi   Kolkata
Kuala Lumpur   Madrid   Melbourne   Mexico City   Mumbai   Nairobi
São Paulo   Shanghai   Taipei   Tokyo   Toronto

Copyright © 2005 by Oxford University Press, Inc.

Published by Oxford University Press, Inc.
198 Madison Avenue, New York, New York 10016

www.oup.com

Oxford is a registered trademark of Oxford University Press

Library of Congress Cataloging-in-Publication Data
Skeel, David A., 1961–
Icarus in the boardroom : the fundamental flaws in corporate America
and where they came from / by David Skeel.
   p. cm.
ISBN-13 978-0-19-517471-7
ISBN 0-19-517471-2
1. Corporate governance—United States. 2. Directors of corporations—United States.
3. Industrial management—United States.   I. Title.
HD2785.S437 2004
338.0973—dc22   2004009677

9 8 7 6 5 4 3 2 1

Printed in the United States of America
on acid-free paper

For Carter and Stephen

Acknowledgments

Thanks go first to David Kairys and Dedi Felman. David, a friend and colleague for well over a decade, first proposed that I write the book in fall 2002, then spent months going back and forth with me on the ideas and structure. Dedi, my editor, also shaped both the initial structure and final version of the book, reading and editing every paragraph of every chapter with extraordinary care and insight. It would be hard to overstate Dedi's and David's influence. They have been collaborators—almost like co-authors—on every aspect of the book.

I was blessed to have several excellent research assistants while I was writing the book. Seth Chertok spent a year plowing through old hearings and other historical information, as well as researching more recent developments. Michael Sherman provided equally able assistance in his final year of law school, before heading off to New York law practice.

Several colleagues and friends read drafts of the entire manuscript. I am especially grateful to Mitu Gulati and Mark West for extensive comments and encouragement throughout the project. Brian Cheffins provided numerous insightful suggestions, both in writing and on a crowded train ride from London to Cambridge. Reuven Avi-Yonah, Jeff Bauman, Sally Benner, Nell Minow, and David Skeel Sr. also offered valuable comments at key points in the writing process.

Thanks also to Bill Draper, Merle Slyhoff, and the staff at the Biddle Law Library at the University of Pennsylvania Law School who cheerfully (and quickly) tracked down even the most obscure source materials. It is hard to imagine that there is a better law library anywhere.

I am grateful to my dean, Mike Fitts, for his ongoing encouragement, to the University of Pennsylvania Law School for generous summer funding, and to Jessica Ryan and Tracy Baldwin for the copyediting and design.

The germs of several of the arguments in the book date back to a short piece Mark Noll and John Wilson invited me to write for *Books and Culture*, and to an op-ed John Timpane commissioned for the *Philadelphia Inquirer*. Thanks to each of them for the invitations.

I am most grateful of all to my family. My parents are ever-encouraging, even when work has interfered with the possibility of visits. My in-laws, Erich and Kay Haegele, live nearby and are always ready to lend a helping hand. To my wife, Sharon, I owe deep gratitude of every kind. The Proverbs say that a virtuous woman is much to be praised; Sharon is that and much more, from scholar to mother and wife and friend. The book is dedicated to our children Carter and Stephen. Watching them grow up is one of the great joys of our lives. My prayer is that they will look back on this time as an era when the fundamental flaws in corporate America were addressed.

Contents

Icarus in the Boardroom

Introduction

Americans have always loved risk-takers, the man or woman with ambition and vision who goes for broke. "Boldness of enterprise is the foremost cause of its rapid progress, its strength and its greatness," Tocqueville wrote as he surveyed the nation's business landscape well over a century ago. Although American business and financial life reminded this French observer of "a vast lottery," he marveled at the extent to which Americans "encourage and do honor to boldness in commercial speculations."[1]

In Tocqueville's era, adventurers set out for the western frontiers to launch trading operations or speculate on land. Closer to home, they invented the steamer, the cotton gin, and a thousand lesser-known inventions. Jay Gould, who became the most famous of the post–Civil War railroad robber barons, got his start by boarding a train to New York to peddle a mousetrap his family had invented.[2] A century later, Hewlett-Packard was started by two friends who hammered out their vision night after night in a Silicon Valley garage, and a subsequent generation of high-tech whizzes raced to create the next "killer app," or what business writer Michael Lewis labels the "New New Thing." "The U.S. has the world's most diverse and efficient capital markets," Thomas Friedman wrote in 1997, "which reward, and even celebrate, risk-taking."[3]

True risk-taking is a gamble. The entrepreneur literally takes a chance. Unfortunately, even the most talented entrepreneur can overstep his or her bounds, taking one risk too many and losing it all. Indeed, the very qualities that make brilliant innovators special—self-confidence, visionary insight, the ability to think outside the box—may spur entrepreneurs to take misguided risks in the belief that everything they touch will eventually turn to gold.

Throughout this book, I characterize these qualities as "Icaran," based on a legendary risk-taker named Icarus whom many of us remember from a high school reading list.

In ancient Greek lore, Icarus was the son of Daedalus, a famous architect who constructed an elaborate labyrinth at the behest of Minos, the King of Crete, to house a ferocious monster known as the Minotaur. The labyrinth was so intricate and subtly constructed that even Daedalus and Icarus could not figure out how to escape. After days of wandering into one dead end after another, Daedalus "made a pair of wings," as an Anglo Saxon poet later put it, "contrived of wood and feathers and a cunning set of springs." As they prepared to test the wings they would use to escape, Icarus's father repeatedly warned him not to fly too close to the sun. The feathers of his wings were attached to their wood frame by wax, which would melt if he flew too high.[4]

At first, Icarus heeded the warnings he had been given. But as he became acclimated to the wings and reveled in his newfound freedom, Icarus thought less and less about the risk, and more and more about the majesty of his powers. He continued to soar upward, ever closer to the sun, until the wax softened, his feathers gave way, and Icarus crashed down into the sea.

In a famous poem depicting the Icarus myth, W. B. Auden imagines the hubristic youth splashing into the ocean within sight of a farmer and a large ship. Neither pay much heed to Icarus's tragic fall. The farmer continues to work, "and the expensive delicate ship that must have seen / Something amazing, a boy falling out of the sky, / Had somewhere to get to and sailed calmly on."[5]

Auden obviously is exaggerating for poetic effect, but the failure of an ordinary American entrepreneur is similar in some respects. When a would-be innovator with a visionary idea puts every dollar he or she has or can borrow into an Internet innovation, but the dream collapses, it isn't headline news. Even if the entrepreneur loses everything, the failure may not ripple much further than a few family and friends.

Put Icarus in the boardroom and everything changes. The ability to tap huge amounts of capital in enterprises that adopt the corporate form, together with the large number of people whose livelihood depends in one way or another on the business, means that the stakes are extraordinarily high if Icarus is running a major corporation. An Icaran executive who takes excessive or fraudulent risks with a large corporation may jeopardize the financial lives of thousands of employees, investors, and suppliers of the business.

As American corporations expanded in the nineteenth century, their size and complexity not only increased the stakes; it also multiplied the opportunities for mischief. Once lawmakers permitted a corporation to hold the stock of other corporations, managers could tuck some of the assets of a business in one corporation and other assets elsewhere. This organizational flexibility often serves legitimate purposes, but it also can be used to mislead investors about the financial health of the business and just what it is up to. Both in the 1920s and with Enron in our era, investors continued to pump money into companies that were headed for a fall, long after the company's misguided risks would have been obvious were it not for their intentionally and mystifyingly complex corporate structure. Only in retrospect did investors learn that the corporate house was full of false doors and hidden rooms.

Although we rightly pride ourselves on the competitiveness of the American markets, competition increases the odds of spectacular corporate failures. In other countries—Germany, for instance, and much of Asia—it is not unusual for one or a small group of corporations to dominate their industry. Americans, by contrast, have always rebelled against concentrated economic power, in favor of industries with a multitude of competing firms. "We entirely disapprove of the incorporation of companies," a trade union representative complained in 1835, "inasmuch as we believe their tendency is to eventuate in and produce monopolies, thereby crippling the energies of individual enterprise, and invading the rights of smaller capitalists." In this kind of marketplace, the success of a business innovator is sure to attract competitors—the more spectacular the success, the fiercer the efforts to get a piece of the pie. Although some innovations can be patented, many, such as financial innovations or novel business strategies, usually cannot. As competitors enter their market, innovators often see their lavish profits begin to slip away. All too often, the innovators respond by taking increasingly misguided and even illegal risks as they attempt to replicate their early success.[6]

These three factors—excessive and sometimes fraudulent risks, competition, and the increasing size and complexity of the corporation—have been at the heart of a series of devastating crises that have punctuated American corporate and financial life for the past hundred and fifty years. The first came with the 1873 collapse of financial genius Jay Cooke, who pioneered a new strategy for selling government debt during the Civil War; the Great Depression saw the crash of utilities magnate Samuel Insull; and the new century brought still another wave of corporate scandals. Throughout the book, I will refer to crashes that fit this pattern as Icarus Effect failures.

Underneath and in between the scandals is an ongoing cat-and-mouse game between regulators and the leaders of America's largest corporations. Ever since the first large-scale corporations emerged in the nineteenth century, the task of regulators has been to rein in the three factors that can lead to Icarus Effect failures, as these tendencies are manifested in each succeeding era. Congress and state lawmakers sometimes target the first, risk-taking, directly, as when they impose penalties for misbehavior, but they also empower market "watchers" such as accountants or securities analysts to scrutinize the decision making of corporate executives. The second factor, competition, is regulated either by increasing the amount of governmental intervention, as with railroad-rate regulation in the nineteenth century and utilities regulation in the twentieth; or by decreasing it, as with the more relaxed antitrust scrutiny and extensive deregulation of recent years. With corporate size and scope, the final factor, lawmakers attempted at first to impose direct size restrictions, then later focused on limiting the complexity of interrelated corporate structures that were made possible once corporations were permitted to own the stock of other corporations.

Although strict regulation can rein in the Icaran tendencies in American corporate and financial life, it also undermines flexibility and innovation. In every generation, American corporate leaders have responded by simply evading existing regulation or by lobbying for changes that give business more flexibility to expand or take advantage of technological innovations. In the nineteenth century, growing businesses chafed at the strict rules that limited the amount of capital they could raise. Larger companies, they argued, are more efficient and produce goods more cheaply than smaller ones. In our era, corporations use complex financing techniques to circumvent regulatory restrictions of various kinds. An insurance company that wishes to insure a larger amount of risk than regulators or its own shareholders will allow can set up a special new entity to assume the risk. This is one illustration of the financial rocket science known as structured finance.

It is a simple fact of interest-group politics that corporate executives wield extraordinary influence over the political process both at the state and federal levels under ordinary circumstances. Corporate managers are intensely interested in the regulatory landscape, and they are backed by the huge coffers of the corporation itself. As a result, they usually get what they want. Ordinary Americans, by contrast, are much less likely to focus on the issues at stake and do not have nearly the same access to political decision makers. Few Americans entertained President Grant in their homes, as Jay Cooke did in the 1870s; nor have many of us received endearing notes from President Bush like the birthday and Christmas cards he once penned to "Kenny Boy," Enron's Ken Lay.

The efforts by American business to sidestep regulatory oversight can quickly spiral out of control, setting the stage for a devastating breakdown in corporate and financial oversight. The most dramatic collapses have occurred in times of market euphoria, often after a period of technological and financial innovation. Unlike in Auden's poem, the result of a true Icarus Effect scandal is far from an "unimportant failure." Thousands of jobs are lost and thousands of lives ruined when an Insull or Enron implodes. And for every Insull or Enron—for every Icarus Effect scandal writ large—there are other companies that follow the same Icarus Effect script. The headline scandals invariably reflect a broader crisis in American business life, a pervasive failure to keep the three Icaran tendencies in check.

As devastating as these failures are, they also have a silver lining. When the empire created by an erstwhile financial genius comes crashing down in a wave of scandal, ordinary Americans awaken from their slumber. Their outrage has often galvanized public opinion in favor of sweeping corporate reforms that would be politically inconceivable—political nonstarters—in a more placid corporate and financial environment. Our most important corporate regulation has always been enacted in the wake of stunning Icarus Effect collapses.[7]

The importance of scandals doesn't mean that lawmakers disappear after the crisis passes, of course. They continue to tinker with corporate and financial regulation, particularly at the state level. But these interim changes usually have corporate America's fingerprints all over them. It is only when scandals handcuff America's corporate leaders that lawmakers take direct aim at the Icaran tendencies in America corporate life.[8]

Corporate scandals are not unique to America, of course. Just about every country with large corporations has had its share of corporate scandals. But the scandals of other countries have tended to take different forms. In Japan, for instance, many of the most notorious scandals have involved rogue traders and midlevel insiders. In 1997 and 1998, executives at fourteen major companies (including Japan Air, Toshiba, and Hitachi) were arrested for paying thugs—sokaiya—to squelch discussion at their annual shareholders' meetings. In each case, the payments were made by a midlevel employee who did not derive any personal profit from the payments. In America, by contrast, spectacular failures usually start at the top and can be traced back to an Icaran executive who kept gambling even after his fortune or skill ran out, using the size and complexity of the corporation to disguise his flight. America's widely held companies and vibrant stock markets seem to be a particularly congenial environment for, and at times even to invite, Icaran excesses.[9]

To understand the three Icaran tendencies—risk-taking, competition, and corporate size and complexity—as well as the historical tug-of-war between regulators and corporate leaders, we need to start with the origins of the American corporation. In chapter 1, I describe the dramatic surge in incorporations in the nineteenth century. Unlike partnerships, corporations were difficult to dissolve, which protected businesses against the possibility that death or a falling out would force a dissolution. By the second half of the century, corporations also provided limited liability. Limited liability meant that shareholders generally could not be held responsible for the corporation's debts, which made corporate stock a very attractive investment. The first businesses to take advantage of this by tapping large amounts of capital from investors were the railroads, the nation's first large-scale corporations. The rise of the railroads also brought the first true Icarus Effect failure, the devastating collapse of Philadelphia banker Jay Cooke and his vast Northern Pacific Railroad project. Cooke's failure, and the excesses of the railroad robber barons, not only led to specific legislative reforms, but also propelled the coalition of farmers and small business owners that became known as American Populism into the national spotlight.

Chapter 2 chronicles the rise of the great corporate trusts of the Gilded Age, as John D. Rockefeller and other business titans outmaneuvered the efforts of state regulators to limit the size and scope of the railroads and other corporations. If the corporate-trust movement had continued, it might, in rather perverse fashion, have eliminated the Icaran tendencies in America's large-scale corporations. Great trusts such as Rockefeller's Standard Oil and Andrew Carnegie's steel empire cut off competition in their industries. The absence of competition removes the pressure to take risks and thus decreases the threat of Icarus Effect failures, since the monopoly business can earn large profits without any serious encroachment from competitors. The prospect of concentrated economic power has always drawn resistance in this country, however. Teddy Roosevelt's trust-busting campaign tapped into the resistance and signaled that there were limits to the amount of concentration that would be tolerated. Although Roosevelt abandoned the effort to directly restrict corporate size, his trust-busting campaign reflected a renewed commitment to industry competition.

The decades leading up to the 1929 stock-market crash saw the most important shift in corporate structure in American business history. Whereas the shareholders of even the largest corporations had actively managed the company and served as its directors in the nineteenth century, the emergence of corporate giants at the end of the century led to a separation of ownership and control. Shareholding became widely diffused, and shareholders played little role in the management of many of the nation's largest corporations. In some industries, J. P. Morgan & Co. and other investment banks continued to seek to combine the principal competitors in order to "rationalize" (their euphemism for forging a monopoly) competition. In the utilities industry, corporate leaders like Samuel Insull manipulated the corporate form, creating complex structures of parent and subsidiary corporations that enabled them both to maintain control with a small ownership stake and to raise money from investors who didn't understand the distinctions among the interrelated corporations.

Although Insull is largely forgotten today, the spectacular Icarus Effect collapse of his Chicago-based utilities empire personalized the need for sweeping reform. After campaigning in 1932 against "the Ishmael or Insull whose hand is against every man's," Franklin D. Roosevelt and the New Dealers restructured American business and financial regulation with a series of reforms that targeted each of the Icarus Effect factors. As described in chapter 3, the securities reforms of 1933 and 1934 required extensive disclosure, added antifraud provisions, and reinforced the role of accountants and securities analysts as watchers, all of which made it more difficult for Icaran executives to take excessive risks. New Deal banking reforms ended the monopoly of Morgan and the Money Trust over American finance; this and aggressive antitrust enforcement reinvigorated competition in some industries, while others settled into a competitive equilibrium. Although the New Dealers' principal curative for abuses of corporate size and complexity was disclosure, they intervened more directly in the utilities industry, forcing a complete restructuring of the industry under the so-called death penalty provision included in the Public Utilities Holding Company Act of 1935.

The New Deal reforms brought both an increasing federalization of corporate regulation and a shift from the rigid, per se rules that lawmakers had used in the nineteenth century to a more nuanced approach to regulation. Like corporate America, corporate and financial regulation had also come of age.

For the next several decades, the Icaran tendencies in American corporate life seemed to go into remission. As described in chapter 4, this all changed in the 1970s and 1980s, thanks to a takeover boom fueled by the junk-bond operation pioneered by Michael Milken and Drexel Burnham Lambert, together with deregulation and decreased antitrust scrutiny. These changes reinvigorated the Icaran tendencies in American corporate life. Managerial risk-taking returned after an era when corporate leaders had functioned more like bureaucrats than entrepreneurs, and competition was reintroduced into industries like telecom and utilities. The 1980s also saw the first hints of the financial innovations which would create new opportunities for manipulation of the corporate structure in the decade that followed.

The final three chapters shift from history to the present. Milken's 1989 indictment and incarceration brought Drexel crashing down in Icarus-like fashion. But Milken's fall differed from previous Icarus Effect failures in important respects and served principally as foreshadowing of the scandals that later followed. Chapter 5 chronicles the rise of charismatic CEOs like Enron's Ken Lay and Bernie Ebbers of WorldCom, the role of continued deregulation, and the use of innovations such as structured finance—the "sale" of assets to separate but often related business entities—to evade regulation and mislead investors. Chapter 6 focuses on the corporate-responsibility legislation that was enacted in response to the outrage provoked by the collapse of Enron and WorldCom and by the crisis of confidence in corporate America. The new legislation attempted to remedy the conflicts of interest that discouraged directors, auditors, and securities analysts from reining in Icaran risk-taking and manipulation. But it did little to alter the underlying incentives for corporate leaders to take excessive risks and left the other two Icarus factors—the competitive structure of industry and the misuse of corporate size and complexity—largely untouched. Chapter 7 explains why the powder keg is still very much in place. Corporate culture continues to reward managers who are willing to take risks and don't second guess the genius of the decisions they make. The competitive structure of important industries is still in turmoil. And regulators have not yet caught up to innovations that companies use to move assets and liabilities around a web of corporate entities.

For much of American business history, the risks posed by the Icaran tendencies in American business and financial life were, for most ordinary Americans, somewhere off in the distance. Although Jay Cooke's principal innovation was to market government debt and then railroad bonds more broadly than ever before, only a few Americans had extra savings to invest in stock or bonds. Even for wealthy investors, the investment of choice was real estate, not the stock market. By the end the nineteenth century, increasing numbers of upper- and upper-middle-class Americans ventured into the stock markets, and this trend intensified in the roaring twenties, when millions of ordinary Americans bought stock or bonds. But for much of the twentieth century, the stock market was still viewed primarily as the playground of the rich.

Not any more. For the first time, more than half of all Americans now own stock, either directly or through mutual funds. This in itself is a stunning development. Equally remarkable is the fact that much of this stake is retirement money and other savings, not money that Americans have intentionally put at risk. The most obvious victims of the Enron and WorldCom collapses, after all, were the thousands of men and women whose retirement portfolios were wiped out. As I argue in the final chapter, these developments have enormous implications for the next generation of corporate reform. Any effort to correct the Icaran tendencies in corporate America must account for the stake that millions of Americans now have in the market.

The long history of Icarus Effect scandals, and of the ever-evolving skirmish between regulators and corporate leaders, is no longer simply a fascinating and at times heart-wrenching historical tale. It is a tale that involves more of us than ever before. The story you are about to read is your story too.

One Jay Cooke and the Birth of America's First Large-Scale Corporations

As the end of the Internet bubble was followed in short order by the collapse of Enron, WorldCom, and other major corporations, the newspapers were filled with stories about the great market bubbles of the past. Five years earlier, in 1996, Alan Greenspan had warned that stock-market valuations were inflated by "irrational exuberance." In 2000, just as the bubble burst, the economist Robert Shiller borrowed Greenspan's phrase for the title of a book that explained how excessive optimism can produce market bubbles or, in his words, natural Ponzi schemes.[1]

The two most famous bubbles of all were the tulip bubble in seventeenth-century Holland and the eighteenth-century South Sea bubble in England. In the former debacle, the delicate beauty of some of the rarest bulbs inspired a frenzied price war. Most prized of all was the "Semper Augustus," which a poet later described as "indeed beautiful, thanks to its sophisticated and at the same time simple harmony of colors: petals impeccably white, and with small, fiery, ruby veins running along them, the bottom of the chalice blue like the reflection of a sunny sky."[2] At the height of the bubble, a single Semper Augustus bulb sold for $5,000, the value of a comfortable house with a sizable yard. In the South Sea bubble, the frenzy was over trade rather than rare beauty, but it burst in similarly spectacular fashion.

Market euphoria manifests itself differently in different countries; it adapts to the soil from which it springs. Since 1873, the most important market crashes in the United States have involved corporations and an Icarus Effect collapse. It began with the emergence of the railroads as America's first great corporations in the nineteenth century. With the first large-scale corporations came the first Icarus Effect scandal and the beginnings of a pattern that has recurred in American corporate and financial history ever since.

At the heart of it all lies the miracle, and the dangers, of the corporate entity.

The Democratization of Corporate Charters

In our era, if you want to start a new corporation, you can do it almost instantly. To set up shop in Delaware, the state of choice for nearly half of America's largest corporations, it doesn't take much more than a telephone call or e-mail message. For less than $200, Delaware incorporators such as Corporation Service Company, CTA Advantage, and CorpAmerica Inc. can have the corporation ready to go within forty-eight hours. Two days and a nominal fee, and anyone can have their own corporation. You need only fill out a simple organizational document—often referred to as the certificate of incorporation or charter. The charter can be as terse as a recitation of the name, address, and business of the corporation, together with the number of shares its directors will be authorized to issue. All of the other rules for running the corporation—rules specifying how many directors the company will have, for instance, and how many days' notice must be given before a shareholders' meeting—can be left for a separate contractual document known as the bylaws. For those who are uncomfortable drafting these documents, the incorporators and often the state filing office itself have sample charters and bylaws to use as a starting point.

As simple as the charter is, it carries remarkable powers, powers such as entity status and limited liability that will be discussed in much more detail below. Collectively, these powers are what we have in mind when we refer to the "corporate form" or to an entrepreneur's desire to obtain a corporate charter. The powers that come with a corporate charter are powers that just about anyone can have.

Things worked rather differently in the nineteenth century. Corporate charters weren't available simply for the asking. Before we explore why corporations were so special, we should consider why they were so rare at first: the story, that is, of the democratization of corporate charters in nineteenth-century America.

The dearth of corporations can be attributed in part to the South Sea bubble in England at the outset of the eighteenth century. Much as the Dutch tulip mania had been fueled by an obsession with rare tulips, the South Sea bubble fed on the proliferation of private joint-stock companies that promoters set up to finance voyages to Asia or South America for trading purposes. These "companies" were contractual in nature and could last for either a single voyage or, in time, a series of such projects. At the end of the voyage or voyages, the cargo—or "stock"—of the ship was divided among the investors who had financed the adventure. In the meantime, stakes in the joint-stock companies could be bought and sold, much like shares of stock today. As the English mercantile empire expanded, investors became less and less selective about the projects they invested in. "Some of [the projects] were of so preposterous a character," a minister told his flock a century later, "that their titles could not be recited here without exciting an unbecoming merriment." Perhaps the most famous "was styled, 'A company for carrying on an undertaking of great advantage, but nobody to know what it is.'" After the promoter collected $2,000, he "quietly withdrew that evening to the continent, and was never heard from again."[3]

The economic crisis triggered by the bursting of the South Sea bubble was so devastating that it poisoned English lawmakers' perception of this form of business enterprise for decades. In 1720, Parliament passed the Bubble Act, which made it illegal for a private business to "presum[e] to act as a corporate Body," thus outlawing joint-stock companies and temporarily thwarting the evolution of the private corporation. The Bubble Act "was widely understood to have been enacted for the benefit of the South Sea Company," as Stuart Banner notes in his important history of securities regulation, "as a means of driving a large swath of alternative investment vehicles from the market, thus channeling more capital into South Sea shares." But once the bubble burst, the Bubble Act served as a general indictment of joint-stock companies. Under the act, the only way to obtain all of the benefits of the corporate form was to petition the crown for a formal charter. It was quite difficult to obtain a charter, which meant that most entrepreneurs were left to muddle through as best they could.[4]

The same stance toward corporations also made its way across the Atlantic to America. From the beginning, the states were the ones who dispensed corporate charters (this tradition explains why so much of corporate law continues to be regulated by the states today); and state lawmakers were quite stingy with this privilege for the first several decades of the nation's existence. Most states granted only a handful each year, and the charters (when they weren't for nonprofit entities like churches or schools) were often for very specific projects. If a state needed a bridge or a canal, it would grant a charter to a bridge- or canal-building company. To encourage entrepreneurs to engage in much-needed activities, states frequently gave them monopoly rights, together with other special privileges ranging from freedom from taxation to exemption from the militia and even the power of eminent domain—the right to force landowners to sell their property to those involved in the corporate enterprise.[5] In practice, these corporations were more like branches of state government—like little administrative agencies—than like the corporations of today.

As the nineteenth century wore on, however, and opportunities to make money in mining, manufacturing, and other areas proliferated, the genteel pattern of carefully regulated state charters began to break down. There were carriage wheels to be made, and railway cars, shipping containers, and farm tools. The number of applications for corporate charters skyrocketed, which made it increasingly difficult for states to review the requests on an individualized basis. One after another, the states gave in, tossing out their old system of special charters and enacting revolutionary new general-incorporation statutes that adopted a "come one, come all" approach. As of 1800, there were 335 corporate charters in the entire country; by 1890, the number would be nearly 500,000.[6]

The Rise of the Corporate Entity

What was so special about corporations? Why were so many entrepreneurs knocking at the statehouse door, asking for a corporate charter?

When we ask this question today, the obvious answer is limited liability—the fact that the shareholders of a corporation are not personally responsible for paying its debts. When an opera singer from my church called me recently to ask about starting a corporation for his singing career, the first thing he wanted to talk about was the benefits of limited liability. Limited liability matters a great deal, for reasons we will consider below. But it really was only the second most important benefit the corporate form offered to nineteenth-century entrepreneurs. The first was entity status, or as it is often called, corporate "personhood."

When entrepreneurs wished to start a business at the outset of the nineteenth century, the most common strategy was to set it up as a partnership. Then, as now, the partnership form was quite simple, and the parties could agree to divvy up the profits of the business (should there be any) however they wished. This works just fine for many businesses, and the partnership turns out to be a great improvement over simply doing business as a sole proprietorship, due largely to the fact that partnership law draws a line between partnership creditors (that is, those who are owed money by the partnership itself) and personal creditors of the partners. Corporate-law scholars Henry Hansmann and Reinier Kraakman refer to this characteristic as "affirmative asset partitioning." They argue that, because the personal creditors have no right to partnership assets until after partnership creditors are paid, it is easier for a business to borrow money if it is a partnership rather than a sole proprietorship. A bank that is thinking about lending money to the partnership knows that it will have first dibs if the business fails, rather than having to compete with the grocery store from which one of the partners bought groceries or the shoemaker who sold shoes to another. Protected by the clarity and security of affirmative asset partitioning, the bank will be more willing to lend—and on better terms—than it would if it faced the prospect of a scrum with everyone to whom any of the partners owed money.[7]

For entrepreneurs who wanted to build a business that would endure, partnerships nevertheless had a huge limitation. They worked well so long as everyone got along and there were no major bumps in the road, but it didn't take much to trigger a dissolution of the partnership. Under traditional partnership law, the partnership was dissolved if any of the partners died, became insolvent, or withdrew from the partnership. Dissolution of the partnership arrangement would not necessarily cause the underlying business to be shut down. But often it would. Unless the partners managed to strike a deal to keep the business going (by agreeing to pay off the creditors of an insolvent partner, for instance), dissolution could force a sale of the business and destroy all of the value that the parties had built up over time.

The corporate form solved this problem by making corporations permanent. Once the parties set up a corporation and give it title to all the assets of the business (the property, equipment, intellectual property rights, and so on), it is very difficult to force a dissolution. The corporation simply keeps on ticking, even if individual shareholders die or file for bankruptcy. Corporate-law scholars refer to this attribute of the corporation as "continuous existence" or "perpetual life." It is also part of what we have in mind when we say that corporations are treated as separate "entities" by the law.

The petitions sent by nineteenth-century business owners to their state capitals, begging for a corporate charter, give a good sense of just how important they thought this permanent entity status was. The promoters of the Schuylkill Coal Company, as Professor Margaret Blair recounts, prepared a pamphlet listing several reasons why they needed to incorporate, rather than setting up the business as a partnership or an unincorporated association. Number one on the list was the promoters' desire "to have the real estate of the Company, consisting of the coal lands which they hold, and such limited additional quantity as they may be allowed to acquire, with the necessary and appropriate improvements for the working of the mines, exempted from the laws of succession or inheritance, which govern the cases of natural persons or individuals."[8]

Further on in the pamphlet, the promoters explain this concern in more detail, emphasizing precisely the issues we have been discussing. "If [the company is set up as a partnership and] one of the partners dies," they write, "his undivided interest will descend by inheritance, or pass by devise to his heirs, who may consist of numerous children, in infancy, or numerous collateral relations, widely spread, and difficult of recognition." In this event, "The operations of the Company must . . . immediately cease, and the joint estate be sold for division, or be otherwise divided between the survivors and the heirs of the deceased member, according to the decree of a proper legal tribunal, perhaps after a tedious suit, involving intricate questions of partnership claims, accounts and settlements."

Entity status provided another crucially important benefit as well. Unlike partnerships and other forms of business enterprise, a corporation could hold property, sue and be sued, and take other actions under the law—all in its own name. If the partners of a partnership wanted to bring suit, for instance, every single partner had to join in the suit in his or her individual capacity. To say that this limitation crimped the partnership's style, and that the corporate entity offered important advantages, is a vast understatement. With a corporation, investors could contribute property, patents, or other forms of intellectual property with the knowledge that they would stay within the corporation and that the corporation could sue or take other actions to protect them in its own name. There was much less of a risk that the patent would be up for grabs once again if one of the investors died or filed for bankruptcy.

The Magic of Limited Liability

The other major benefit of obtaining a corporate charter is the one we think of first: limited liability. When investors buy stock in a corporation, the amount of money they spent on the stock is usually all that they have at stake. Unlike the partners of a general partnership, shareholders are not personally responsible for the corporation's debts even if the corporation itself is unable to pay them. When Enron, WorldCom, or United Airlines collapsed, there wasn't much hope for their shareholders' stock, but shareholders weren't called on to pay any of the losses or liabilities.

At first, entity status was of primary importance. In the early years of the nineteenth century, it was not even a forgone conclusion that limited liability came with the territory. Many states did not limit the liability of corporate shareholders at all. When Massachusetts enacted an 1809 statute authorizing general incorporation for manufacturing businesses, it explicitly subjected shareholders to full liability. It would be another thirty years before the shareholders of Massachusetts corporations would be insulated from liability. A common alternative to either fully protecting shareholders from liability or fully exposing them to it was to provide for so-called double liability. If a state corporate-law statute authorized double liability, shareholders might be forced to pony up more money down the road, but the assessment could not exceed the amount they had originally paid for their shares.[9]

For many nineteenth-century businesses, unlimited liability wasn't nearly so frightening a prospect to shareholders as it is now. Businesses faced a much narrower range of risks in the nineteenth century. Until the great expansion of heavy industry in the mid-nineteenth century, there was little risk of liability for workplace injuries and the like. And it would be another century before the advent of mass tort litigation such as the asbestos lawsuits that have led to dozens of corporate bankruptcies in the past two decades. A century and a half ago, an opera singer such as my friend would have had little need for limited liability unless, say, he planned to go into real-estate speculation on the side.

But as businesses expanded in the second half of the nineteenth century, limited liability became an increasingly important attraction of the corporate form. With unlimited liability, shareholders needed to keep close tabs on the management of the business, because they were on the hook if it ever became insolvent. As a shareholder, you needed to make sure that the business wasn't borrowing too much money and that it was being run well. You also needed to pay close attention to the identity of the company's other shareholders. Each shareholder was responsible for all of the company's debts, not simply the stockholder's proportionate share. (This rule is referred to as "joint and several liability.") As a result, if the other shareholders were or had become unable to contribute, or disappeared, one wealthy shareholder could be forced to make good on all of the company's unpaid obligations.

Limited liability changes this calculation dramatically. With limited liability, an investor no longer needed to worry about being held liable for the corporation's obligations. It also did not matter nearly so much who the other shareholders were. This made it possible for the investor to buy stock in a variety of different companies and thus diversify his or her investment. Even if one or two of the companies failed, the investors would still do fine if the other companies thrived. From the perspective of the corporation, the implications were even more profound: since anyone could invest in a corporation, there was almost no natural limit on how much capital a successful corporation could raise by selling securities to the public.

Financing the Railroads,
America's First Great Corporations

So long as corporations remained small, the Icaran tendencies in American business life stayed somewhat muted. Only when corporations begin to tap large amounts of money, and extend their tentacles into hundreds or thousands of lives, does the full force of the phenomenon come into play. With the advent of large scale corporations came the central theme in Amerian corporate and financial life: the ruinous effects of Icarus Effect failures, and the regulatory responses they inspire.

The corporations that emerged as America's first large-scale business enterprises were the railroads. The railroads were the forerunners of modern enterprise, as business historian Alfred Chandler explains: "By bringing many units under its control [the railroad] began to operate in different locations, often carrying on different types of economic activities and handling different lines of goods and services. The activities of these units and the transactions between them thus became internalized. They became monitored and coordinated by salaried employees rather than market mechanisms." As the railroads expanded, revolutionizing transportation and at the same time benefiting from the markets created by this revolution, they adopted increasingly hierarchical business structures, with a class of middle managers between the railroad's workers and its executive officers. The innovations began in the 1840s, when the Western Railroad, which connected Worcester, Massachusetts, and Albany, New York, became the first to introduce full-time salaried managers. David McCallum, a civil engineer who ran the Erie Railroad, developed a much more elaborate organizational structure (complete with "one of the earliest organization charts in an American business enterprise") in the 1850s, and the other railroads soon followed suit.[10]

Although these developments were driven by the technological demands of constructing and running railroads, the railroads' corporate charters also lent an important helping hand. So long as shareholders enjoyed limited liability, it wasn't necessary that they actively manage or oversee the business, which made it much easier to separate ownership from management and to develop a specialized class of managers. Limited liability also made it possible to tap large amounts of money from many different shareholders. And the perpetual life of the corporation reduced worries that a disruption such as a death or falling out might jeopardize the ongoing business. It is no accident that although some important businesses (such as Singer typewriters) with a small group of core owner-managers and a relatively limited need to tap outside capital continued to operate as partnerships even late in the nineteenth century, America's first truly large-scale businesses—the railroads—were invariably set up as corporations, just as nearly every large business is today.

In addition to the core attributes of the corporation, early corporate law supplied several additional protections for shareholders. The first was par value. Par value was the company's best estimate of the value of its stock; shareholders were required to pay at least this amount for each share of stock the company issued. (The par value rules were concerned only with the initial sale; once an investor paid at least the par value for a share of stock, the stock could be sold to subsequent investors for any price.) Second, preemptive rights gave shareholders the right to purchase a pro rata amount of any new stock the company issued. Par value was designed to assure investors that other shareholders had paid the same price for stock as they did, and preemptive rights tried to prevent corporate managers from diluting the voting power of existing shareholders by flooding the market with new stock. Both protections eventually proved ineffectual and exist only in watered down form today, but they signaled that at least some courts would be willing to step in to protect investors.[11]

Before roughly 1850 these investors generally came from the local community. "At first," as Chandler recounts, "investors were merchants, farmers, and manufacturers, who initially promoted and financed their roads in order to improve the economic fortunes of their particular city or region." A prominent farmer who bought stock in a railroad that had been proposed for his region was contributing to a project that could open new markets for his harvest; a merchant was investing in access to new sources of goods for his store. "It was the practice," according to an early twentieth-century history of railroad finance, "to begin with subscriptions to share capital by persons interested in local manufacturing or commercial enterprises or by local investors who had accumulated savings or inherited small estates."[12]

This local finance was supplemented by a helping hand from Uncle Sam and from the states. Starting in the 1830s, Congress exempted the railroads from duties on imported iron, and in 1850, it began a program of granting lands to railroads, some of which they used for their track and some of which could be sold to help defray the costs of construction. By the time the dust settled, Congress had given almost two hundred million acres of land to a total of seventy-nine railroads. States and municipalities also got into the act by guaranteeing the obligations of railroads and sometimes borrowing money to purchase railroad stock in order to help finance the road.[13]

During the first half of the nineteenth century, then, most of the railroads' private capital came from the sale of its stock to a group of locally prominent citizens who hailed from the region that the railroad was intended to serve. As the railroads grew, this financing pattern started to change in two crucial ways. The first was an expansion of their financial horizons beyond the immediate locale of the railroad. Although local interests were still an important source of funding, they were increasingly "supplemented by [capital] from the nation's oldest and largest commercial centers." As the railroads became more regional in scope and began to develop strategic alliances, they "began to rely for funds on such eastern capitalists as the Vanderbilts, the Forbeses, Erastus Corning, Moses Taylor, John N. A. Griswold, William Osborn, and Henry Villard."[14] The capitalists would take a significant stake in the railroads, and the voting rights that came with their ownership stake gave them a major say in the railroad's future.

The second change was that other investors increasingly shifted their focus from stock, which represented a permanent ownership interest and a right to any dividends if the railroad was profitable, to bonds, which were a temporary investment that would be repaid with interest over time. Holding the stock of a new railroad in the 1840s and 1850s could give an investor vertigo. Stockholders profited handsomely if the railroad was built as planned, at something like the projected cost, but there was no guarantee that the investors would ever see a return. If the railroad failed, the bondholders and other creditors were entitled to be paid before the stockholders saw a dime. As recounted in the railroad-finance history noted earlier, "failure to build within estimates, calls for assessments to put in proper condition the inferior work turned over by contractors, and delays in the payment of dividends, eventually led investors to regard railroad shares as of uncertain value, and to put their savings into railroad bonds."

It would be a mistake to suggest that Americans from every neighborhood and town bought corporate stock or bonds. Most ordinary Americans had little or no extra savings, and for those who did, the investment of choice was real estate. Land was the great speculative investment of the nineteenth century, dwarfing corporate securities by any conceivable measure. Before the 1860s, in fact, no one thought of marketing securities of any kind to ordinary citizens. But by the end of the Civil War, this had changed. It started with government debt, and one man showed the way. His banking and railroad empire rose with one of the great bubble markets of the nineteenth century. Its Icarus Effect collapse would trigger both the century's most devastating economic depression and a major political and regulatory effort to rein the railroads in.

The Rise of Jay Cooke

In 1861, Pennsylvania lawmakers passed an act authorizing the sale of $3 million of government bonds to the public, but there was a great deal of skepticism as to whether anyone would sign on. Pennsylvania already had more than $40,000,000 in debt outstanding, much of which had been sold to banks and the states' wealthiest citizens in more auspicious times. The state had struggled to make its interest payments on the bonds, and there had already been a lively debate as to whether these existing obligations should simply be repudiated.[15]

The commission for selling the bonds was given to Drexel & Co., the leading Philadelphia Bank, and Jay Cooke, a thirty-nine-year-old Philadelphia banker who had only recently opened his own bank, Jay Cooke and Company. These were desperate financial times, and they called for desperate—or, at the least, unprecedented—measures. While Drexel & Co. used the usual techniques—trying to round up the major banks and the state's wealthiest investors, Cooke cast his net far more broadly, sending a small army of agents across the state to knock on the doors of local banks, insurance companies, and private investors. Cooke's first stroke of genius was to wrap his appeals in the American flag. Cooke suggested that, by readily purchasing the bonds, Pennsylvanians would demonstrate the financial health and commitment not just of Pennsylvania, but by extension of all the Union states in the escalating Civil War against the Confederacy. Subscribing to a loan "for so large a sum as three millions," he told one initially reluctant bank, "would strike terror to the rebels and greatly help the United States government in selling bonds [at their full face value]."[16] Cooke's other great innovation was the creative use of advertising, which he supplemented by persuading (and at times, essentially bribing) the media to run flattering stories about his campaigns. The strategy was an enormous success. Cooke astonished nearly everyone by selling the entire $3 million loan at par almost immediately.

It didn't take long for Cooke to move on to bigger game. Cooke's brother Henry owned several newspapers in Ohio and through this had become friendly with Salmon Chase, the secretary of the Treasury and later chief justice of the Supreme Court. As secretary of the Treasury, Chase was the one who decided which banks would be authorized to sell government bonds on behalf of the U.S. government to finance the Union cause in the Civil War. In 1861, at the same time as his Pennsylvania triumph, Cooke peppered Chase with offers to help raise money. After Chase succumbed and brought him on board, Cooke almost single-handedly took charge of the nation's financing needs. Starting with a $50 million loan that Chase assigned to him that summer, Cooke perfected his revolutionary new technique for selling government debt on a door-to-door basis, to ordinary Americans. From a twenty-first-century vantage point, Cooke's tactics seem high pressure, and even a bit corny. Flyers for the loans—which promised 7.3% interest and became known as "7-30s"—proclaimed that the government was "The Working Men's Savings Bank," that the loans would be "forever safe," and that they offered the "BIGGEST INTEREST!" It was as if Barnum & Bailey had gone into the banking business. But it worked. Through his war-bond sales, Cooke showed that investment banking could be done on a retail basis—by tapping the funds of ordinary Americans—rather than just on the traditional, wholesale basis of selling primarily to banks and other financial institutions.

By the time the Civil War came to an end, Cooke had become a national hero. On March 3, 1865, Congress passed a bill authorizing the sale of $600 million of new 7-30 bonds. After General Lee surrendered on April 9, 1865, the bonds sold rapidly. "The great success of the 7-30 loan," a characteristic newspaper account gushed, "must always be looked upon as one of the most powerful evidences of the strength of the United States Government. . . . In the three months that the loan has been in charge of Mr. JAY COOKE, over five hundred million dollars [of subscriptions have been sold]." When the loan closed at the end of July, Cooke had placed an astonishing $830 million of government securities.[17]

Cooke had single-handedly created a new market for governmental debt. In his door-to-door sales, saturation advertising, and manipulation of friendly media, he had helped the American investment-banking industry to find a vast new market.

The Wild, Wild World of the Railroads: Corporate Governance Comes of Age

It may have taken a financial genius to see—as Cooke did—the previously untapped potential for investment by ordinary Americans. But it didn't take a genius to see the relevance of Cooke's strategies for financing private corporations such as the railroads. Like the U.S. Treasury during the Civil War, the railroads had a mission—expanding across the country—that called for enormous amounts of cash. It was only natural that railroad entrepreneurs would apply Cooke's bond-selling techniques to their campaigns to finance the rapidly growing railroads.

And they did. Once the Civil War was finally over, the U.S. markets took off, and a great speculative frenzy was unleashed. Much of it centered on the railroads, which both transformed American life and precipitated America's first great corporate-governance scandals when the bubble burst a few years later in 1873.

The grandest project of all was the quest to build a railroad that spanned the entire country, from one ocean to the other. Congress played a pivotal role in this quest, granting federal charters to the Union Pacific Railroad to build westward from the Missouri River and to the Central Pacific, which would start on the west coast and build eastward. In the same 1862 legislation, the Pacific Railway Act, Congress also gave huge subsidies to the railroad project. The Union Pacific was allotted twelve million acres of land and $27 million in government bonds bearing 6% interest. The subsidy to the Central Pacific totaled nine million acres of land and $24 million in government bonds. ("I give no grudging vote," proclaimed Senator Henry Wilson of Massachusetts. "What are $75,000,000 or $100,000,000 in opening a railroad across regions of this continent, that shall connect the people of the Atlantic and the Pacific, and bind us together. . . . Nothing! As to the lands, I don't begrudge them.")[18]

Although the Union Pacific succeeded in linking the nation from shore to shore, the project also epitomized the dangers of American corporate governance gone amok. The directors of the railroad set up a company known as Crédit Mobilier, a corporation that they owned and controlled, to handle much of the construction of the Union Pacific project. The directors then contracted with Crédit Mobilier to clear the land and lay down the railroad track. The directors thus stood on both sides of the contracts, since they controlled both companies. As the project went on, the price that Crédit Mobilier charged for the construction of each mile of track rose higher and higher, from $80,000 to $90,000 and then $96,000, fully double the costs that had been projected by the Union Pacific's engineers. In theory, these prices might simply have reflected unexpected costs of constructing the railroad, but there were increasing rumors that the railroad's directors were using Crédit Mobilier to line their own pockets, either by overcharging the Union Pacific—which would inure to their benefit, because they had a greater ownership stake in Crédit Mobilier than in the railroad—or simply by stealing money.

"By chance," as a historian later recounted, "the Union Pacific in 1864 had as its chief engineer Peter A. Dey, an able and honest technician":

He estimated the cost of building the first hundred miles at $30,000 per mile, and for the second hundred miles $27,000 per mile. Durant, vice-president and active head of the company, objected strenuously to such estimates, and Dey unwillingly raised his estimate to $50,000, then suddenly resigned. The contract was given over to one Hoxie, who followed Dey's first specification carefully, but "expended" about three times as much cash as he called for! Here alone, one may account for the disappearance of $6,000,000 in two hundred miles of construction.[19]

Although Congress had chartered and subsidized the Union Pacific and thus bore significant responsibility for its oversight, lawmakers refused to intervene as rumors swirled around the project throughout the 1860s. There was an obvious reason for this. The Union Pacific "had received the political benediction of statesmen of both parties," many of whom had been given stock in Crédit Mobilier, the Union Pacific, or both. The point person for these transactions was Oakes Ames, a Congressman from Massachusetts, who distributed stock to his fellow lawmakers for little or nothing; his goal was to ensure that the stock would end up "where," as he put it, "it will do most good for us." "We want more friends in this Congress," he wrote to a friend. "There is no difficulty in getting men to look after their own property."[20]

When the Union Pacific and Central Pacific came together at Promontory Point, Utah, on May 10, 1869, there was a national celebration. "Chicago held a parade several miles long," according to one account; "in New York City the chimes of Trinity were rung; and in Philadelphia the Old Liberty Bell in Independence Hall was tolled again."[21] For the moment, at least, the railroads were the toast of the nation.

The building of the Union Pacific had involved a concerted effort to link the nation from shore to shore. Elsewhere in the country, by contrast, the railroad boom was far more helter-skelter. Railroad owners could make enormous profits by taking control of important segments of track and charging as much as the market would bear. The swashbucklers who played this game, men like Jay Gould, Daniel Drew, and Jim Fisk—have been long been known as "robber barons." Their most infamous swordfight of all was the battle over the Erie Railway, the "Scarlet Woman of Wall Street," which connected New York to the west. Prior to this struggle, Cornelius Vanderbilt had put together a link from New York to the west by taking control of the New York Central and two smaller railroads, the Harlem and the Hudson River. In 1867 Vanderbilt launched an effort to acquire the Erie and thus to eliminate any competition for trans–New York traffic.[22]

The principal obstacle in Vanderbilt's way was Daniel Drew, who for some years had been both a director and the treasurer of the Erie. Drew was a notorious speculator of whom wags claimed: "Daniel says 'up,' Erie goes up, Daniel says 'down,' Erie goes down. Daniel says 'wiggle-waggle,' it bobs both ways!"[23]

When Vanderbilt started buying Erie stock, Drew, who had allied himself with Jay Gould and Jim Fisk, responded by dumping millions of shares of new Erie stock into the market, thus diluting Vanderbilt's interest so that he would not have enough voting shares to assert control. After an apparent truce between the factions, Drew once again thwarted Vanderbilt, this time by inducing the Erie's board of directors to issue $10 million of bonds that could be converted into still more stock. At this point, Vanderbilt took his campaign to the courts. Carefully selecting his judge— Judge George C. Barnard of the New York State Supreme Court, who was a favorite of the Tweed ring that dominated New York politics—Vanderbilt asked for and received an injunction prohibiting the Erie from issuing any more stock. Vanderbilt's victory was only temporary, however. Jay Gould managed to persuade—with both words and money, by all accounts— another New York State Supreme Court judge to issue conflicting injunctions. Vanderbilt then asked Judge Barnard to arrest Drew, Gould, and Fisk. Tipped off that the police were coming, Drew and his allies hurried across the Hudson River to New Jersey, setting up their operations in a Jersey City hotel, just beyond the reach of New York law enforcement.

The final battle began with another round of bribes. Several weeks after Drew, Gould, and Fisk ensconced themselves in Jersey City, "Jay Gould suddenly departed for Albany upon a secret mission of tremendous importance. He bore with him a big valise containing $500,000 in greenbacks." Gould's objective was to persuade the legislature to legalize the sale of the Erie's convertible bonds. Vanderbilt sent his own agents, with their own briefcases, to argue the other side of the issue. "Never," according to a later account, "had such bounties been offered for the goodwill of State senators." Some were said to have received as much as $100,000, and Gould himself "admitted afterward having overpaid one man 'in whom he did not have much stock' by $5,000." In the end, Vanderbilt relented, and the Erie legislation was enacted, effectively legalizing all of the securities that Drew's faction had issued in the course of the battle.[24]

The Erie was the most dramatic of the battles, but there were many more to come. The opportunistic careers of the robber barons illustrated, in almost caricatured form, the worst possible abuses of a large-scale corporate enterprise. Taking control of an important railroad gave Gould and Fisk, who ran the Erie as partners until Fisk was murdered in 1872 by a jealous lover of his buxom mistress Josie Mansfield, access to a capacious corporate treasury. The corporate treasury could be used to buy influence and fend off regulatory or judicial interference. Contemporary accounts compared Fisk—a beefy man who best rode Wall Street bedizened in a "scarlet-lined cape" with touches of awe, horror, and hyperbole—to a "fiery meteor, or a great comet . . . plunging with terrific velocity and dazzling brilliance across the horizon, whirling into its blazing train broken fortunes, raving financiers, corporations, magnates and public officers, civil and military, judges, priests and Presidents." Gould was as quiet as Fisk was flamboyant, which gave him an air of mystery. Henry Adams described him as "small and slight in person, dark, sallow, reticent, and stealthy, with a trace of Jewish origin." (the opt-hinted at Jewishness was, as it turned out, imaginary).[25] In an era when there was little effective regulatory oversight, and even the judicial system was suspect, they demonstrated that even blatant bribery and misappropriation were a plausible business strategy.[26]

At first, Jay Cooke had resisted the railroad frenzy of the post–Civil War era. But after a resounding success applying his marketing techniques to a Minnesota railroad, the Lake Superior and Mississippi, Cooke agreed to help finance the Northern Pacific, a railroad project that would provide a northern alternative to the Union Pacific. The Northern Pacific would run from Minnesota to Seattle, and it was being built eastward from the west coast and westward from Minnesota. In the words of his brother Henry, if they could pull it off, the Northern Pacific would be "the grandest achievement of our lives"—even grander than their success selling the government's Civil War debt.[27]

But Cooke had bitten off more than he could chew. Cooke's agents fanned out all over Europe, trying to persuade Rothschild and other major European banks to participate in the financing, but not one of them signed on, in part because of the uncertainty created by the onset of the Franco-Prussian War. To continue on with the financing, even after the most prominent banks in the Western world had declined to participate in the risk, was an act of stunning hubris. Even today, banks routinely syndicate major loans, bringing in other banks so that no single financial institution bears too much of the risk that the loan will not be repaid. Bond issuances are often divided up in somewhat similar fashion. For a banker to attempt almost single-handedly to raise all of the money for so large a project would be unusual now; in the nineteenth century, it was unprecedented.

Not only did Cooke run the risk that he would be unable to sell the bonds, but he magnified his risks still further by taking a large portion of the bank's commission for the bonds he did sell in stock rather than cash. This meant that Jay Cooke and Company was not just the underwriter for the Northern Pacific project. It was also the controlling shareholder. He and the bank were running a major corporate enterprise.

As the railroad inched forward, the construction was bedeviled by acrimony among the Northern Pacific's managers, by rumors of fraud, and by the kinds of lavish expenditures we now associate with scandal-ridden executives like WorldCom's Bernie Ebbers and Tyco's Dennis Kozlowski. Despite all the hints of trouble, Cooke refused to turn back. Cooke's "gigantic successes since 1861 had given him a feeling of invincible power," in the words of an otherwise admiring biographer, "and although beset with difficulties that would have deterred and utterly discouraged other men, he had scarcely begun to develop the plans which he expected to execute before he should be willing to confess defeat."[28]

Cooke took greater and greater risks with the Northern Pacific leviathan, continuing to push forward and eventually acquiring a majority of the corporation's stock. Cooke's desperation was stoked by increasing competition from other investment banks. In June 1871, J. Pierpont Morgan and Anthony Drexel, two of Cooke's principal competitors, joined forces, forming Drexel, Morgan & Co. (Drexel, Morgan was the predecessor to the bank that eventually became J. P. Morgan & Co. The London office, J. S. Morgan & Co., was headed by Pierpont's father, Junius Morgan, who gradually transferred control over the Morgan banks to Pierpont in the decades before his death in 1890.) Together, they held themselves out as an alternative to Cooke when the government was looking for a bank to sell its bonds. Although Cooke had pioneered the strategy of selling bonds to ordinary investors, he had no way to prevent other bankers from imitating his innovation. To make matters worse, Morgan and Drexel actively undermined the Northern Pacific itself, often taking advantage of the *Philadelphia Ledger*, a major Philadelphia newspaper that was financially dependent on Drexel, to sow doubts about the project. The gentlest of the criticisms lampooned the Northern Pacific as Cooke's "banana belt" empire (the name was inspired by the flowery advertisements claiming that the Northern Pacific would traverse land of unparalleled beauty) and suggested that the project was as speculative as ventures that collapsed in the era of the South Sea bubble.[29]

By 1872, Cooke's own partners were begging him to back off. "No enterprise of such magnitude has ever before been so entirely dependent upon one house, or rather upon one man," H. C. Fahnestock wrote. "I claim that it is in every respect unwise to make such an undertaking dependent upon the strength of one house, or on the life of one man. . . . [We] must squarely look in the face all errors of the past and see what is now best for the road and ourselves. Enthusiasm alone will not be sufficient. It must be combined with the soundest judgment. . . . Radical and immediate changes are necessary," Fahnestock concluded, "to save the company from ingloriously breaking down within the next year and involving us in discredit, if not in ruin."[30]

But Cooke refused to listen, still certain that he could make the project work. In late 1872, after it became increasingly difficult to sell enough bonds to keep the Northern Pacific construction afloat, Cooke turned to Congress once again looking for help—for a new land grant to supplement a massive grant that the Northern Pacific had been given in 1870. But by this time, the Crédit Mobilier scandal had broken. Two factions within Crédit Mobilier had been "at loggerheads over their shares of the rich building contracts," and in 1872 one faction took the squabble to the courts. The litigation exposed Congressman Ames's efforts to dole out stock to influential lawmakers. As the scandal exploded, and with a Congressional investigation finally underway, lawmakers had no interest in going anywhere near a troubled railroad.[31]

Unable to make any headway in Washington, Cooke tried to organize a syndicate to sell $9 million of bonds that remained unsold from an earlier $30 million issuance. But by May 1873, there were no real takers. Many banks were losing deposits, in part to concerns about pervasive corruption in the railroad industry. In the first two weeks of September, New York Warehouse & Security Company and Kenyon, Cox & Co., two banks that were, like Cooke, closely tied to railroads, collapsed. Although Jay Cooke and Company was thought to be sound, it was increasingly unclear whether the bank had enough funds to pay the anxious depositors who wanted to withdraw money. Far too much of its assets were tied up in Northern Pacific stock and unsold bonds.[32]

The bottom fell out for the bank and the Northern Pacific corporation to which its fortunes were hitched on September 18, 1873. By then, Cooke had nowhere else to turn. After entertaining President Ulysses Grant at his Ogontz mansion on the outskirts of Philadelphia the night before, he took a carriage into the city and ordered the doors of Jay Cooke and Company shut. "The news spread like fire on the Northern Pacific's own dry prairies," according to one account. The New York office of Jay Cooke and Company "was surrounded by a crowd of men, women and children, who were shouting and gesticulating wildly." In the New York Stock Exchange, "messengers fled every which way with the story of ruin, and down came the stock all along the line." Several blocks away, "a little newsboy who shouted an 'extra'—'All about the failure of Jay Cooke'—was arrested and taken to a 'station house' by a policeman who was not early apprized of the disaster, so wholly unbelievable did it seem to be to all classes of people."[33]

The shock of Cooke's failure was magnified by the fact that

he, unlike Gould and other railroad speculators, had been viewed as a model of probity. The implosion of the empire of a man who had so recently been a financial hero suggested that American corporate life was fundamentally unsound. With Cooke's collapse, the nation's first Icarus Effect scandal, the economic depression known as the 1873 Panic, was unleashed. There was no central bank to pump money into the staggering economy, and one company after another failed as they were unable to meet obligations incurred in the flush years after the Civil War.

The Scandal in Daily Life and on the Political Stage

The impact of Cooke's collapse on those who had invested in railroad stock or bonds was immediate and severe, as the value of railroad securities plummeted. Investors knew that railroad bonds weren't risk-free, but many had thought these bonds—which were secured by mortgages on railroad land and property—would be left standing even if, as Cooke put it in a letter to an investor several months before his collapse, the skies should fall. Cooke's failure devastated many of these investors. "At the request of Eliza ——," one man wrote to Cooke in early 1874, "a poor blind woman who holds a $500 Northern Pacific bond . . . , I write to state to you that this is all her earthly wealth, and the loss of it will oblige her to go to the poorhouse."[34]

The ripples of the failure were felt even across the Atlantic. "The all-absorbing topic of conversation among Americans in this city," wrote a Paris correspondent for the *New York Times*, is the financial crisis in the United States. . . . When the first news came that Jay Cooke & Co. had suspended payments, and that other houses might follow, there was general consternation. . . . A Senator and a Chief Justice are among the losers here," the correspondent noted, "but, of course, such persons can always obtain money from friends. It is the people of moderate fortune who suffer. . . . Several ladies in Dresden claim to have been left utterly destitute. One gentleman has just telegraphed as follows. 'For God's sake help me out or I shall be arrested here. I was behind in my payments—waiting for money from home—and have just got Jay Cooke & Co.'s draft.'"[35]

For most Americans, the effect of the Cooke scandal was more indirect than direct. The "people of moderate fortune" who bore the immediate brunt of the collapse were far removed from the average American who worked on a farm or in a small factory. Most of our ancestors were more likely to be working as share-croppers or raising cattle than depositing money in Cooke's bank or investing in the Northern Pacific enterprise. But his failure was not solely an affair of the rich, as illustrated by the Eliza letter quoted above, and it dealt a staggering blow to the American economy.

Two years later, thinking back on the impact in Ohio, a Cleveland reporter recalled that the "chill of Jay Cooke's failure [was] felt in thousands of honest hearts and pockets, the panic had overspread the country, and even Republicans [were] alarmed and disgusted with the course of public affairs."[36] This alarm and disgust echoed through the American political world and would have enduring effects on the regulation of American corporate life.

The Politics of an Icarus Effect Scandal

Under ordinary circumstances, corporate managers have a great deal of influence on the laws that are or aren't passed to regulate corporations. Ordinary citizens, on the other hand, have almost no influence, due to the simple realities of interest-group politics. Managers and their companies have a much greater stake than an ordinary citizen does; for a nineteenth-century railroad, for instance, obtaining a local or Congressional subsidy might mean millions of dollars of land or other property for the railroad. The cost of the subsidy would in a sense be borne by the American public, of course, but the expense to each individual citizen would be quite small. Even if the corporate handouts (or freedom from regulation or other corporate benefits) cost Americans as a whole far more than they helped the railroad and its managers, ordinary citizens were usually too poorly organized to make a difference.[37]

Access to the corporate kitty has a feedback effect on the conditions that can trigger an Icarus Effect scandal. Not only does the ability to tap huge sums of capital in a corporation magnify the potential consequences of Icaran risk-taking, this same capital can be used to influence the lawmakers or regulators whose task it is to prevent risk-taking that edges toward market manipulation or fraud and to oversee the competitive structure of the American markets. The extent to which these objectives could be compromised was most graphically illustrated by the Erie Railway debacle, when judicial decisions were bought and sold with a brazenness that far exceeds the corruption that attended the privatization of Russian industry during the 1980s. But even Jay Cooke had actively traded Northern Pacific stock for favors in Congress.

Writing in 1869, prominent nineteenth-century social critic Henry Adams worried that the railroads, with their rapidly increasing corporate treasuries, would prove impossible to keep in check. "With the prodigious development of corporate and private wealth," he fretted, as he considered the nationwide scope of the Union Pacific, "resistance must be vain." Although Adams had good reason to worry, there is one circumstance when the political calculus is transformed: a full-blown corporate scandal. When public opinion is galvanized by corporate misbehavior, lawmakers suddenly stop answering the phone—as Cooke's friends did after the Crédit Mobilier debacle and as President

Bush and Congress did when Enron collapsed—and they spring into action on the legislative or judicial front. With the Icaran collapse of an American business hero like Cooke, whose failure seems emblematic of a breakdown in American corporate life, just about any regulatory response that takes aim at Icaran risk-taking is temporarily on the table.

Railroad and Corporate Reforms after the Cooke Collapse

The most obvious response is simply to outlaw the most egregious behavior, the actions or transactions that seem to epitomize how everything went amok. Each Icarus Effect scandal has prompted this kind of "tit-for-tat" response, and the depression— the 1873 Panic—that followed Cooke's failure was no exception. All of the corporate governance breakdowns had involved railroads—Cooke's Northern Pacific, the Erie, and the Crédit Mobilier Scandal—and so too did the principal responses.

At the state level, several states revamped legislation—much of it dating to an earlier wave of railroad collapses, in 1857—that was designed to get the states out of the business of subsidizing railroad expansion. To prevent future corruption, as well as honest but overenthusiastic subsidization of business, several states simply turned off the spigot altogether. Pennsylvania amended its state constitution to prohibit the legislature from authorizing any political subdivision "to obtain or appropriate money for . . . any corporation, association . . . or individual."[38] These statutes were, in a sense, a very early illustration of a legislative effort to limit corporate influence over the political process, a issue that would take center stage by the end of the Gilded Age after Teddy Roosevelt's first presidential election campaign.

As challenges to the abuses of the railroads percolated through the judicial system, the courts also helped to reshape the regulatory environment. Most striking was the courts' treatment of contracts between a corporation and its own managers, the arrangements that Crédit Mobilier had used to siphon off hundreds of thousands of dollars from the Union Pacific. The courts simply adopted a blanket rule prohibiting corporations from entering into any contract with their own managers. "It is among the rudiments of the law," the Supreme Court explained in the most important of these decisions, that the "same person cannot act for himself and at the same time, with respect to the same matter, as agent for another, whose interests are conflicting. . . . Hence, all arrangements by directors of a railroad company [to enter into contracts between the company and themselves] will be condemned whenever properly brought before the courts for consideration."[39]

Although the impulse to enact strict prohibitions in response to a corporate scandal is powerful in every era, it was particularly strong in the nineteenth century. There was no army of regulators to audit corporate behavior, and corporate accounting was still so primitive that the railroads themselves often did not have a clear grasp of the finances of the company. In this environment, clear, simple rules were the only plausible way of protecting investors. But there is a significant price to be paid for rigid rules. Strict rules prevent the entrepreneurial spirit from spiraling out of control, but they also can severely constrain companies that are engaging in perfectly appropriate business activity. The prohibition against any transaction between a company and its managers is a good example. Although Crédit Mobilier demonstrated the dangers of self-dealing contracts, managers themselves are sometimes the best source of financing or supplies for a growing company. By the end of the nineteenth century, as courts were confronted by the benign cases, rather than just the most atrocious ones, things would be much more complicated. Courts started carving out exceptions to many of the strict rules that characterized nineteenth-century America cor-

porate law, including the par valve and preemptive right requirements described earlier. But the first response of both judges and
lawmakers after the Cooke collapse and the railroad abuses that
preceded it was to outright prohibit the behavior that Americans
most closely associated with the scandals.

The Grange and the Rise of American Populism

The explicit legal responses were just the tip of the iceberg. Far
more important in the long run was the jolt that Cooke's
failure and the 1873 Panic gave to American politics. The outrage
launched American Populism, a previously diffuse movement of
farmers and small merchants in the south and west, to the fore-
front of American politics. Farmers and small merchants had
depended heavily on the railroads from the beginning, since the
railroads were their only link to the markets and suppliers of the
Northeast. Starting in the 1840s, they had begun organizing local
associations, which became known as the "Grange" or Granger
movement, to protest the railroads' pricing practices and to call
for regulatory oversight. A particular source of ire was the fact
that costs varied dramatically from one route to the next. Although the organization of a group as scattered and diffuse as
farmers was remarkable in itself, this proto-Populist movement
had achieved only limited success prior to 1873.

The Cooke collapse and the 1873 Panic ignited this popular in-
surgency that would eventually lead to the nomination of Populist hero William Jennings Bryan as the Democratic presidential
candidate in 1896 and 1900. The most important of the great
Populist campaigns was a debate over monetary policy that went
well beyond the railroads or corporate law, but was closely intertwined with the efforts to rein in the nation's first large-scale
corporations.

With a great deal of lobbying by Cooke and others, Presidents

Johnson and Grant had kept a strict rein on the nation's monetary supply, backing each dollar with gold and guaranteeing repayment of the nation's Civil War debts. Only by "fully funding" the government debt—that is, paying it in full—Cooke insisted, could the stability of the nation's finances be assured. "I consider the agitation on this subject," he wrote in a long letter published in the *Philadelphia Inquirer* in March 1868, "namely, the payment of our [debt] in anything but gold, as an unnecessary and injurious attack upon the public credit. No possible good can come from it. Much injury to the credit not only of the nation but the whole business community must ensue from the bare discussion of such a question."[40]

This policy was hard on farmers and other debtors, since a strong currency made dollars and thus repayment costly. In 1874, in the wake of the Cooke scandal, the debtor class swept to power as the Democrats wrested control of the House in the midterm elections. With the leaders of business weakened, debtors and their advocates campaigned for "free silver"—that is, for an inflationary monetary policy, later enshrined in the Bland-Allison Act of 1878, based on large purchases of silver by the government to pump more and more silver dollars into circulation. The free-silver debate would continue to dominate American politics until the end of the century. "Upon which side will the Democratic party fight," Bryan asked in his famous "Cross of Gold" speech, "upon the side of the 'idle holders of idle capital' or upon the side of 'the struggling masses?'"[41]

The Debate over Railroad Regulation

Second only to the monetary issues on the Populist agenda was reining in the railroads. After the Crédit Mobilier scandal and shortly before the Cooke collapse, the Second National Agricultural Congress adopted a series of resolutions, a manifesto that graphically illustrates their concerns about railroad governance. The longest of the resolutions accuses the railroads of looking to local investors and local government for financing, then forcing the original shareholders out at depressed prices. *"Resolved,"* the resolution begins, that

> the system adopted and now practiced in the building of
> railroads, viz.: the soliciting of stock subscriptions from
> individuals, corporations, and counties, and after receiving
> these subsidies to depress the value of said stock by forcing
> it upon the market and depreciating its value to such an
> extent as to enable a few speculators to secure control of
> the road, thereby depriving those who aid in its construc-
> tion of all voice in its management; increasing the cost
> four or five times above the amount it would have cost if
> those managing it in the outset had had the foresight to
> have the funds on hand at the start . . . operates most
> injuriously to the best interests of the farming class,
> and calls loudly for reform and restraint by adequate
> legislation.[42]

The most frequent complaint, figuring in nearly all of the ten resolutions, is the concern about discriminatory pricing. *"Resolved,"* the second resolution says, that "railroad corporations in many instances have been exorbitant in their charges, have discriminated unjustly between localities, and have failed to respond to the generous grants of power and moneys that have been given them by our national and state governments."

One solution both to the farmers' and merchants' concerns and to the reckless competition in the railroad industry that was personified by the robber barons' fight over the Erie Railroad in 1869 might have been for Congress simply to take over the railroads and develop them as governmental corporations. Like water and utilities, the railroads can be seen as a natural monopoly— an industry where coordinated development by one or a small number of producers sometimes makes more sense than relying on private production due to economies of scale—the fact that large companies can often produce goods or services more cheaply than smaller ones because the average cost of making or transporting a large amount is lower. Competition in an industry that is most efficiently run by a small group of companies can be extremely destructive, as corporate executives race to be one of the survivors, one of the companies that will dominate the market and thus be in a position to charge high rates and earn enormous profits. The slash-and-burn strategies of the railroad robber barons were of course an exaggerated illustration of this danger.

In many other countries, railroads have always been run by the state, largely for these reasons (and indeed, even now, Amtrak is a quasipublic railroad that is kept afloat by huge Congressional subsidies). Government ownership addresses two of the three Icarus Effect factors: it dampens both Icaran risk-taking and the effects of competition by taking the industry out of the private sphere altogether. Government-owned companies are not immune from fraud and other misbehavior, of course. But the misbehavior is likely to take different forms in that context. We do not generally see the managers of government-owned companies taking extraordinary risks, gambling on a new innovation or business strategy.

Although some Populists called for complete government ownership, Congress never seriously considered taking this step. The debates centered instead on regulatory oversight and controls on the rates that the railroads could charge. Buoyed by the outrage created by Cooke's collapse and the 1873 Panic, the Grangers persuaded several state legislatures to enact strict railroad-rate regulation. Although most of these laws were later struck down by the Supreme Court, Populists would eventually persuade Congress to pass the Interstate Commerce Act of 1887, which introduced the first extensive federal regulatory oversight of the railroads. Whether rate regulation ever achieved its objectives has long been a matter of dispute, but it clearly diminished some of the worst excesses of railroad competition. Regulatory oversight made it harder for railroad buccaneers to profit by buying key segments of the railroad network and then charging exorbitant prices to everyone who needed to pass that way.

As with government ownership, the railroad-rate regulation takes aim at Icaran risk-taking and the possibility of inefficient competition by reducing the possibility of profiteering by the winners in the scramble to dominate this transportation network. Rate regulation does not directly address the third factor—the burgeoning size of the railroads and their use of the huge amounts of capital they amassed within the corporation—but this too was a major concern. The battle over corporate expansion became a central theme in American corporate life, and, with the advent of the great corporate trusts of the Gilded Age, it soon extended well beyond the confines of the railroad industry.

Two The Gilded Age and the Crisis of Competition

In the heart of the seaport town of Newport, Rhode Island, Cornelius Vanderbilt II, grandson of the Commodore and son of the railroad baron William Vanderbilt, built himself a summer cottage. Like many of us, he longed for a quiet retreat, a place to escape from the chaos of the city during the heat of the summer. Vanderbilt's getaway was, however, quite different than the average bungalow. Designed by Richard Morris Hunt, one of the leading nineteenth-century American architects, it fans out over seventy rooms. There are ceilings adorned with stained-glass designs created by LaForge; the bathtub in one of the bathrooms is carved out of a single block of Italian marble; and Vanderbilt's coat of arms—oak leaves and acorns—is a recurring motif in the paintings that festoon nearly every room. The Breakers, he called it, naming his getaway for the waves that slap against the rocks at the edge of its vast manicured grounds.

Newport has the greatest concentration of these houses, but others are scattered across the country—the Rockefeller house in Hyde Park, New York, the Biltmore in Asheville, North Carolina. Their owners were the closest thing that we have ever had to American royalty, the barons of American business who accumulated great fortunes during the Gilded Age, the era when many of America's largest corporations were launched and Congress hadn't yet put an income tax in place.

After Cooke's collapse and the 1873 Panic, Congress stopped directly subsidizing the railroads, and for the most part the states did too. But the travails of the railroads were far from over. There would be another wave of failures in 1883, when the next economic depression hit the American markets. Both before and after this time, the railroads continued to consolidate. The first of the great railroad systems was the Pennsylvania, which started purchasing adjoining railroads to fend off a threat from Jay Gould in 1868. After the Pennsylvania, the system-building strategy quickly spread through the industry, with the Baltimore & Ohio and several southern and western railroads building major networks. This same strategy also caught on in other industries, where men like Rockefeller and Andrew Carnegie cobbled together great, monopolistic trusts from the warring corporations in their industries. The new business titans defended the consolidation as "rationalizing" American business by taming the fierce competition among the industries' small and medium-sized corporations. They also extolled the superior efficiency of the great combinations. Before they could assemble their corporate behemoths, however, Rockefeller, the railroad barons, and their peers had to circumvent the state lawmakers, and state corporate laws, that stood in their way.

The State Law Limitations on Corporate Bigness

Unlike the corporate laws of today, which cater to the needs of large-scale corporations, nineteenth-century corporate-law statutes were designed with small corporations in mind. In part, lawmakers were simply legislating based on what they saw: until the railroads, large-scale private corporations were scarce, so it was only natural that the concerns of small enterprises would occupy the attention of lawmakers. But the state corporate laws of the nineteenth century also reflected an implicit suspicion of large corporate enterprises, a desire to limit the size of any given corporation, and, perhaps more to the point, the amount of capital that could be amassed in the corporate treasury.

In characteristic nineteenth-century fashion, many of the key restrictions on corporate size were framed as simple, rigid prescriptions or prohibitions. Many states imposed both minimum and maximum limits on the amount of corporate capital—that is, the cash or property that shareholders put into the corporation in return for its stock. If you set up a mechanical, mining, or manufacturing corporation in Massachusetts, for instance, the total shareholder contribution had to be at least $5,000 in capital, but no more than $1,000,000. The maximum, $1,000,000, was a great deal of money in 1882, when this particular provision was put in place, but even then it didn't make for a corporate behemoth.[1]

In addition to the capital requirements imposed by many states, courts enforced a long-standing judicial rule known as the *ultra vires* doctrine. Under the *ultra vires* doctrine, corporations were prohibited from conducting any business that was not specifically authorized in their corporate charter. If a flour mill started manufacturing tires, for instance, a shareholder could ask a court to step in and bring a halt to the tire-making. The rule was designed to protect the company's shareholders and creditors by ensuring that the managers did not change the company's focus, but it also had the effect of limiting expansion by the business into new areas.

Stop for a moment to consider the Icarus Effect implications of these restrictions on size and diversification. If they were completely effective, the restrictions wouldn't prevent Icaran entrepreneurs from taking excessive or even fraudulent risks, the first Icarian tendency. Nor would they eliminate competition and the possibility that competitive pressures will magnify an entrepreneur's incentives to go for broke, the second factor. Quite to the contrary, size restrictions can be expected to increase competition, since they reduce the ability of any given company to dominate its industry. But if the size and complexity of corporations are limited, and thus the third Icarus Effect factor is neutralized, the risk of a true Icarus Effect collapse is sharply diminished. The failure of a single, moderately sized corporation, or even a group of such corporations, does not have nearly the same ripple effect on the lives of hundreds or thousands of Americans as the collapse of a behemoth like Jay Cooke's Northern Pacific. Nor is the manager of such a company likely to have the larger-than-life quality that characterized Cooke and the Icaran heroes who would follow. It is the combination of genius and size that produces both the shock and devastation of a full-blown Icarus Effect failure and the subsequent demand for reform. Take away corporate size and the pattern would look very different.

The problem with size limitations, of course, is that they sharply curtail the flexibility of American business. Restricting a Massachusetts mining corporation to $1 million in capital may be highly inefficient, for instance, if the most effective new mining technology calls for large operations and expensive equipment.

The trade-off between giving corporate enterprise the flexibility to expand and consolidate, on the one hand, and keeping the dangerous potential effects of this expansion in check, on the other hand, was the central theme of American corporate life in the closing decades of the nineteenth century. The cat-and-mouse game between crafty business leaders and the lawmakers who wished to rein them in started, like just about everything else, in the railroad industry.

The Battle over Bigness in the Railroad Industry

The capital limitations didn't usually apply to railroads, but *ultra vires* did. This doctrine became a battleground in the 1880s, after a wave of consolidations swept over the railroad industry, triggered in part by the speculative activities of Jay Gould. "No man," as Alfred Chandler puts it, "had a greater impact on the strategy of American railroads than Jay Gould, [the 'Mephistopheles' of Wall Street], the most formidable and best known of the late nineteenth century speculators."[2] After he solidified his control of the Erie, Gould started plotting to take control of the western railroads that were then allied with two other railroads, the Pennsylvania or the New York Central, in order to "assure traffic for the road and at the same time weaken a major competitor." Gould's threat underscored the instability of the alliances that the Pennsylvania and other railroads had formed to prevent opportunists from buying up a crucial link of road between, say, Pittsburgh and Chicago and charging exorbitant rates to other railroads that had no choice but to send passengers or freight over the opportunist's track. In the face of this threat, and the other difficulties with holding a cartel together, the major railroads largely abandoned their informal alliances in the 1870s and 1880s and started purchasing adjoining railroads or building their own, parallel lines, instead.

This is where the *ultra vires* doctrine came in. Corporate law prohibited one corporation from owning the stock of another, so the railroads sometimes used long-term leases to achieve essentially the same effect. If the Pennsylvania wished to acquire an adjoining line, for instance, it might lease all of the other railroad's facilities for a period of, say, a hundred years. (Ninety-nine-year leases are still used today for other reasons, such as the tax benefits available when property is leased rather than owned.) This stratagem was challenged on *ultra vires* grounds, and more often than not the Supreme Court agreed. According to the Court, the lessor railroad—that is, the one that was giving up its facilities—didn't have the power to do this under a corporate charter that characterized the company's business as running a railroad.[3]

If the battles were taking place today, conservatives would no doubt be cheering on the railroads, defending them as they grew bigger and bigger, whereas liberals would view big business as a threat. But in the late nineteenth century, many conservatives (including a majority of the Supreme Court, as the *ultra vires* decisions suggest) viewed large-scale corporate enterprise with deep suspicion. When free marketeers dreamed of markets, they imagined individual entrepreneurs and small businesses contracting with one another. The large railroads and the great corporate trusts didn't fit neatly within this conception; they seemed more like little bureaucracies than real markets. It didn't help when a socialist like Edward Bellamy praised precisely the attributes that made big business worrisome to conservatives. The increasing consolidation, Bellamy argued, "is a result of the increase in the efficiency of capital in great masses." "The few economists who still seriously defend the competitive system are heroically sacrificing their reputations in the effort to mask the evacuation of a position which, as nobody knows better than our hard-headed captains of industry, has become untenable."[4]

Most conservatives would come around by the end of the nineteenth century, and many of the legal obstacles to consolidation would drop away, but the emergence of large-scale business in America was a rocky transition even for these eventual allies of "our hard-headed captains of industry."

The Rise of J. P. Morgan as Market Intermediary

The consolidation of American business wasn't effected entirely by railroad barons and the captains of industry like John Rockefeller and Andrew Carnegie whom we will consider in more detail below. Investment banks—most prominently, the Morgan banks, J. P. Morgan & Co. in London and Drexel, Morgan in the United States—pitched in by providing both financing and corporate expertise for many of the consolidations. After gradually taking over for his father Junius Morgan in the late 1870s and 1880s, J. Pierpont Morgan (usually known as J. P. or Pierpont Morgan) would become the greatest and most feared banker in the history of American finance. From middle age onward he "wore a drooping grizzled mustache," in the words of a recent biographer, "and his overgrown eyebrows arched up like wide-angled Gothic vaults." Most startling of all was his nose, which had been turned into a "hideous purple bulb" by a disease known as rhinophyma. These features were combined with a piercing stare that the photographer Edward Steichen later described as "like looking into the lights of an oncoming express train."[5]

The ascendancy of the Morgan banks began in earnest after the end of the Civil War. For much of the 1870s, the Morgans competed with Jay Cooke and Company for supremacy in the market for selling government bonds. In 1879, the Morgan partners shut down their government-bond operation altogether, and the bankers turned all of their attention to the railroads.[6]

As much as American securities markets had grown since the early nineteenth century, they were still quite illiquid and undeveloped, and enormous information problems remained. "Rumor was the nectar of Wall Street on which traders and journalists alike fed," one historian notes, "the former to nourish their schemes and the latter to spice their columns."[7] The contribution of Morgan and a small group of other investment banks was to provide a substitute to investors for direct information about the market. Although investors couldn't know for sure what was going on in any given railroad or industrial corporation, Morgan offered an implicit promise that it marketed—or, to use the investment-banking term, "underwrote"—only the securities of railroads (and later, other corporations) that could be trusted. The Morgan bankers put the banks' reputation on the line every time they offered an issuance of stock or bonds for sale. If the managers of the corporation turned out to be swindlers, investors would keep this in mind the next time a Morgan partner hit the streets hawking another corporation's stock or bonds.

In its early years, the Morgan bankers particular specialty was marketing American railroad bonds in Europe. As the railroads expanded, their cash needs were far too great to be satisfied solely by the local investors who had financed the earlier roads, and or even by the wealthy investors in the major east coast cities. They needed to tap the European market as well. If the ups and downs of Wall Street were baffling even to American investors, it is easy to imagine the trepidation with which European investors viewed the chaotic American securities markets. Wall Street was foreign in every sense of the word, much as Asia and other emerging markets seem foreign to us today. As in Asian markets, there were profitable securities to buy on Wall Street, but it was hard to tell from a distance what was what. This is where the Morgan partners came in. The original bank was in London, where Pierpont's father Junius had set up shop with George Peabody in 1854, and it used this office to help European investors separate the wheat from the chaff.

The Morgan partners' seal of approval didn't guarantee that everything would turn up roses, of course. Even if Pierpont Morgan's men steered investors toward quality railroad bonds, some of these railroads would later fail. This was unavoidable in a market where as much as 20 percent of America's track was in default at various points in the late nineteenth century. But the decision of the Morgan banks to market a corporation's securities meant that the odds of being taken to the cleaners were much lower than average, and the odds of success high.

Morgan and his partners were more than simply the Warren Buffett or Peter Lynch of their time, however. They weren't just picking stocks for investors. The Morgan bankers took an active interest in the governance of a company even after they had sold its stock or bonds to investors. Morgan partners regularly served as directors of their clients, and if the company failed, the bankers stepped in to help restructure its obligations. They also were a great believer in consolidation. Morgan partners seemed to roam to and fro across the world of American business, looking for railroads and other businesses that could be combined into larger enterprises. In the 1890s, when railroad competition was at its fiercest, Pierpont Morgan and his partners intervened to rescue the Northern Pacific, which was controlled by railroad magnate Henry Villard; brokered a deal to end a battle between the Pennsylvania and the New York Central, two of the nation's major trunk lines; and attempted to arrange an industry-wide truce in 1888, shortly after the enactment of the Interstate Commerce Act. The list of non-railroad trusts with the banks' fingerprints on them was long and eventually included the Steel Trust, the Harvester Trust, and the Shipping Trust.

In effect, the Morgan banks and their peers, which were later dubbed the "Money Trust" by hostile Progressives like Louis Brandeis, served as the first "watcher" of America's large-scale corporations. The Morgan partners kept a tight rein on the managers of the companies in their corporate stable and, as a result, sharply reduced the likelihood that an Icaran manager would take excessive risks with the company's assets. Nowhere was this influence more colorfully in view than in the banks' relationship with Thomas Edison, which we will discuss in more detail in chapter 3. Morgan partner S. B. Easton concluded that Edison's quest to establish centralized electricity plants, rather than relying on a network of scattered local plants, was too risky, a disagreement that provoked a pitched battle within the company that eventually became General Electric. Pierpont Morgan and his partners preferred industry consolidation and steady growth rather than bold and risky schemes. In the vast majority of the companies that the powerful banks financed—including, in the end, GE—this was the strategy that prevailed.

The Great Merger Wave and America's Giant Trusts

During the 1880s and thereafter, the consolidation trend reached nearly every American industry. No one figured more prominently in the efforts to evade the obstacles that stood in the way than John D. Rockefeller. "At night," when Rockefeller was young, "he had read the Bible, and retiring had the odd habit of talking to his pillow about his business adventures." He was "handsome," according to one account, "his eyes small, birdlike; on his pale bony cheeks were the proverbial side-whiskers, reddish in color." From his earliest years in Cleveland, Rockefeller plotted to become rich, starting in the produce business before turning to oil.[9]

Both by contract and by intimidation, Rockefeller brought many of the nation's independent oil producers together under one roof, the Standard Oil Company trust, in 1882. Inspired by Rockefeller's example, the H. O. Havemeyer family linked together seventeen different sugar refineries into a single entity, American Sugar Refining, in 1887. (Not one to leave matters to chance, Havemeyer also benefited from a protective tariff, courtesy of Congress, as well as a collusive arrangement with the customs officials charged with weighing the sugar for taxation purposes.) By the end of the decade, there were already "approximately 100 such associations, in whiskey, sugar, tobacco, cattle feed, beef, wire nails and even bicycles and electric appliances."[10]

Populists—and, as noted earlier, even some conservatives—
viewed the emergence of the trusts with great alarm. State corporate law put a variety of hurdles in the way of the consolidations,
as we have seen, but the hurdles weren't stopping "our hard-
headed captains of industry" and their banks from forming their
monopolies. Indeed, the trust mechanism itself was vivid evidence of their ingenuity. State law prohibited corporations from
owning stock in another corporation, so Rockefeller's lawyers
achieved essentially the same effect by arranging for the controlling stockholders in each of the companies in a cartel to contribute their stock to a newly established trust. In return, the
stockholders were given trust receipts, which functioned just like
stock in a combined corporation would.

In 1890, Populist lawmakers and their allies persuaded Congress to enact the Sherman Act, which thrust Congress into the
antitrust business for the first time. The heart of the act consists
of two admirably succinct sections, which are worth quoting directly. Section 1 states that "every contract, combination in the
form of trust or otherwise, or conspiracy, in restraint of trade or
commerce among the several States, or with foreign nations, is
declared to be illegal." And section 2 states that "EVERY person
who shall monopolize, or attempt to monopolize, or combine or
conspire with any other person or persons, to monopolize any
part of the trade or commerce among the several States, or with
foreign nations, shall be deemed guilty of a felony."

As these sections suggest, the Sherman Act was framed in the
broadest of terms. Rather than attempting to spell out the boundaries of permissible and impermissible combinations, Congress
simply declared that combinations "in restraint of trade" (section
1) and monopolization (section 2) were illegal. In other sections,
the statute provides for triple damages and the payment of plain-
tiffs' attorneys fees, both of which are designed to encourage private parties to enforce the act. The statute was a tremendous
manifestation of the long-standing American hostility to concen-

trated economic power and a signal legislative victory of the American Populist movement. What was far less clear—and has continued to generate debate ever since—was how courts would interpret the key terms of the act. What exactly counted as a "restraint of trade" or an "attempt to monopolize"?[11]

The first great Supreme Court decision interpreting the Sherman Act came five years later. In 1895, the Court decided the *Knight* Sugar case, a challenge to the American Sugar Refining Company monopoly. The sugar trust had a monopoly that was nearly as pure as Dove soap—it controlled more than 98% of the nation's sugar refining after acquiring the stock of every one of its significant competitors. It is hard to imagine a more complete monopoly. Yet the Supreme Court held that the trust was beyond the reach of the Sherman Act. The Court conceded that the sugar trust functioned as a restraint, but the Court drew a sharp line between restraints on manufacturing and restraints on commerce. Because most of the trust's refining capacity was located in a single state, Pennsylvania, and because the contracts used to create the trust were contracts to purchase the stock of competitors, rather than contracts "to buy, sell, or exchange goods to be transported among the several states," the sugar trust did not directly interfere with "commerce among the states," as the Sherman Act required. "The object was manifestly private gain in the manufacture of the commodity," as the Court put it, "but not through the control of interstate or foreign commerce."[12]

The *Knight* decision struck a devastating blow to those who had hoped for aggressive enforcement of the Sherman Act. Despite the facts that the Sherman Act was enacted with the trusts in mind and that the sugar trust completely monopolized American sugar refining, the Court declined to intervene. In the words of a later observer, the *Knight* case "had shown once for all that the government had no intention of prosecuting the Trusts. . . . In the next five years, there were three thousand such monopolies formed, many of which sprang almost at birth to giant size."[13]

Now, the *Knight* case did not mean that America's industrialists could simply ignore the Sherman Act as they consolidated their industries. Indeed, some commentators conclude that the decision was an attempt by the Court to preserve state authority over antitrust issues, not an assault on the idea of prohibiting monopolies.[14] The Court had emphasized that the trust's manufacturing capacity was centered in the state of Pennsylvania and that the only contracts that implicated more than one state were contracts to purchase stock of companies incorporated in different states. It was still possible that contracts involving the operations of competitors located in different states, rather than just the sale of their stock, would be viewed as affecting interstate commerce. And the Supreme Court soon concluded precisely this, ruling in 1896 and 1898 that companies that entered into agreements to fix prices or divvy up the market in an industry had violated the Sherman Act if the companies were not located in a single state.[15]

The Role of State Corporate Law

The Supreme Court's interpretation of the Sherman Act created a division of labor of sorts between Congress and the states when it came to antitrust matters. If the competitors in an industry made a deal to fix prices, this would qualify as a contract in restraint of trade and would thus be fair game for enforcement under the Sherman Act. But if the monopoly was assembled under a single corporate umbrella—as a single corporation and its subsidiaries, as with Rockefeller's Standard Oil, rather than contracts among separate corporations—it fell into the lap of state lawmakers. Only if both the federal government and its state counterparts aggressively patrolled their side of the antitrust line would the trust movement be brought to a halt.

As it turned out, state lawmakers—or at least, lawmakers in the states that mattered—sided with the trusts rather than with those who opposed them. Under traditional corporate-law statutes, as noted earlier, corporations could not own stock in other corporations, which precluded would-be consolidators from using a holding-company structure consisting of a parent corporation and a series of subsidiaries. New Jersey had fixed this problem by changing the rule in 1889 (it was no accident that Standard Oil was incorporated in New Jersey), an innovation whose significance in the subsequent history of American business is hard to overstate. Once corporations were permitted to own stock in other companies, the corporate entity could be shaped in an almost infinite variety of ways, from a single corporate entity to vast webs of interconnected entities. As important as this rule was for the nineteenth-century trusts, it would become far more significant—for both good and ill—in the century that followed.

In 1896, New Jersey enacted a revolutionary new corporate-law statute that gave corporations almost complete flexibility to structure their company however they pleased. In addition to giving them the right to hold stock in other corporations, New Jersey permitted corporations to define their business broadly, which diminished the significance of the *ultra vires* doctrine (once you're permitted to define your corporation as "doing any lawful business," nothing the corporation might do will be out of bounds). The New Jersey statute also eliminated any requirement that the directors be New Jersey residents, and it authorized corporations to hold their meetings wherever they wished, in state or out. The New Jersey changes reflect a pattern that has continued to characterize American corporate and financial life ever since: much more than Congress, state lawmakers, particularly in leading corporate states, tend to accommodate the perceived needs of America's largest corporations by adjusting the regulatory framework to keep pace with changes in the business world.

New Jersey's defenders argued that the state was simply giving corporations the same treatment as natural persons were entitled to. In a speech to the American Bar Association, Edward Keasbey, a prominent corporate lawyer, explained that New Jersey "adopts the principle that men, when associated as partners or in joint-stock companies under the name of corporations, should be allowed all the liberty that is consistent with public safety and order; that freedom of contract is an essential part of the liberty of the citizen, and that the largest practicable freedom of the individual is for the best interest of the community."[16] (This same emphasis on "freedom of contract" would be used in the early twentieth century to strike down Progressive-era legislation that was designed to improve working conditions for American employees. Employees should have the right, the reasoning went, to agree to work sixteen-hour days or seven-day weeks in stultifying factories if they "wanted" to.)

There is of course a simple political explanation as well. So long as the rights and obligations of the shareholders and directors of a corporation are defined by the state where the corporation is incorporated, as they are under a doctrine known as the "internal affairs" doctrine, attracting corporations can be a lucrative business. The state can receive "franchise" taxes from the corporations it charters, in return for an implicit promise that the state will be mindful of the concerns of the corporations that fly under its flag.

During the heyday of the great trusts, several other states competed with New Jersey to attract corporations in general and to offer a haven for the new trusts in particular. Virginia, according to an early critic, "became a 'Snug Harbor' for roaming and piratical corporations," and West Virginia did its best to establish itself as a "Mecca of irresponsible corporations." But the clear winner was New Jersey, the "Mother of Trusts." In the first seven months of 1899 alone, 1,336 corporations set up shop in New Jersey.[17]

Woodrow Wilson and the Progressive Movement

When we think of corporations today, New Jersey isn't usually the state that comes to mind. Delaware is. Let me jump ahead for a moment to explain why: the reason for the switch, which would come a little more than a decade into the twentieth century, was Woodrow Wilson and Progressivism.

At the outset of the twentieth century, the Progressive movement emerged as a counterpart of sorts to Populism. Progressivism had much more of an aristocratic cast—many of its advocates were well-to-do men and women in the Northeast—but it focused attention on the plight of those at the same end of the economic spectrum as did the Populists. Progressives campaigned for a wide range of laws that were designed to improve the living and working conditions of lower-class workers, such as child labor and maximum-workweek laws.

Wilson, who was closely identified with the Progressive movement, was persuaded to run for governor of New Jersey by prominent Democrats who believed the Princeton president had presidential potential. After his election in 1910, Wilson took aim at the corporate trusts, proposing a group of laws known as the "Seven Sisters" that were designed to give New Jersey state regulators more power to crack down on monopoly. By the time the laws were enacted in early 1913, Wilson was the nation's president-elect.

America's great corporations, most of which were incorporated in New Jersey, took one look at the restrictive new laws and said, in effect, thanks but no thanks. They hopped on the turnpike and drove down to Delaware to reincorporate. Delaware had been grooming itself to serve as New Jersey's understudy for some time—by adopting a replica of New Jersey's statute in 1896, for instance—and was more than happy to step into the spotlight. Delaware welcomed the exiled trusts with open arms and has maintained the embrace ever since.

The Shift to Investor Capitalism

As the nation's business leaders devised ways to maneuver around the strictures imposed by the Sherman Act and by state law restrictions on corporate expansion, corporate America unleashed a merger wave that was unprecedented and never again equaled until the go-go years of the late twentieth century. Between 1897 and 1903, "more than 1,800 firms disappeared and well over half of the resulting consolidations absorbed over 40 per cent of their respective industries."[18]

The great merger wave dramatically altered American investment patterns in two crucial ways. The first effect was quite similar to the effect that the railroads' expansion had had on railroad ownership several decades earlier. The corporations that joined forces to create a new industry juggernaut were often local companies that were controlled by a local individual or family and the remainder of whose stock was owned by local investors. Once the firms were merged, this local orientation began to disappear. The new, bigger business was now owned by shareholders from a variety of locales. Moreover, the manager-owners who had controlled a local company, but would not be running the new larger enterprise, often sought to sell some or all of their shares after the merger. Investors snapped up the stock as it became available, at least in part because they anticipated that the newly consolidated companies would enjoy monopoly profits in their industries.

The second effect was a shift from real estate to corporate stock and debt as the investment of choice for relatively well-to-do Americans who had extra money to invest. For much of the nineteenth century, most Americans who had a taste for speculation dabbled in land. The famous Massachusetts Senator Daniel Webster, for instance, was forever buying new plots of western land in the hope of striking it rich. Land was plentiful, and the westward expansion of the nation meant that well-situated property was likely to be increasingly valuable.

Plenty of gambling took place on the stock market, too, but almost the only stocks and bonds traded on the New York Stock Exchange were railroad securities. "The very term 'industrials,'" as two business historians note, "did not come into use until [nearly 1890], and even then it generally appeared in quotation marks." But by the turn of the century, several dozen industrial corporations were traded on the New York Stock Exchange, which gave investors more securities options than ever before. These years "marked an abrupt change in the trend of investments, for thenceforth and continuing down to the present, industrial stocks gained increasing prominence as an investment for the nation's savings."[19]

As with real estate, investors who bought industrial securities knew that their money was at risk—there was no guarantee of success. But as the depth of the stock market increased—with a wider variety of stocks to buy and sell, and shares changing hands more frequently—the volatility of market prices declined. (Wild price swings occur less frequently and the risk of manipulation by speculators like Daniel Drew or Jim Fisk decreases when stock changes hands all the time. Economists refer to this quality as market "liquidity.") This increased stability attracted increasing numbers of Americans to the markets and signaled the dawning of the age of investor capitalism.

The advent of investor capitalism complicated the politics of corporate and financial regulation. As more Americans participated in the markets, they strengthened the constituency that supported the growth of large corporations. The new corporate behemoths were worrisome, but an increasing number of Americans—most of them relatively wealthy but some of them ordinary Americans as well—now had a stake in the stability and success of corporations like U.S. Steel, International Harvester, and AT&T.

Teddy Roosevelt's Trust-Busting Campaign

The battle over corporate combinations didn't end after New Jersey rolled out the red carpet for the great corporate trusts. The first decade of the twentieth century saw the greatest challenge yet to the hegemony of America's Gilded Age industrialists. In 1901, President William McKinley was felled by an assassin's bullet. McKinley, who had twice defeated Populist Democratic candidate William Jennings Bryan, had grown increasingly concerned by the explosive tensions between America's corporate empires and the nascent labor movement. (The Knights of Labor waged successful strikes against several major railroads in the 1880s, but suffered a steep decline in membership after a deadly standoff with police in Haymarket Square in Chicago in 1886. Thereafter, the less radical American Federation of Labor, headed by Samuel Gompers, became the leading labor organization.) But McKinley hadn't taken any concrete action to rein in the trusts. With McKinley's death, all eyes turned to Theodore Roosevelt, who had achieved fame leading the Rough Riders in the Spanish American War and since then, in the words of one business historian, was "considered to be happily 'shelved' in the vice presidency." Born of New York aristocracy, Roosevelt traveled in the same circles as Pierpont Morgan, John D. Rockefeller, and the other corporate titans. But during his tenure as governor of New York, Roosevelt had established a reputation as a Progressive and a reformer after taking on Jay Gould in a fight over control of New York's elevated trolley system.[20]

After Roosevelt took over, "all possible pressure was brought on the White House from quarters near and far." Mark Hanna, the powerful head of the Republican party, warned Roosevelt to be "close-mouthed and conservative" and to "go slow." Hanna and his allies were soon disappointed. Before his first year in office had come to a close, Roosevelt started making secret plans to attack the "malefactors of great wealth," the "mighty industrial overlords of the country"[21] who now controlled so much of the nation's production. In the public mind, the greatest malefactor of all was the just-formed Northern Securities Corporation, a veritable who's who of American finance and industry. After a battle between the nation's two transcontinental railroads, Cooke's old Northern Pacific Railroad (which was now controlled by Jim Hill and Pierpont Morgan) and the Union Pacific (which featured E. H. Harriman, John D. Rockefeller, and prominent investment bank Kuhn, Loeb), the warring factions had come to an agreement in the fall of 1901. A corporation was formed in New Jersey (which was still, at this point, the land of corporate opportunity), and the two sides exchanged their stock for stakes in the new holding company, Northern Securities Corporation. Almost before the ink on the stock certificates was dry, Roosevelt jumped in. In January 1902, shortly after Minnesota brought a state law action to force the dissolution of the Northern Securities Corporation, Roosevelt's attorney general followed suit under the Sherman Act. At first, Morgan treated the litigation as an unfortunate misunderstanding. "If we have done anything wrong," he reportedly told the president, "send your man [meaning the attorney general] to my man [naming one of his lawyers] and they can fix it up." Roosevelt refused to "fix it up." ("That is a most illuminating illustration of the Wall Street point of view," he marveled. "Mr. Morgan could not help regarding me as a rival operator, who either intended to ruin all his interests or else could be induced to come to an agreement to ruin none.") And his Justice Department fought it out in the courts for two years, before the Supreme Court finally handed down a 5-4 decision ordering that the Northern Securities Corporation be dissolved. Roosevelt had won.[22]

For his part, Morgan never forgave Roosevelt's impudence. Some years later, upon learning that Roosevelt was taking a hunting trip to Africa, Morgan commented to a friend that "I hope the first lion he meets does his duty."

Teddy Roosevelt's Foray into Campaign Finance

Although the trust-busting campaign is Teddy Roosevelt's best-remembered challenge to the increasing dominance of corporate America, he led another important charge after the 1904 election. In his 1905 state of the union address, Roosevelt announced that the time had come for election reform. The flagrant bribery and "sales" of securities to newspapermen and politicians of the early railroad years had disappeared—or at the least were less prevalent—but the nation's largest corporations seemed to be achieving similar objectives by helping to finance the political process. Corporate largesse had dominated the 1904 election and seemed to make a mockery of the democratic process. Distancing corporations from American politics, Roosevelt made clear, would be a major objective of his new term. The subjects of regulation should not have so much influence over their regulators.

Despite his reputation as a corporate reformer, Roosevelt was an unlikely champion of campaign-finance reform. He was the one who had benefited most from the fact that, as a congressional reformer put it several years later, "some of the great corporations of this country, in order to corrupt the electorates of this Republic, took from their treasuries in the last national campaign many thousands of dollars."[23] As unhappy as the corporate trusts were with Roosevelt, they still much preferred him to Judge Alton B. Parker, the Democratic candidate for president, and most of the contributions went to Roosevelt's Republican party. Indeed, Parker made corporate contributions a major issue of the 1904 campaign, accusing corporate America of buying influence with the president and Congress, each of which was in Republican hands. Roosevelt hadn't helped matters by choosing George Cortelyou, a former secretary of commerce and labor, to lead the Republican National Committee. Cortelyou's new post put him in the position of raising money from the same corporations he had previously regulated.[24]

Like Bill Clinton in our own time, Teddy Roosevelt knew a parade when he saw one. He didn't let his status as a beneficiary of the corporate largesse stop him from jumping on the campaign-finance bandwagon as soon as the election was over. In his sixth annual message, on December 3, 1906, campaign-finance reform was the first item on Roosevelt's agenda. "I again recommend a law prohibiting all corporations from contributing to the campaign expenses of any party," he told the assembled lawmakers. "Let individuals contribute as they desire; but let us prohibit in effective fashion all corporations from making contributions for any political purpose, directly or indirectly."[25]

The following year, Congress answered Roosevelt's call by enacting America's first major campaign-finance legislation, the 1907 Tillman Act. The Tillman Act, which inspired similar state legislation in many states, prohibits corporations from making contributions directly to political candidates. Nearly a century later, as we wrestle with campaign finance anew, these prohibitions, which were extended to labor unions as well in the late 1940s, still lie at the heart of our regulation of corporate campaign contributions.

Roosevelt proposed to diminish corporate influence over the regulatory process—over regulators' efforts to rein in the Icaran tendencies in American business—in another way as well: by shifting the regulatory mantle away from New Jersey and other states. "It can not be too often repeated," Roosevelt said at the conclusion of this sixth annual address,

that experience has conclusively shown the impossibility of securing by the actions of nearly half a hundred different State legislatures anything but ineffective chaos in the way of dealing with the great corporations which do not operate exclusively within the limits of any one State. In some method, whether by national license law or in other fashion, we must exercise, and that at an early date, a far more complete control than at present over these great corporations. . . . This will tend to put a stop to the securing of inordinate profits by favored individuals at the expense whether of the general public, the stockholders, or the wageworkers.[26]

If Congress took over the regulation of corporate law—deciding whether to permit businesses to incorporate and regulating their conduct—the nation's largest corporations might be subject to much closer scrutiny. Not only does Congress have broader regulatory authority than any of the states, but it also would not curry the favor of corporations. But the more stringent regulation would also come with a cost: Congress would be less likely to keep pace with business innovation.

Surprisingly enough, many businesses supported federal incorporation after the Panic of 1907, hoping that this strategy might stabilize the business environment. But farm and labor leaders complained that the proposed bill would insulate big business from antitrust scrutiny, and many lawmakers worried that it gave too much power to the federal government. The proposal proved to be too radical for its time, and nothing came of it during the Roosevelt era.[27]

Historians have long debated the efficacy of Roosevelt's efforts and of the Progressive movement of which he was so visible a representative. His trust-busting obviously didn't end the hegemony of the great American industrialists or eliminate corporate America's influence over the political process. The Progressive movement had an enormous impact in the first decade of the twentieth century—ushering in the income tax and reforms of American work life in addition to the corporate campaigns we have discussed—but it began to fade thereafter. Roosevelt, according to a Depression-era assessment of the corporate industrialists, had "placed himself at the head of the extraordinary mass movement of protest, which after 1901 swept the country in a great wave, a wave that had swept it before, like the cyclones of Kansas, the grasshopper pests of the Northwest or the droughts, quite native to the climate, but leaving it afterward fundamentally unchanged and as much like itself as before."[28]

This is a trifle unfair. Roosevelt's trust-busting campaign helped, at the least, to slow the monopoly movement. It was followed, in 1911 and 1912, by a scandal in New York and several weeks of high profile hearings scrutinizing the involvement of insurance companies and other financial institutions in the governance of large corporations. These hearings, conducted by the House banking and Currency subcommittee under Louisiana Congressman Arsène Pujo attempted to document the existence of a "money trust." Louis Brandeis, a well-known Progressive lawyer and future Supreme Court justice, seized this opportunity to write a series of magazine articles, later published as the influential book *Other People's Money*, which pointed out that Pierpont Morgan's partners sat on hundreds of corporate boards. Chastened by the firestorm of protest, Morgan's partners stepped down from all of the boards, though the Money Trust continued to dominate American corporate finance. Although the trust-busting campaign, the Pujo hearings, and other Progressive efforts had only a limited effect in the short run, they laid the intellectual groundwork for the more sweeping and effective reforms of the New Deal era.[29]

The end of the Roosevelt era saw a major shift in the ongoing dance between lawmakers and the leaders of American business. Rather than attempting to directly control corporate size or complexity—the third Icarus Effect factor—Roosevelt increasingly focused on policing corporations' use of the capital they amassed.

In Roosevelt's vision, the government rather than Pierpont Morgan's banks would be the principal watcher of the nation's largest corporations. The government would prevent monopoly, but it would tolerate enough consolidation to reduce the risk of excessive competition. Both Icaran risk-taking and the danger that corporations would use their vast capital to buy influence would be controlled by close regulatory oversight.

The vision was a plausible one but it was only partially implemented. In part this was due to the limited capacity of the federal regulatory apparatus at the outset of the twentieth century; in part it reflected the lack of political stomach for more extensive governmental intervention. In the meantime, the relationship between the ownership and management of the nation's largest corporations was rapidly changing. The stage would soon be set for the next great Icarus Effect failures and general crisis in American corporate life.

Three Icarus Meets the New Deal

In the late 1920s, Samuel Insull was a corporate superstar. After starting as Thomas Edison's assistant in the 1880s, he had purchased an electricity company in Chicago, revolutionized the delivery of electricity, and built a vast utilities empire. At the turn of the century, he managed to lower prices for his consumers almost every year. During World War I, Insull lent his expertise to the U.S. government, selling more than a billion dollars of government bonds to help finance the war effort; and a decade later, he almost single-handedly raised the money to finance the new forty-two-story home of the Chicago Civic Opera Company. In the minds of many, Insull was living proof of the proposition that one could do both good and well in the optimistic world of 1920s America.[1]

By 1932, as the nation struggled with the effect of the 1929 Crash and the Depression that followed, Samuel Insull stood for a very different proposition. In one of his most famous speeches,

Franklin D. Roosevelt railed against the "Ishmael or Insull whose hand is against every man's." During the summer of 1932, shortly before Roosevelt's presidential contest with Herbert Hoover began in earnest, Insull's vast empire had collapsed, and his collapse seemed to epitomize the excesses of American business, excesses that manifested themselves in mystifying new manipulations of the corporate form.

If captains of American industry like Insull were one major target of Roosevelt's ire, the other was the Wall Street banks that continued to dominate American finance. What the nation needed, Roosevelt argued, was to completely restructure corporate America, to make it safe for ordinary Americans to return to the market. By the end of the New Deal, Roosevelt would achieve his wish. The New Deal reformers would transform American business and finance with a series of legislative initiatives that took aim at all three Icaran factors, risktaking, competition, and the misuse of corporate size and complexity. But it took a complete breakdown of American corporate life, punctuated by Insull's spectacular Icarus Effect collapse, to make the reforms possible.

The Rise of the Berle-Means Corporation

The roots of the corporate and financial crisis that dominated the 1932 presidential campaign went much further back than the 1929 Crash, of course. Corporate wealth was increasingly concentrated, and control of this wealth was being placed in fewer and fewer—and sometimes unscrupulous—hands. Shortly before the campaign heated up, Adolf Berle and Gardiner Means, a Columbia University law professor and economist, respectively, offered some historical perspective and an unsettling diagnosis concerning one important part of the problem—America's giant corporations—in *The Modern Corporation and Private Property*, a book that is universally viewed as the most important book ever written about American corporate law.

Looking out over the corporate landscape of the first two decades of the twentieth century, Berle and Means found a startling pattern. In a remarkable number of the nation's largest corporations, there was a vast separation between the shareholders, who theoretically owned the corporation, and the managers who ran it. In the nineteenth century, a corporation's shareholders and managers had usually been the same people, as is still true of most small businesses today. But even in companies with professional managers, like the railroads, shareholders invariably exercised significant managerial oversight. Corporate voting was a direct democracy, the business equivalent of a New England town meeting. Indeed, until well into the twentieth century, it was illegal to pay the directors of the corporation. Courts assumed that the directors would all be substantial shareholders and that their shareholding stake was the directors' real interest in the business.[2] When Berle and Means surveyed the nation's largest corporations, however, they found that corporate democracy didn't look much like democracy anymore.

To be sure, shareholders still were the ones who elected the company's directors, but Berle and Means didn't believe that these elections amounted to much. Who nominated the company's preferred directors? Well, the managers, of course. Who sent the notice of the shareholders' meeting, described the issues to be considered, and requested that the shareholders send in proxy forms supporting the managers' candidates? The incumbent managers, once again.

The shareholders, moreover, had become as weak as the managers were strong. In 1901, American Telegraph had a total of 10,000 shareholders. By 1931, the number had soared to 642,180, and the largest shareholder owned only 0.34% of AT&T's stock.

The story with America's other large corporations was less dramatic, but similar. Since most shareholders had only a tiny stake in the company and since the managers "controlled the proxy machinery," shareholders simply did what the managers told them. "As his personal vote will count for little or nothing at the meeting," Berle and Means concluded, "the shareholder is practically reduced to the alternative of not voting at all or else of handing over his vote to individuals over whom he has no control and in whose selection he did not participate."[3]

It wasn't just an accident that no one had noticed the separation of ownership and control that Berle and Means documented. The Berle-Means corporation—as corporations that fit this profile have come to be called—was quite new. The great merger wave at the end of the nineteenth century had played a central role in the transformation. When the competitors in an industry merged, the manager-owners of the companies that were being acquired, the little fish in the transaction, were often paid with common and preferred stock, rather than cash. Over time, these managers often sold much or all of their stock, thus helping to scatter its ownership. As corporations needed new capital, moreover, they often raised it by selling still more stock.[4]

In the early decades of the twentieth century, then, all roads led to a radically new corporate ownership profile. "Within [America's corporate system]," Berle and Means warned, "there exists a centripetal attraction which draws wealth together into aggregations of constantly increasing size, at the same time throwing control into the hands of fewer and fewer men. The trend is apparent; and no limit is yet in sight."[5] What Berle and Means didn't pay quite as much attention to in their book is how these great corporations were structured: many consisted of a vast, confusing array of subsidiary corporations. The malleability of the corporate form, the ability to set up as many new corporations as the managers desired, was used, as it turned out, to perpetrate a series of spectacular frauds on American investors.

Icarus and the Berle-Means Corporation

In the empirical phase of their analysis, which focused on America's two hundred largest corporations, Berle and Means found that only 11% were either privately held or had a majority shareholder.[6] Control of all of the other companies was either scattered or held by a minority block of shareholders.

This, of course, is a recipe for disaster. Left unchecked, the Berle-Means corporation is a breeding ground for Icarus Effect failures. If a financial genius can raise millions of dollars by selling stock and other securities and hold onto control with only a small ownership stake, with little oversight from shareholders, the stage is set for Icarus Effect excesses if the company's fortunes take a turn for the worse. The market euphoria of the 1920s magnified the Icaran tendencies in American corporate and financial life both by encouraging American business leaders to believe that they were financial geniuses and by making it easier than ever before to raise huge amounts of capital—both legitimately and through sleight-of-hand manipulations of the corporate entity.

The 1930s saw a wave of stunning failures that fit the Icarus Effect pattern. One of the most spectacular was Ivar Kreuger, the "Swedish match king," who at one time had supplied 75% of the world's matches and later acquired banks, railroads, film companies, and gold mines. The "three central beams of the Kreuger house"—Kreuger and Toll, Swedish Match, and International Match of New York—had been used to disguise, as the poet and statesman Archibald MacLeish put it, "a mesh and tangle of spiderweb subsidiaries. Some of the subsidiaries were real, some were a set of books, some were a name." Kreuger used these fraudulent subsidiaries to obscure his financial condition as he raised money to expand the Kreuger empire throughout the 1920s. The thread that eventually pulled the web apart was a fraudulent bookkeeping entry discovered by auditors for IT&T when Kreuger was negotiating to acquire IT&T through an exchange of stock with one of Kreuger's companies. In their review of Kreuger's books, IT&T's accountants discovered a major entry that was listed as an asset but appeared to be little more than a "claim" against other Kreuger entities. When Kreuger couldn't offer a credible explanation for the accounting, the IT&T deal fell through, Kreuger's access to credit dried up, and his empire quickly unraveled. In March 1932, Kreuger calmly shot himself in the heart in his Paris house. "It was the shot that was heard across the world," a *Toronto Star* reporter later wrote. "He had conned bankers, finance ministers, hundreds of thousands of shareholders in a gigantic fraud involving claims running into billions of dollars." "Few of the few who knew him could describe him well," MacLeish recalled. "What survived was not a head but a manner—an embarrassing trick of talking with the mouth drawn back in a kind of canine grin, a way of twisting the neck, a gracious, gentle courtesy in speech; a man who could talk figures in the four languages of the world."[7]

But it was another crash that exemplified America's crisis more than any other. The crash that spurred Congress into action was Samuel Insull and Middle West Utilities. When Roosevelt railed in 1932 against "the Ishmael or Insull whose hand is against every man's," he lumped Insull with the "reckless promoter" and "unethical competitor" against whom "the Government may properly be asked to apply restraint."[8] That isn't how Insull started. Until things went sour, Insull had been hailed as a business genius, as the leader of what investors thought was the safest of industries, electric power.

The Rise of Edison's Right-Hand Man

Just who was this Insull, this man who epitomized corporate chicanery and greed in the 1930s, the Enron and WorldCom of his era? By birth Insull was an Englishman, but his life and domicile were transformed by a pair of indirect encounters with Thomas Edison. When Insull was barely nineteen, he read a breathless article in *Scribner's Monthly* about Edison's genius as he was preparing for a literary society discussion of self-help; Insull was hooked. Some months later, after having searched out and studied every account of Edison's inventions he could find, Insull responded to an advertisement seeking help for an "American banker." The "banker" turned out to be Edison's European representative. Through him, Insull subsequently met Edward Johnson, Edison's chief engineer. Johnson was so impressed with Insull's acumen and his encyclopedic knowledge about Edison that he maneuvered Insull into Edison's inner circle. Shortly after Johnson was called back to New York in 1881, he persuaded Edison to send for Insull as well.[9]

Starting as Edison's secretary and as "personal flunky of the Great Man," Insull won Edison's confidence and eventually became his principal tactician and advisor. By 1892, Edison's most brilliant inventions were behind him, but the marketability of his patents had skyrocketed, and several rivals were challenging Edison for supremacy in the electricity business. Edison's bankers—the House of Morgan, of course—decided it was time to "rationalize" competition. Toward this end, the Morgan bankers engineered a merger between Edison General Electric and Thomson-Houston Electric Company, its most aggressive competitor. Although he was invited to remain as a second vice president after the merger—the only Edison manager who would retain a high-level post—Insull had no intention of sticking around. He was distinctively underwhelmed by the management of Thomson-Houston, and he had developed a lifelong disdain for the Morgan partners as a result of the merger and an earlier proxy fight between Edison and the bankers. By the time the dust settled and the company we now know as General Electric was born, Insull was gone—off to Chicago.

Although Insull was not an inventor, he too proved to be

an innovative genius. What Edison had been to the discovery of electricity, Insull was to its modern distribution. His initial insight was quite simple; like many brilliant ideas, it seems obvious in retrospect. For several decades, it made him a corporate hero.

Unlike other products, electricity can't be squirreled away for later use. This means that an electric company's plant must be big enough to generate the amount of electricity that is needed at the period of highest demand. Because Insull's residential customers used large amounts of electricity in the morning and evening, but relatively little in between, his plants sat around for much of the day before booming into action in the early evening. Much of the plants' capacity was simply being wasted. Insull's customers didn't really stop using electricity after they left their homes in the morning. During the day, they rode the trolley and rail lines to and from work and throughout the city. But in Chicago, as elsewhere, the urban transit lines produced their own electricity with their own generators. Insull realized that, if he persuaded the transit lines to let him supply their electricity for them, he could keep his plants humming around the clock. Insull loaded up his briefcase with projections proving that, by operating his plants all day, he could generate electricity much more cheaply than could the transit companies themselves. One by one, the companies came into his fold. (Long before historians mistakenly attributed the phrase to Henry Ford, Insull referred to his strategy of maximizing output in order to reduce per unit costs as "massing production.")[10]

At the same time, Insull vastly expanded his residential customer base by selling electricity at lower and lower prices. The average rate for Insull's residential customers was roughly 20 cents a kilowatt hour in the early 1890s, then fell to 10 cents by 1897, to 5 cents in 1906, and to 2.5 cents in 1909. "By the turn of the century," Insull's biographer writes, few men in the industry could be regarded as his equal. "By 1910, all men in the business walked in his shadow; others in the industry sometimes spoke of him, as did his employees, as 'The Chief.'"[11]

Around Chicago, Insull cut a figure as large as his business empire. With his distinctive white moustache—which he grew to disguise the fact that "when he was startled or puzzled, . . . he inadvertently curled his upper lip, as if sneering"—Insull could be seen at every performance of the Chicago Civic Opera Company; and in the 1920s, he would finance and build a forty-two-floor office building on the bank of the Chicago River to house a new home for the opera—a building that Chicagoans referred to as "Insull's throne." He also took up yachting. As with Enron's Kenneth Lay in Houston seventy years later, if there was an important Chicago charity event, Insull was likely to be there.[12]

Insull and the Holding-Company Strategy

But Insull could never simply stand still. No doubt this stemmed in part from a built-in thirst for expansion, for new financial adventure. Insull's biographer also attributes his restlessness to a decision in 1912 by his wife Gladys, a beautiful former actress who didn't like sex, that they would never again make love.[13]

But as with Jay Cooke before him and each Icarus Effect failure since, Insull also was driven by constant external pressures. To lock up control of the Chicago-area electricity market, Insull had to diffuse the political opposition that his steadily increasing power provoked. Insull devoted much of his energy to heading off reforms that might otherwise open up the market; this often meant greasing a well-placed palm. To fend off an initiative to end his monopoly on urban transit in 1930, for instance, Insull set aside $500,000 to be "deliver[ed] to the appropriate politicians" in connection with the vote.[14]

Insull also faced challenges from other utility companies. Insull's strategy for outmaneuvering potential competitors, and for maintaining his extraordinary profits, was to buy up many of the smaller electricity companies around him. By 1907, Insull had acquired twenty additional utilities as he tried to swallow each new competitor, like the pac-man in the 1980s computer game. In addition to enlarging Insull's electricity empire, the acquisitions also drew him into other industries. "Since so many local plants provided gas, water, streetcar or ice service as well as electricity," his biographer notes, Insull "often found [himself] wandering into these businesses while buying an electric plant." By the end of World War I, the tentacles of his empire reached into thirteen states.[15]

Notice the Icaran pattern in Insull's rise. The success of his innovations fed his already gargantuan ego, and Insull used the enormous capital of his enterprise to quite literally buy off the lawmakers who were supposed to be exercising oversight over the utilities industry. Insull was a throwback to the robber-baron era, to the business titans who bribed lawmakers who were responsible for preventing manipulation and fraud and for policing the competitive conditions of the marketplace. But Insull also used a very up-to-date strategy to maintain control over his empire.

On paper, Insull actually owned only a minority stake in his utilities conglomerate. The vulnerability of this status was merely hypothetical until Cyrus Eaton, a well-known investment banker, started buying stock in Insull's companies in late 1927. When Insull learned that Eaton had acquired 80,000 shares of stock, he became convinced that Eaton was gearing up for a hostile raid to take control of the Insull empire. In the face of this threat, Insull took several drastic steps. The most direct was to buy back Eaton's stock at a handsome premium. First, however, Insull ratcheted up a process he had begun before Eaton entered the scene—turning his empire into a network of interconnected corporations or "pyramid." Near the top of Insull's pyramid were four main companies: Middle West Utilities (a corporation that

Insull had formed fifteen years earlier to consolidate part of his empire), Commonwealth Edison (the core of his early Chicago electricity holdings), Peoples Gas (the largest Chicago gas company), and Public Service. Insull owned a large but minority stake in these companies, and each of the companies controlled still other companies themselves. During the Eaton crisis, Insull transferred his stakes in each of the four major companies to a pair of trusts, Insull Utility Investments and Corporation Securities Company of Chicago, and used voting agreements with the friends and family members who also held stock to begin assembling a controlling interest in each of the two trusts.[16]

Insull's pyramiding arrangement was complex, but the basic idea is quite simple: if an entrepreneur controls the company at the top of a pyramid, and this company has a controlling stake in the subsidiary corporations at the next level of the pyramid, and so on, the entrepreneur can end up controlling a large empire with a surprisingly small stake. Ordinarily, the entrepreneur will need a 51% majority at each level, but if the stock is held by thousands of small stockholders, a much smaller stake may be enough to assure practical control. Think of the corporate structure as a marionette. So long as the entrepreneur holds the strings at the top, he can control how all of the other pieces move. "This control," as Congressman Sam Rayburn explained in a subsequent congressional hearing, "is exercised through a maze of intercorporate relationships quite confusing to the understanding of ordinary men. In fact, these arrangements are often made for the very purpose of avoiding the understanding and scrutiny of the common man."[17] By setting up a web of separate subsidiaries, Insull could sell securities in each of the independent entities without jeopardizing his overall control. The ordinary investors who bought stock or bonds thought they were dealing with the overall Insull enterprise, but in reality many had invested in a financially precarious subsidiary. They didn't realize it, but they were playing a shell game.

The business titans of the 1920s had John D. Rockefeller to thank for this strategy, of course. By persuading New Jersey to permit corporations to own stock in other corporations back in 1889, he had created the opening that invited the holding-company excesses of Insull and other business leaders of the 1920s.

Now, there were and are legitimate reasons for permitting corporations to set up separate subsidiaries for different parts of their overall business. A manufacturer of cameras can use a separate subsidiary to develop software applications, for instance, so that the risks of the new software project are kept separate from the camera business, and vice versa. So long as the company's shareholders and creditors are aware that the corporate entities are distinct, keeping them separate can benefit everyone. Creditors can specialize in monitoring one part of the business or the other, and the corporate boundaries make it harder for managers to shuttle money back and forth. But holding companies can also be used to obfuscate. Corporate disclosure obligations were quite limited in the 1920s, and it was all too easy for Insull and other utility executives to play bait-and-switch. They set up separate subsidiaries so that they could continuing raising huge amounts of cash even after their business had begun to founder. "So lucrative was the holding company structure that their number increased from 102 to 180 between 1922 and 1927," according to one account. "By 1932, only eight holding companies controlled almost three-quarters of the investor-owned utility business. Perhaps best of all for the holding companies, their operations usually were exempt from the investigation of state regulatory commissions, since so much of their business crossed state boundaries."[18]

Insull's failure to retain a full 50 percent stake at the top as he extended the tentacles of his empire made it possible for Eaton to give him a brief scare. But Insull learned his lesson; he was careful to tighten his grip from then on.[19]

The Fall of the House of Insull

In the 1920s, Insull's expansion reached a feverish pitch. The euphoric conditions of the market made it uncommonly easy to finance each new venture. For a time, it seemed that everything he touched would turn to gold. The utilities industry was booming, and, like Ken Lay and Enron, who would use an even more sophisticated manipulation of the corporate form to keep their corporate treasury flush in the 1990s, Insull was the star. In 1927, the House of Morgan entered the picture. Pierpont's son and successor, the second J. P. Morgan, who had assumed the reins after Pierpont's death in 1913, decided that the time had once again come to "rationalize" the utilities industry, this time by assembling it under a single roof, the United Corporation. The United Corporation would be the Morgan partners' greatest monopoly yet, with a total capitalization twenty times as large as U.S. Steel. Insull, who still despised the Morgan bankers and their methods, would have none of it. He girded for battle and, in an enormous tactical blunder, launched an acquisitions spree that included two large utilities holding companies whose operations spanned the Northeast, a territory far from Insull's home base.

By 1929, Insull's empire was creaking under an enormous debt load and struggling with the fallout from his ill-advised foray eastward (an "invasion," in the words of his biographer, that "proved to be as successful as Napoleon's invasion of Russia"). Had he slowed down at that point and focused on paying off some of the debt, perhaps scaling down his empire, he might have weathered the crisis. He could have turned from the sun before it was too late. But "one of his most deep-rooted traits," as with Jay Cooke sixty years earlier, "was that he was absolutely unable, save on an abstract and purely intellectual level, to imagine the possibility of his own failure; he entirely lacked the sense of caution of those who doubt themselves." He "looked from day to day," according to an article in the *New Republic* in late 1932, "for the miraculous return to prosperity." But prosperity didn't return. Pinched by the Morgan competition and by the effects of his increasingly risky acquisitions, Insull came crashing down.[20]

In 1932, Insull's banks marched in and took control. To sort out the details, the banks brought in a then-unknown accounting firm, Arthur Andersen, which would rise to national prominence as a result of its sterling performance throughout the investigation and subsequent trial. Arthur Andersen himself was a Northwestern University professor who had founded the accounting firm in 1913 and who was known for his resolve and willingness to stand up to his clients. ("To preserve the integrity of his reports," Andersen said in a characteristic 1932 speech, "the accountant must insist upon absolute independence of judgment and action.") What Andersen's accountants found as they picked through the empire's financial statements was a welter of confusion and obfuscation. They also discovered evidence of "one corporate indiscretion after another—particularly in the form of intercorporate loans made during Insull's last-ditch efforts to save his companies."[21]

Criminal charges soon followed. The government's twenty-five-count indictment alleged that Insull had committed mail fraud by "devis[ing] a fraudulent scheme whereby, through 'false pretenses, representations, and promises,' [he] defrauded thousands of persons of money by inducing them 'to buy the worthless stock of this corporation [Corporation Securities Company of Chicago] at highly inflated and fictitious prices.'" But accounting fraud is extremely difficult to prove, and Insull never did go to jail. During Insull's 1934 trial, which came after Insull had fled to Greece and then was hauled back to the United States, Insull's attorney was able to defend many of the accounting procedures that Insull had used. Most dramatically, he forced a key government witness to admit that the corporation's treatment of stock dividends as a capital expense, rather than as a charge against income, a technique that appeared to inflate the corporation's reported income, was the same approach that the federal government itself recommended for income tax purposes. In the end, Insull was acquitted. But those who remember Insull remember the scandal, much more than his genius, his revolutionary innovations, or even his acquittal.[22]

Utility Bonds and the American Investor

Who financed Insull's disastrous flight? As we have seen, it was American investors. The securities of America's utilities were one of the most popular investments in middle-class America as the markets heated up in the 1920s. According to subsequent congressional testimony, "three-fourths or more of the [utility holding company] securities are represented by preferred stocks and bonds which are held directly by the general public." The sheer number of investors who had invested a portion of their savings in utilities meant that the collapse of Insull and other sprawling utilities companies was destined to have dramatic consequences both for the investors' financial stability and for their perception of American business. But dollar amounts alone can't adequately capture the shock of Insull's collapse. Most shocking of all was the fact that many investors—especially those who invested in bonds—thought they were buying a safe investment. They weren't like the stock-market investors who bought stock knowing that there was a risk involved. The utilities were viewed as a safe haven for investors' money, not as an investment at risk.[23]

A speech by the chairman of Illinois Bell Telephone in 1923 nicely sums up the perception that utility bonds were nearly as dependable as government securities like savings bonds or treasury bills. "As to the safety of investments in securities of gas, electric light and telephone companies," B. E. Sunny (his real name) explained, "it can be said that issues of bonds and notes in the hands of the public have made an almost perfect record, in that there seems to be no default by any of them so far as inquiry among those well informed on the subject is concerned." Sunny attributed this to the fact that the utilities were carefully regulated, stable businesses.[24]

By the late 1920s, some of the investors who put money in utilities were speculators, but many thought they were parking their savings in a secure haven. These were the hardest hit when Insull and other utilities empires collapsed. "One day," an Interstate Commerce Commission official later testified before Congress, "I stood and watched those holding securities and obligations of these companies coming in and filing them. They were just the average run of people—clerks and school teachers there in Chicago, small shopkeepers in Illinois, farmers from Wisconsin—and what they brought in, of course, was worth nothing. They had lost every penny." "It was the fellow in the sticks," according to another official, "who got the worst drubbing in the selling of these securities."[25]

In the shock to these investors of losing apparently safe investments lay the seeds of the market reforms that Roosevelt would start rolling out as soon as he arrived in Washington.

The Solution as Problem: J. P. Morgan and the Money Trust

I do not mean to suggest that there were no checks on the excesses of Icaran executives in the years leading up to the great market Crash. As we saw in chapter 2, many of the nation's largest corporations were subject to a very important check: J. P. Morgan & Co., the successor to the two Morgan banks, and the other leading investment banks. Insull, in fact, was one of the few managers of the nation's largest corporations who steered clear of Wall Street. Insull's principal banker, as well as friend and advisor, was John J. Mitchell of the Illinois Trust and Savings

Bank. Insull's first rule for financing his empire, according to his biographer, "was that New York was out of it. The second was that the financing would always be done in Chicago when Chicago could and would accommodate him."[26]

When other large corporations needed access to capital and a liquid market for their stock, they usually turned to the Wall Street banks for help. The House of Morgan had contacts and clout, and it always delivered on the sales it promised. If the Morgan partners agreed to underwrite a company's stock or bonds, the company could be quite sure that the securities would be sold and the money raised. A company that looked to one of the Money Trust banks for help was expected to submit to the bank's oversight. Having the Morgan partners or their peers around dramatically reduced the likelihood of an Icarus Effect failure. Indeed, the Morgan bankers had precisely this effect with Thomas Edison. As much as Edison and Insull chafed at the bankers' restraints, Morgan curbed Edison's enthusiasm for risk-taking and built a company that remains dominant even today— the company we know as General Electric.

But Money Trust oversight came at a steep price. We have already seen that the investment banks' modus operandi was to create monopolies in order to minimize the effects of competition, and they themselves held a firm monopoly over large-scale corporate finance. The banks also operated behind a great shroud of secrecy, and the stock-market Crash and Depression made all too clear that investors could be devastated by the things they didn't know.

The New Deal Debate: Competition or Federal Control?

When the Roosevelt administration launched its famous First Hundred Days in 1933, Insull epitomized the duplicity of corporate America. Not just Roosevelt, but politicians across the country had pointed their finger at Insull in their 1932 campaigns, saying "never again." There also was a deep and growing hostility toward the Wall Street banks. The market and governance crisis gave Roosevelt a license for reform.

It is sometimes assumed that Berle and the other members of Roosevelt's Brain Trust spoke with a single voice and mapped out a neat New Deal agenda, as they geared up for the remarkable run of corporate and financial legislation that Congress enacted in the 1930s. The reality was much more complicated and contentious. Roosevelt's advisors agreed on the diagnosis—the Money Trust was a problem, as were Insull and the utility holding-company pyramids and managers' dominance of other large corporations—but they had sharply different views as to the proper cure. In particular, there was deep disagreement about how best to address the second Icaran factor, competition in America's major industries.

One group was deeply influenced by Louis Brandeis, and like Brandeis believed that corporate governance should promote competition—in particular, competition by numerous, small, and medium-sized "Main Street" businesses rather than domination by a few corporate colossi. Berle—who, it turns out, had written Roosevelt's famous "Ishmael or Insull" speech—stood on the other side, as did Means and Rex Tugwell. Berle believed that it was too late to turn back the clock on the growth of big business. Rather than fragmenting the nation's great corporations, he insisted that corporations should be subject to extensive federal oversight; the giants should be treated as quasipublic entities, privately owned but with close federal involvement.[27]

Notice that both views have important implications for the three Icaran tendencies in American corporate and financial life: risktaking, competition, and the misuse of corporate size and complexity. In a perfect Brandeisian world, with smaller corporations and a more competitive marketplace, the Icarus Effect threat wouldn't disappear—hubris and competition would continue to mix. But the consequences of an Icaran disaster would be less draconian, since the size and complexity of American corporations would be held in check. Brandeis would fetter the corporate treasury by keeping corporations small and rely on disclosure and added governmental oversight to control risk-taking and police competition within any given industry.

Berle and Tugwell's vision of giant but pacified corporations would take aim at the Icaran tendencies in American business in much the same way as true government ownership of an industry does: by bringing competition to an end. This, in turn, would snuff out Icaran risk-taking, since one or a small group of corporations would firmly control any given industry. There would be little room for brash upstarts to challenge their dominance. Like the abominable snow monster in the children's Christmas show "Rudolph the Red-Nosed Reindeer," who becomes a "*humble bumble*" when his teeth are removed, America's giant corporations wouldn't disappear, but they would be tamed by vigorous governmental oversight.

Although the Brandeisian view is often seen as having won out overall, and his vision does indeed underlie several of Roosevelt's major legislative initiatives, it is more accurate to describe the New Deal reforms as a split decision. The New Deal certainly didn't signal the death knell of giant corporations in America. The nation's largest corporations were alive and well when all was said and done. And the utilities industry was restructured along very Berlean lines, with close regulation of large but simplified utility companies. But other key reforms, including both the banking reforms that launched the New Deal and the securities acts that soon followed, had a distinctively Brandeisian emphasis on disclosure and competition. The three sets of reforms I have just mentioned—banking, securities, and utilities—would transform the regulation of American corporate and financial life. Each is worth considering in some detail.

The End of the Money Trust

A friend of mine is often complimented on his lovely teeth. They are straight and white—not unnaturally white like those of an actor or television reporter, but noticeably straight and white. If you remark on his teeth, and aren't in a rush, he'll tell you the whole story. As a child, his teeth and jaw caused him endless trouble. The jaw was seriously out of alignment and eventually had to be fixed. The operation itself was no picnic: the doctors broke his jaw, reset it, and wired his mouth shut. My friend then spent six weeks drinking his meals through a straw. But the wires are a distant memory, and he now has lovely teeth and no longer wakes up at night in pain.

The New Dealers' approach to Wall Street's role in American business and finance was quite similar. J. P. Morgan & Co. and the investment banks were a response to the Icarus Effect problem. They were effective watchers, monitoring the managers of companies whose stock they underwrote and restructuring the company's obligations if it ran into financial trouble. But their oversight was deeply dysfunctional. The Money Trust promoted monopoly, had a near monopoly over large-scale finance, and was surrounded by secrecy. The only way to fix American corporate governance, the reformers concluded, was to completely restructure the framework for overseeing America's largest corporations. The jaw needed to be broken and reset, the Money Trust had to give way to a new oversight model. Watchers would still be necessary, of course, but the watchers should have less power and more accountability than J. P. Morgan had.

These concerns came to a head in a highly publicized series of

1932 hearings known as the Pecora hearings. (Pecora was the eventual chief counsel for the Congressional committee that staged the hearings.) Grilling the managers of National City Bank, one of Morgan's principal Money Trust partners, the investigators elicited testimony about CEO Charles Mitchell's enormous salary and about the bank's efforts to sell the securities of companies to which it had made loans. Although the investigators didn't find any outright fraud when they questioned J. P. (Jack) Morgan, Americans learned that Morgan's partners had paid almost no taxes in recent memory and that the bank kept a "preferred list" of customers who received stock at much more favorable prices than the investing public. (They also saw, plastered on the front page of nearly every major newspaper, a photograph of Jack Morgan, with a dwarf woman sitting in his lap and a quizzical look on his face, a media stunt that added to the carnival atmosphere and the perception of Morgan as dangerous and out of touch.)

The Pecora hearings set the stage for all of the New Deal banking and securities legislation, including the law that most directly targeted the Money Trust: the Glass-Steagall Act. Glass-Steagall, which lasted for nearly seventy years, until its repeal in 1999, prohibited banks from combining both commercial and investment banking. They had to choose one or the other. (After much deliberation, J. P. Morgan & Co. decided to stick with commercial banking. It spun off its investment-banking arm, which became Morgan Stanley. Kuhn, Loeb, on the other hand, remained in investment banking.) The Glass-Steagall Act struck a blow for all of the local banks across America that couldn't compete with J. P. Morgan & Co. and the other Wall Street titans. It was much harder for the Money Trust to dominate if they were limited to either commercial or investment banking.

Glass-Steagall wouldn't have leveled the playing field by itself, however. Because the Wall Street banks were so much bigger than anyone else, they were much less likely to fail than Jimmy Stewart's building-and-loan in *It's a Wonderful Life*. The giant sucking sound that local bankers heard during the bank failures of the early 1930s was the sound of depositors fleeing to the safety of Wall Street banks. To give local banks a chance and to end the bank runs that forced Roosevelt to declare "bank holidays" on several occasions during his first term, the New Deal reformers put deposit insurance in place under the Banking Act of 1933. Deposit insurance means that none of us will ever have to worry about losing our money (for accounts up to $100,000) if a bank fails. It also meant that local banks would have a fighting chance to attract deposits, since they were now just as safe for depositors as the Wall Street giants.

The reformers also took aim at the Wall Street banks through reforms that didn't seem to have a great deal to do with banking at first glance. Lest the Money Trust banks that opted to stay in investment banking—as did Kuhn, Loeb—think they could continue to dominate American corporate governance, the New Deal reformers sharply reduced the influence of a company's investment bankers through a pair of reforms later in the decade. An extensive revision of the bankruptcy laws in 1938 destroyed the equity receivership technique that J. P. Morgan had used to restructure many of the nation's railroads and large corporations. Investment banks would no longer run the process; instead, a court-appointed trustee would take charge of any large corporation that filed for bankruptcy. And the Trust Indenture Act of 1939 prohibited companies from issuing bonds that could be restructured pursuant to a vote by the bondholders, which made it difficult for the investment bankers who underwrote an issuance of bonds to oversee a restructuring outside of bankruptcy.

By the end of the 1930s, the Money Trust just wasn't what it used to be. The jaw had been broken and was in the process of being reset. Jack Morgan was still cruising on his enormous yacht and instantly recognizable in the Wall Street community. But the Money Trust was no longer the only game in town when it came to American corporate governance.

Deposit Insurance and Savings at Risk

We have just seen how deposit insurance contributed to the New Deal destruction of the Money Trust. The success of this reform is important to our story for another reason as well: it underscores the distinction in American financial life between ordinary savings and savings at risk. By the 1920s, ordinary Americans were much more likely to put their spare dollars in financial assets than to invest in land or other real estate, as their nineteenth-century predecessors had done. Among the financial options, there was a subtle but important distinction between those that were assumed to be sure things—a safe harbor with little or no risk—and those that involved a higher risk along with the possibility of greater reward. Bank accounts and bonds (particularly bonds backed by mortgages) in stable industries like utilities fell into the first, safer category, and investments in the stock market were viewed as riskier—as what we would now call risk capital.

The genius of the New Deal corporate and financial reforms is that Roosevelt and his advisors recognized the importance of this distinction. Ordinary Americans never dreamed that the money they put in banks might be savings at risk. The horror of the 1930s bank closings was the horror of thousands of Americans waking up to the possibility that savings they thought were absolutely secure might all be lost. The enactment of deposit insurance guaranteed that this horror will never again be repeated. When Americans put money in risky investments, they know there is a chance they will lose the investment. But the money we put in bank accounts is completely safe.

Taking the Utility Pyramids Down

As they debated the utilities industry crisis, it was clear that the New Dealers' response would involve major new federal oversight—indeed, Roosevelt had promised as much back on the campaign trail. State regulators, who traditionally had primary responsibility for utilities regulation, were hampered by their inability to cross state lines; and the utilities were simply too large for state regulators to control. So the feds would take charge— the Securities and Exchange Commission, as it turned out. But the scope of the regulators' mission was very much up for grabs. The simplest solution would be to impose careful controls on rates and disclosure, but leave the utilities' corporate structure more or less intact. A far more dramatic strategy would be to force the utilities to restructure or even to outlaw holding companies altogether.

Roosevelt threw his support behind the latter solution.[28] Although the administration did not propose to abolish holding companies altogether, it called for a dramatic simplification of the existing structures. It wasn't enough to simply clean up around the edges. As with the Money Trust banks, the New Deal reformers concluded that the utilities industry needed structural change. The convoluted holding-company structure helped men like Insull parlay a small stock interest into vast control and made it impossible for investors to figure out what they were up to.

The utilities industry lobbied fiercely against the proposed legislation. In addition to offering to submit to greater control by state securities regulators—an obvious ploy to fend off much more sweeping regulation from Washington—the utilities arm-twisted their employees to criticize the legislation and launched an all-out public relations campaign against the proposed re-structuring. "We are receiving literally thousands of letters from stockholders who are protesting against this bill," one utility executive said. "They tell us they are greatly frightened over the provisions of this bill." Another witness, who spoke as a "representative of the middle class," warned that "this legislation [would] mean the beginning of the end of our democracy." The debate in Washington was far more contentious than with most of the New Deal reform package, but Roosevelt eventually got what he wanted. The Public Utilities Holding Company Act (PUHCA) passed Congress in late August 1935.[29]

The cornerstone of the legislation was a provision that opponents dubbed the "death penalty." Under this provision (section 11 of the act), utility holding companies can have only two levels—a company on top that owns one or more operating companies underneath. No more webs and mazes of the sort that Insull had mastered. This provision also required holding companies to divest themselves of any assets that were not geographically connected. No more patchwork of companies, some nearby, some far away. Insull was once again an illustration, of course, with his foray into Northeastern utilities far removed from the base of operations in Chicago. The goal was to dramatically simplify the industry, a goal that was supplemented by extensive new disclosure obligations and a requirement that every interstate utilities company register with the SEC.

In Icaran terms, PUHCA took most direct aim at the third factor, misuse of corporate complexity. Although the decision to limit utilities to a single layer of subsidiaries imposed an obvious cost—it reduced the flexibility of the corporate structure—it ensured that the utilities would no longer be able to use structural complexities to mislead investors.

Simplifying the corporate structure and confining the utilities to a contiguous geographical region also had obvious implications for both Icaran risk-taking and for the competitive structure of the industry. Given the enormous economies of scale for utilities—as Insull showed, it is quite inexpensive to produce each additional kilowatt of electricity once the plant is in place—it was almost inevitable that a single utility would dominate any given market. Restrictions on entry into other markets limited the ability of utilities executives to gamble with the firm's assets, and the monopoly conditions minimized competition.

It is worth pausing to underscore the political significance of the holding-company reforms—a significance that has been largely forgotten in the intervening decades precisely because the reforms proved to be so successful. Under ordinary circumstances, the prospects for a reform that would bring some of the nation's largest corporations to their knees, and force them to completely restructure, would be infinitesimally small. The lobbying might of corporate managers, and the power of their political contributions, is too great for even relatively minor reform to succeed. But corporate and financial scandals change the political calculus. They galvanize the political might of the middle class. There are few more vivid illustrations of this principle than the Icarus Effect collapse of Insull's empire and the utility reforms it inspired.

Sunlight and a Boost for the Green-Eyeshade Crowd

It's not for nothing that we think of the New Deal reforms as the most sweeping intervention into the American markets in our history. The banking and utilities reforms responded to the two most glaring problems in American corporate governance—the Money Trust and the governance manipulations personified by the Insull scandal—by completely reengineering each of the offending industries. By themselves, however, these reforms raise an obvious question. Once the temple had been swept clean, who would step in and take over for the Money Trust as the principal watchers of America's giant corporations? The answer to this question lies in a less spectacular but equally revolutionary set of reforms that came during the same burst of activity in Roosevelt's first term: the Securities Act of 1933 and the Securities Exchange Act of 1934.

Masterminded by Harvard law professor and future Supreme Court Justice Felix Frankfurter, the securities acts personified one aspect of the Brandeisian gospel, the view—actively shared by President Roosevelt—that "sunlight is the best disinfectant." "Turn on the light," Roosevelt had shouted in his "Ishmael or Insull" speech, and a few moments later, "Again, 'let in the light.'" Although the securities acts did not promote Brandesian competition, they made it much harder for companies to keep investors in the dark.

As implemented and gradually expanded after the New Deal, the two securities acts call for detailed disclosure at every stage in a large corporation's life. The 1933 act applies primarily to a company that is selling its stock to public investors (that is, ordinary investors like you and me) for the first time. Under the 1933 act, these companies must issue a prospectus—complete with extensive disclosure about the company and its stock—before the company can go public. Once the company has sold the stock and thus gone public, the 1934 act imposes a variety of ongoing disclosure requirements. When newspaper stories refer to a company's "10-K," they are alluding to one of these obligations—the requirement that publicly held companies issue a yearly report that includes the information specified in form 10-K. Publicly held companies are also required to provide quarterly disclosure (their "10-Q"), as well as additional disclosure (an "8-K") of major events.

To function effectively, the disclosure regime also needed someone to a police it and tools for punishing cheaters. The 1934 act created the now-familiar Securities and Exchange Commission and authorized the SEC to serve as top cop of America's markets and stock exchanges. The securities acts then gave the

SEC, and in some cases investors too, a variety of weapons, including several very broad antifraud provisions. The best known of these antifraud provisions, such as the prohibition against insider trading, are in the 1934 act.

Think back to why J. P. Morgan & Co. and the investment banks rose to prominence in the first place. As America's markets grew and the railroads emerged as the first large-scale corporations, it was impossible for investors to determine which were promising companies and which were rotten to the core. Morgan served as a substitute for the information that investors didn't have. By the 1930s, there was much more information about the ins and outs of Wall Street, but ordinary investors still could easily be misled. There was far too little information to make sense of complicated enterprises such as Insull's Middle West Utilities. The securities act, as fleshed out by the SEC, filled the void by forcing companies to make significant disclosures about their operations. More information coming directly to investors reduced the need for an information substitute such as the Money Trust.

Investors couldn't do it all on their own, of course. Someone needs to look over the company's shoulders when it produces all of this information. If it's not going to be the government, someone else needs to step in. Here, too, the securities laws, together with the rules that were and are promulgated by the SEC, provided an answer, though they did so almost by accident. The annual disclosure from each company must include a variety of audited financial statements; under the current rule, this means balance sheets for the company's last two fiscal years and three years' worth of income statements. Because the audits must be done by outside auditors, the securities acts—which built on a New York Stock Exchange rule that was put in place a year earlier, in 1933—paved the way for accounting firms to become one of the principal watchers of Wall Street.

The accounting industry didn't suddenly emerge out of

nowhere—like Athena springing forth full-grown from the head of Zeus—after the securities laws of 1933 and 1934. There were accountants long before 1933. Arthur Andersen had been founded twenty years earlier. Indeed, in retrospect, the removal of J. P. Morgan & Co. and its peers from their perch atop American corporate and financial life is sometimes seen as inevitable, as a natural consequence of the increasing sophistication of the accounting industry. Unlike in the nineteenth century, when the railroads themselves often had only a dim understanding of their own finances, new accounting techniques had begun to make the previously invisible visible.

At the least, the New Deal reforms dramatically hastened the changing of the guard; and at the most, they completely altered the direction of American corporate and financial life. In the accounting industry, the biggest beneficiaries would be a small handful of major Wall Street accounting firms that rose to the top as industry leaders—the accounting firms known as the Big Eight, the Big Five, and now the Big (or Final) Four. Perhaps the biggest beneficiary of all was Arthur Andersen, which came to symbolize unyielding integrity after its accountants picked through the wreckage of Insull's Middle West Utilities.

The accountants' job was to make sure that a company's disclosures were legitimate, that they looked more like GAAP (or generally accepted accounting principles) than GIGO (or garbage in, garbage out). But that still leaves the matter of processing the information that was disclosed. Anyone who has ever looked at a stock prospectus knows that the average investor isn't likely to read and digest all of the information. It's simply too complicated. The New Deal reformers assumed that securities analysts would step up to the plate to fill this role, and that's exactly what eventually happened. There were securities analysts within the investment banks, as well as independent analysts of various kinds, and these analysts became increasingly important under the new disclosure-oriented securities laws.

The Taming of Icarus: Summing Up the New Deal

Never before or since has an administration enjoyed so great a mandate to reform corporate America as did Roosevelt during the New Deal. And the New Dealers took full advantage of the invitation they had to fix some of the most unseemly aspects of American corporate governance.

The New Deal reforms targeted each of the three factors that can lead to Icarus Effect scandals and cripple American corporate and financial life. The extensive new disclosure requirements made it more difficult for Icaran entrepreneurs to gamble the corporation's assets right under investors' noses. Accountants and securities analysts both had an incentive to sleuth for dubious behavior, and their private efforts would be supplemented by the oversight of the SEC. The securities reforms also curbed abuses of the third factor, corporate size and complexity, since it was harder to manipulate the corporate structure in order to raise capital from unsuspecting investors. With the second factor, competition, the New Deal reforms reintroduced competition in the financial sector. The New Dealers initially experimented with centralized planning in other industries under the National Recovery Administration, rather than promoting competition, but they eventually shifted their emphasis to antitrust. In 1941, the Temporary National Economic Committee called for "the vigorous and vigilant enforcement of the antitrust laws," a call that antitrust regulators would answer in the years to come, as we shall see.[30]

In the utilities industry, PUHCA imposed direct restrictions on the corporate form, prohibiting the use of complex corporate structures. The benefits of giving corporate managers flexibility in their design of the overall corporate structure, the reformers concluded, were outweighed by the potential costs. The reformers also limited both risk-taking and competition by providing, in effect, for local utility monopolies, since utilities were prohibited from acquiring operations that were not geographically contiguous. A leading local utility no longer needed to worry that outside competitors would establish a beachhead in the local utility's region. The intuition behind this regulatory strategy was that in some industries—industries with significant economies of scale—unbridled competition can be counterproductive.

Notice that all of the reforms we have discussed are federal in nature. The New Deal reforms reflected the most extensive incursion of federal regulation into American corporate life in American history. Some of the reformers, such as Berle himself and SEC chair and subsequent Supreme Court Justice William Douglas, wanted Roosevelt to federalize corporate law altogether by enacting a new federal incorporation statute. But the proposed federalization of corporate law never found traction in Congress—in part because Roosevelt linked it to a bill that would have imposed draconian penalties on antitrust violators. As a result, state lawmakers retained a central role in the oversight of corporate law, a role that would put Delaware squarely in the national spotlight in the 1970s and 1980s.[31]

Recent decades have seen a great deal of revisionist history about the legacy of the New Deal reforms. Everyone agrees that sunlight is a good thing. But skeptics of the securities laws point out that the New York Stock Exchange had begun to impose disclosure obligations on companies listed on the exchange even before the 1933 act was enacted; and they argue that companies will let the sunlight in themselves if this is what investors want. Other critics question whether there was as much fraud and manipulation in the markets on the eve of 1929 Crash as reformers claimed. And one occasionally hears suggestions that there should be less protection of bank deposits than has traditionally been the case.

But much of the criticism is misguided (more on this in the endnotes),[32] and the legacy of the New Deal reforms is beyond serious dispute. In the decades after the nation climbed out of the Depression, the American securities markets became by far the most liquid and transparent in the world. It became much harder for an Icaran entrepreneur to disguise what he was doing and to take desperate gambles. For a time, at least, Icarus had been tamed.

Four "I Want to Be Like Mike": LBOs and the New Corporate Governance

In 1974, International Nickel Company, an established and successful company, launched a takeover bid for ESB, another established and successful company. Quarterbacking the takeover effort was Morgan Stanley, the blue-chip investment bank that had been formed when Glass-Steagall forced J. P. Morgan & Co. to sever its commercial- and investment-banking businesses. The takeover wasn't astonishingly large as takeovers go, nor especially dramatic. Kohlberg Kravis Roberts and Company's (KKR) acquisition of RJR-Nabisco in 1989—the takeover immortalized in the book and movie *Barbarians at the Gate*—makes the ESB takeover seem almost trivial by comparison on both counts. But it was ESB that launched the revolution. Before ESB, established corporations didn't wage hostile-takeover battles against one another; and a top-drawer investment bank like Morgan Stanley certainly didn't dirty its hands in such an unseemly endeavor.

The ESB takeover broke all the rules that had characterized

large-scale American corporate governance since the end of the New Deal. In the corporate world of the 1950s, everyone knew their place. The CEOs of companies like IBM or General Electric didn't simply appear out of nowhere. They worked their way through the ranks, starting at the bottom; rising to CEO was almost invariably the culmination of a career spent in the same firm.

In Icarus Effect terms, the class-based code of this era wasn't entirely bad. Because the CEOs of America's largest corporations were elevated from within and reached the top after a long apprenticeship within the firm, there weren't many Jay Cookes or Samuel Insulls running American corporations. The qualities that were rewarded in most major companies were dependability and loyalty, not creativity. The most prominent CEOs were more likely to be corporate bureaucrats than entrepreneurial geniuses. This was not an era when Icaruses were flying too high and sending major American companies spiraling out of control.

But it was also a time when shareholders had little say over the direction of large-scale business, and companies tended to grow bigger rather than more innovative and efficient. The ESB takeover signaled that the foundations of this era were crumbling. In little more than a decade, the Icarus Effect would be back, spurred by a bank that fancied itself as the next House of Morgan.

"What's Good for GM Is Good for America"

The world that was about to crumble is hard to remember or even imagine now. Flush with postwar success, many of America's most prominent corporations enjoyed steady profits throughout the 1950s, and corporate-governance issues seemed to fade into the background as the American markets expanded and the Cold War took hold. At "Big Blue"—as IBM became known—workers could count on a lifetime of employment. In 1953, Charles Wilson, the president of General Motors and Eisenhower's nominee to serve as secretary of defense, announced, with no apparent irony, that "what's good for GM is good for America."

The 1950s was also the heyday of unionism. The Wagner Act of 1935 and the more pro-manager Taft-Hartley Act of 1946 had ushered in a period of union strength—roughly 40% of industry was unionized. Although management and unions were often at loggerheads, unionism served as an additional check on managerial risk-taking, since unionized employees had a stake in the long-term viability of the companies they worked for. After concluding that the "only thing standing between the corporation and virtually limitless profits was the possibility of labor unrest," David Halberstam writes in *The Fifties*, GM signed a historic labor agreement, the "treaty of Detroit," with Walter Reuther and the United Auto Workers in 1948: "In effect it made the union a junior partner of the corporation, tying wages not merely to productivity but to such other factors as inflation as well. The agreement reflected the absolute confidence of a bedrock conservative who saw the economic pie as so large that he wanted to forgo his ideological instincts in order to start carving it up as quickly as possible." Even in nonunionized companies—IBM is once again a prime example—stability was the watchword. By emphasizing loyalty and length of service, internal tenure and promotion practices reinforced this mission.[1]

The birth of America's great conglomerates in the 1960s took the impulse toward size and stability to a whole new level. In managerial circles, conglomerates—corporations that brought a variety of different kinds of businesses under the same roof—were seen as the pinnacle of corporate evolution. The modern corporate executive, according to this view, was a skillful administrator who nimbly shuttled funds from one business to another within the corporate enterprise as circumstances dictated. Based on this kind of reasoning, the nation's largest corporations grew larger and larger. Antitrust law prevented them from buying up their competitors and achieving a monopoly in their industry, but it didn't put any obstacles in the way of expansion in other directions, so they moved into new and often unrelated areas. The stock market soared during the 1960s, and this helped too, by inflating the value of the stock that many of the conglomerates used to acquire new businesses.

It's easy to see why corporate managers loved the conglomeratization movement. The only thing better than running a big company is running an even bigger company, and that's what the conglomerates offered. The managers of a conglomerate also didn't need to worry much about pesky shareholders, since the larger the company became, the more likely its shareholders were to be widely scattered and unable to coordinate to keep tabs on the managers or participate in corporate decision making. And the fact that conglomerates were diversified offered still more insulation for managers. Even if one of the company's businesses did badly, its other businesses could pick up the slack.

With the start of the takeover boom in the 1970s, this world was about to come under siege. Takeovers weren't suddenly invented in 1974, of course. There were takeovers throughout the 1950s and 1960s. But these had always taken place outside of the Gentleman's Code that governed the white shoe banks, law firms, and their corporate clients. "The leading takeover lawyer, Joe Flom of Skadden, Arps, Slate, Meagher, & Flom, had pioneered hostile takeovers in the 1950s," according to one business historian, "when Skadden, Arps was still a humble, four-man operation." Flom was Jewish, and this was an era when Jews were regularly told they need not apply for jobs in the top-tier New York law firms. Many Jewish lawyers who wanted to practice corporate law had to go it alone or work for small firms. Flom created a niche for himself as a smart, hard-nosed lawyer who was willing to represent corporate "troublemakers." "For twenty years, he thrived on the scraps from law firms that were too haughty or too dignified to conduct hostile raids."[2]

Unfortunately, Gentleman's Code corporate governance tended to produce mediocre companies. The biggest didn't usually lose money, but they weren't run nearly as efficiently as they could be if the managers spent less time socializing with their peers and more time focusing on the bottom line. There was a lot of money to be made by raiders who bucked convention and invaded the cozy bastions of corporate America. As a result, the norm against participating in hostile takeovers became increasingly costly to the parties who upheld it. By turning their back on hostile takeovers, banks and law firms were giving up the possibility of lucrative fees.

By 1974, the economic pressure on those who refused to participate in the corporate takeover market had mounted. When Morgan Stanley's longtime client International Nickel asked Morgan Stanley to help it raise money for a hostile raid on ESB, the bankers were torn. The "nearly forty Morgan Stanley partners . . . debated whether to spurn [International Nickel] or defy a code that had governed the world of high finance for almost 150 years. The argument of inevitability was probably the decisive one," according to a biographer of the bank. "As one partner recalls, 'The debate was, if we don't do what our clients want, somebody else will.'"[3]

Highly Confident Michael Milken

In the half decade after Morgan Stanley threw its hat in the takeover ring, the rest of Wall Street's blue-chip banks followed suit. Once exotic, hostile bids quickly became part of the standard Wall Street repertoire as the Wall Street banks fell all over each other trying to get a piece of the action.

It wasn't until roughly 1982, however, that the takeover market really took off. Until then, hostile bidders' need for secrecy and speed—taking the victim by surprise has always been the key to piracy, after all—had put serious limits on the amount of money that a hostile bidder could raise. Bidders couldn't knock on doors asking for money if they were trying to keep their intentions secret. As a result, nearly all of the early raids involved relatively small targets. It simply wasn't possible to line up enough money, quickly enough, to take on a whale.

Until Michael Milken and Drexel Burnham figured out how. In the space of less than a decade, the rise of Drexel would bring a radically new era in American corporate life.

The Milken story has been told many times before. This intense young son of a middle-class accountant found himself in college at Berkeley during Berkeley's heyday as a hotbed of campus activism. Milken had a life-transforming experience in the mid-1960s, an experience perhaps similar in intensity but utterly different in kind from that of his fellow students. For Milken, the epiphany was a book by W. Braddock Hickman entitled *Corporate Bond Quality and Investor Experience*. First published in the 1950s, Hickman's book is not exactly bedtime reading. It consists of an exhaustive study of the performance of corporate bonds from 1900 to 1943. Hickman's central finding is that investors who bought the bonds of companies that were on the verge of default did much better than one might expect. Overall, the troubled bonds actually performed better than the bonds of more stable companies.[4]

As he poured over Hickman's findings, Milken realized that subinvestment-grade bonds—such as the "fallen angels" that had lost value because the company's fortunes had deteriorated—were a potential gold mine. Although it would be foolish to put all of your money in the bonds of a troubled company—this was why investors avoided them—things look quite different if you assemble a diversified portfolio of these bonds. Because of the risk involved, this debt carried a very high interest rate. At such high rates, Milken reasoned, an investor who bought a basket of different bonds (which Milken called "high yield" but the rest of the world came to know as "junk") could make a great deal of money, even if a few of the companies later failed.

From then on, Milken preached his junk-bond gospel to whoever would listen. He started investing in high-yield debt—both for himself and for a few of his father's clients—even before he graduated from college. At Wharton Business School, his next step, he wrote papers on high-yield debt for his classes and even published an academic article with one of his professors after he graduated. Once he had his Wharton degree in hand, Milken took a job with Drexel Burnham (which was then known as Drexel Harriman Ripley) in New York. Within a couple of years, he would be doing high-yield debt, all the time.

When Milken first joined Drexel, it was a bank whose best days seemed behind it. Its roots dated back to Philadelphia, where it was founded in 1838, and was one of the nation's leading banks when Jay Cooke burst on the scene in 1861. As we saw in chapter 1, Drexel linked up with the predecessor to J. P. Morgan & Co. after the Civil War, and it continued as the Philadelphia outpost of the Morgan empire until Glass-Steagall forced the two banks to go their separate ways. Although Drexel still counted a few of the nation's most elite companies as its clients, it was caught between this illustrious past and a more precarious future.

Starting out as an ordinary bond trader, Milken quickly mastered the arcane world of high-yield debt. Although he was treated as a "leper" by some of his colleagues, the "high-grade bond guys" who feared that Milken's immersion in low-grade debt would tarnish Drexel's reputation as a high-end bank, Milken's growing profits assured that no one would interfere with his operation. In 1973, Milken earned a 100% return on the

$2 million he was given to invest, at a time when the rest of the firm was barely breaking even. Milken insisted that he be given control over a completely separate high-yield bond unit, and in 1978 he moved the entire operation to the Los Angeles area, where he and his wife were from. By then, he had built up a loyal group of clients who bought the bonds he recommended—clients that included mutual-funds and insurance executives such as Saul Steinberg and Lawrence Tisch.[5]

By the time he moved the show to Los Angeles, Milken was far more than simply a bond trader. With his growing network of client relationships, he could sell new bonds or restructure a company's existing debt with a couple of phone calls. Drexel's fees for these services were astonishingly high; the bank sometimes charged 3% or 4% of the face amount to underwrite high-yield bonds, a nice improvement on the less than 1% that the underwriters of investment-grade debt received. But Milken was a magician. No one else could sell the bonds he sold and raise the money he raised. Milken's group, according to business reporter Connie Bruck, "was not unlike a cult: intensely secretive, insular, led by a charismatic and messianic leader whom many of his followers came to see as larger than life."[6]

Until the early 1980s, Milken's junk-bond juggernaut and the upswing in hostile takeovers that began in the previous decade were separate developments. They were like the "two great tastes" in the old Reese's Peanut Butter Cups commercial—the chocolate and the peanut butter—that no one had thought to put together. But the separate tastes came together in 1982.

Drexel Reinvents the LBO

It started innocently enough, with Drexel's participation in several leveraged buyouts (LBOs). Leveraged buyouts are called "leveraged" because the buyer—either the managers of the company being taken over or outsiders—finances nearly all of the purchase price with debt. The large amount of debt, or leverage, enables the buyer to acquire a company without contributing a great deal of cash. Most of the funding came from commercial banks, and their loans were secured by the assets of target company, much as home mortgages are secured by the house being bought. Drexel's job was to sell unsecured junk bonds to complement the money provided by the senior lenders.

The early LBOs were usually friendly rather than hostile. In theory, at least, there was no reason why the same financing techniques couldn't be used in hostile transactions. The problem, as recounted by Milken's colleague and Drexel CEO Fred Joseph, was that "you can't tell people you're going to do the deal, and you don't know if you're going to need the money [you raise], and you don't know how much money you're going to need, because you may have to raise the price."[7] From a financing perspective, hostile bids were full of caveats and conditions, uncertainties and unknowns.

As they mulled over the problem, Milken and his colleagues hit on a brilliant solution, an invention that would launch a thousand pirate ships—the "highly confident letter." Drexel wouldn't actually raise the money before a raider made his takeover bid. Instead, for an appropriate fee, Drexel would opine that it was highly confident the money could be assembled on short notice. Originally known as the "air fund," because the promise was backed by nothing but air, Drexel's highly confident letter was the modern-day equivalent of the South Sea bubble venture styled as "a company for carrying on an undertaking of great advantage, but nobody to know what it is." In effect, the highly confident letter was nothing more than Drexel's statement that its partners had assessed the proposed takeover and that they were confident that they could persuade bank lenders and private investors to put up the necessary cash.

As insubstantial as highly confident letters were, Milken's

labyrinthine web of clients—individuals and institutions who bought whatever he handed to them—made his promise remarkably credible. Drexel rolled out the strategy for the first time when Carl Icahn made a hostile tender offer for the giant oil company Phillips Petroleum. Never before had a bidder made a tender offer without having its funding already in place, but the "look Mom, no hands" strategy worked like a charm. In the end, Phillips bought peace with Icahn; a few months later, Icahn would successfully take over TWA.

With the advent of Milken and Drexel's highly confident letter, the takeover craze of the "go-go '80s" was truly under way.

Savior or Curse? The Skinny on Takeovers

In late-twentieth-century America, there was no better indication that a person or phenomenon had captured the American imagination than Oliver Stone's decision to make a movie about it. In 1987, in the midst of the hostile-takeover boom, Stone released *Wall Street*, a scathing, hugely successful portrayal of the arbitrageur and raider Gordon Gekko (played by Michael Douglas) and his would-be disciple Bud Fox (Charlie Sheen). In the movie's best-known scene, Gekko insists that "greed is good" before taking over a company, breaking it up and firing many of the employees.

Stone wasn't just making this all up. Although Gekko's speech could easily be mistaken for characteristic Oliver Stone bombast, Stone found his inspiration in an actual speech by takeover raider Victor Posner. *Wall Street* brilliantly captured the popular perception in the 1980s that takeover bidders aren't nice people. They're people who will happily lie, cheat, or steal if the price is right.

That's one side of the story. But there's another side of the story as well. Keep in mind just who the very first "victims" of takeovers were. The first people to lose their jobs after a takeover were the managers of the target company. The managers whose companies were most likely to be taken over were the ones who spent most of their time on the golf course and who treated the chief executive's office as a sinecure. When the buyout firm Kohlberg, Kravis, Roberts and Company (KKR) took over RJR-Nabisco in 1988, there weren't many tears shed for CEO Ross Johnson, who had moved the company to Atlanta because he preferred the weather there to New York's and bought a company Lear Jet and an Aspen condominium for his own private convenience.

This same intuition had been put in more abstract, theoretical terms by Henry Manne in a pathbreaking 1965 article. Manne, who later became dean of the George Mason law school and started a summer camp designed to teach judges and law professors to think like economists, argued that takeovers, or the "market for corporate control," are corporate democracy at its best, a solution to the Berle-Means separation of ownership and control. Takeover bidders search for poorly run companies, buy up a controlling stake, and use their voting power to replace bad managers. Even the possibility of a takeover can have beneficial effects. Managers will work harder and pay more attention to their shareholder, if poor performance might attract a takeover bid.

Takeovers also often had a simplifying effect on corporate structure. In many of the early takeovers, the raiders took control of a conglomerate, then sold off some of its constituent parts. A key objective was to identify a "core competence" and to eliminate the subsidiaries or divisions (a division is a line of business that is not housed in a separate subsidiary) that did not fit this competence. The company that emerged was often more streamlined both in its operations and in its formal corporate structure.

So which is it: are takeover raiders heroes or villains? By the mid-1980s, most corporate-law scholars viewed them—or, at the least, saw takeovers—as heroes. In the most important corporate-law debate since Berle and Means, two University of Chicago law professors, Frank Easterbrook and Daniel Fischel, insisted that target companies should never resist a takeover offer in any way. This corporate surrender strategy or "passivity thesis," they argued, would lead to more takeovers and new managers for more poorly managed companies. Two other professors, Harvard's Lucian Bebchuk and Ron Gilson of Stanford, said, in effect, "no, no, no—this has it all wrong." Target companies should be permitted to resist a takeover, they argued in separate articles, but only so long as their goal was to create a bidding contest that increased the price for the benefit of the target's shareholders. The debate was heated, and still is, but all four of the scholars agreed, as did most other corporate-law experts, that takeovers are a consummation devoutly to be wished.[8]

We need to make serious qualifications before we accept this conclusion, however. Takeovers were a welcome corrective to the corporate fiefdoms of the 1950s and 1960s, but the complaints about takeovers weren't entirely unfounded. This was especially true later on in the 1980s, when the most obvious targets had been raided and "there was too much money chasing too few deals."[9] In addition to layoffs and disruptions, many companies sharply reduced their research and development after being taking over, because all of their available cash had to go to repaying the takeover debt. Takeovers also transformed the corporate ethos in ways that would unleash each of the three Icaran tendencies in American corporate and financial life.

High with a Little Help from Your Friends

The takeover mania of the 1980s wasn't entirely a creation of Michael Milken's fertile mind, of course. While Milken's revolutionary financing techniques took takeovers to a new level, the go-go '80s wouldn't have been possible without three closely related contributions from Uncle Sam.

The first was a shift in antitrust policy. Under the previous five administrations, dating back to Kennedy, regulators at the Federal Trade Commission and the Justice Department, the two agencies with antitrust enforcement power, kept a close watch on the market power of companies within any given industry. Starting in the 1970s, prominent conservative scholars like Robert Bork of the University of Chicago argued that the traditional enforcement strategy didn't understand markets or what's really best for consumers. Bigger is often better, they contended, because of the efficiencies that come with size (or what economists refer to as economies of scale). If consumers have a choice whether to buy the product, moreover, even a company that dominates the market can't get away with charging outrageous prices. Consumers simply won't buy the cereal or bananas or whatever if the price is too high. The bête noir of the Chicago school was cases like the Supreme Court's 1962 decision in *Brown Shoe v. United States*, which struck down a merger between two companies that, together, would have controlled only 5% of the industry's capacity. The Reagan administration was deeply sympathetic to the suggestion that regulators didn't need to intervene so aggressively in the market, and almost as soon as Reagan entered office in 1981 regulators started pulling back the regulatory troops. In Icarus Effect terms, Reagan-era regulators took an increasingly hands-off stance toward the second Icaran factor, the competitive structure of the markets. Business leaders' contention that the market is a more efficient regulator than Washington bureaucrats won out not just in the Reagan administration, moreover, but increasingly in the courts as well.[10]

The effects were most striking in the treatment of horizontal mergers—that is, mergers between two companies in the same industry. (A "vertical" merger, by contrast, is a merger that brings together a manufacturer and one of its suppliers, as would a merger between a car manufacturer and a tire company.) Before the 1980s, regulators would have jumped up and down if a company that had 30% or 40% market share sought to acquire another company in the industry and thus to push its market share even higher. Reagan-era regulators were much more likely to cast an approving eye on these same-industry mergers, which was an enormous stimulus to the takeover market. A significant number of the takeovers were precisely the kind of horizontal mergers that would have been stopped in their tracks by regulators in an earlier era.

The Reagan administration's second, closely related contribution was a four-square commitment to deregulation. Deregulation certainly didn't begin with Reagan. Jimmy Carter, after all, was the one who first deregulated the airline and trucking industries, in response to concerns that government control was stifling innovation and that competition would spur companies to provide superior and more efficient service. But Reagan took deregulation to a new level, continuing the existing efforts and scaling back government oversight in a variety of new areas as well.

Much of the Reagan-era action involved the oil and gas industry. In natural gas, a feeding frenzy was unleashed when the price controls that had long organized the industry were scaled back. After Drexel-financed takeover raider Irwin Jacobs launched a takeover for Internorth, a leading gas pipeline company, Internorth paid a call on the managers of Houston Natural Gas, its leading competitor. Internorth's CEO proposed a merger that would give shareholders of HNG $71 per share at a time when the market price of the stock was $25, and he suggested that HNG's CEO should run the show after the merger. When HNG agreed, an industry-dominating natural-gas pipeline company was born. Shortly after the merger, the CEO used the proceeds of junk bonds (sold, of course, by Michael Milken and Drexel) to finance a restructuring of the company, and a few years later he would give it a new, trendier sounding name: Enron.[11]

Uncle Sam's final contribution was to conjure up a new buyer for the junk bonds that were used to finance so many of the takeovers of the 1980s—the savings and loan industry.[12] In the early 1980s, Congress responded to festering problems in the S&L industry by enacting several major reforms that would pull the S&Ls into the very heart of the takeover wave.

The S&L crisis arose in large part from a serious mismatch between the S&Ls' assets and their liabilities. Because their assets (the mortgage payments owed by homeowners to whom the S&Ls lend money) are paid out over long periods of time, but their liabilities are short term (consisting of deposits that depositors can withdraw at any time), the S&Ls were extremely vulnerable to changes in interest rates. If interest rates rose, S&Ls would be stuck with a lot of mortgages with comparatively low interest rates, while they had to pay increasingly high rates for deposits. Starting in 1966, regulators tried to solve this problem with "Regulation Q," which prohibited the S&Ls from offering more than 5.5% interest on deposits. Unfortunately, the restriction exacerbated the S&Ls' problems when interest rates shot through the roof in the late 1970s. S&L depositors moved their money to money-market funds that offered two or three times as much interest as S&L deposits, while the S&Ls were stuck with the mortgages they'd given before the interest rates exploded.

With the S&L industry on the ropes, Congress tried to fix the problem by enacting two separate pieces of legislation, the Depository Institutions Deregulation and Monetary Control Act of 1980 and the Garn-St. Germain Depository Institutions Act of 1982. The reforms eliminated Regulation Q, so that S&Ls could offer market rates of interest; authorized S&Ls to obtain deposits from anywhere, not just their own geographic area; increased the deposit insurance ceiling from $40,000 to $100,000; and explicitly authorized S&Ls to invest in junk bonds. (Several states, including California, gave state S&Ls even broader authority to invest in junk bonds.) The S&Ls immediately took advantage of each of these changes by ratcheting up their interest rates, paying "deposit brokers" to round up deposits from all around the country, and diving into the junk-bond market. When Milken turned his financing revolution to hostile takeovers, the S&Ls were right there with him, buying the bonds. Although many bought only limited amounts of junk bonds, a few high flyers became outposts of the Drexel revolution. The most prominent, Columbia Savings and Loan, replaced nearly all of its mortgage portfolio with junk bonds, much to the chagrin of federal regulators (who chafed at Columbia's abandonment of the traditional S&L role of lending to home buyers) and to the delight of Milken (who added Columbia to his stable of dependable bond buyers and eventually held a sizeable minority stake in Columbia's stock).

In retrospect, it is clear that regulators should have shut down the insolvent S&Ls while they had the chance, rather than deregulating and hoping that the S&Ls could simply grow out of their troubles. It turned out to be a several hundred billion dollar mistake. In the meantime, the S&Ls added fuel to the 1980s takeover fire.

"Stuck in the Middle with You": The Role of Outside Directors

C lowns to the left of me, jokers to the right," runs the refrain of a 1970s pop-music classic: "Here I am, stuck in the middle with you." As the takeover market exploded, fueled by deregulation and the junk-bond financing that made every firm a possible takeover target, "stuck in the middle" was precisely the position that outside directors—the directors who were not also officers of the company—found themselves in. When raiders came knocking, the managers of the target company almost always wanted to dig in their heels and fight, to act as "defenders of the corporate bastion," as the Delaware Supreme Court put it in one of the most important cases of the 1980s. Raiders, on the other hand, claimed that they came bearing gifts. The target's shareholders would be much better off if the company were taken over, the raiders insisted, since the raiders promised to pay them much more than the current market price for their stock. The question was, who should the directors be listening to, and what should they do when a takeover bidder showed up?

These aren't questions that the post–World War II business world had prepared anyone to answer. Before the New Deal, directors often were not even paid for serving on a board of directors—other than the gold coin many found waiting on their chair when they arrived for a board meeting. The assumption, left over from the nineteenth century, was that every company was run by shareholders who owned a large stake and also served as directors. The directors who served as officers would be paid for managing the company and outside directors would profit if the value of the company's stock increased. There was thus no need to pay either for serving as director. But as the ownership of America's largest corporations dispersed, enforcing the prohibition against directorial pay would have required companies to rely on true volunteers. By the 1950s, the lingering hostility to paid directors had begun to die out, and a new model of the corporate board took hold. This model is sometimes described, following the terms used by corporate-law scholar Melvin Eisenberg, as the "managerial board." The role of the managerial board is, quite simply, to run the corporation. The outside directors would not only serve as a check on inside directors like the CEO; they also would directly participate in managing the company.[13]

The problem with this model is that outside directors who set foot in the company only six or eight times a year for board meetings are hardly in position to run the corporation. In practice, the outside directors simply went along with their CEO's wishes in all but the most extraordinary circumstances. This "go along, get along" mentality was reinforced by the process by which the outside directors were chosen. The CEO decided who would be nominated, and in true Berle-Means fashion, the manager's nominees were invariably elected. Who were these nominees? Studies of corporate boards show that nearly all of the directors were acquaintances of the CEO or people with a business relationship with the firm. If you wanted to serve on a company's board of directors, your best bet was to be a college roommate or lifelong buddy of the future CEO.

When the raiders showed up in corporate America, outside directors tended to side with their friend, the CEO. At first, it didn't matter a great deal what the outside directors thought, since a takeover bidder could make a tender offer directly to the target company's shareholders, and the shareholders themselves could decide whether to accept the offer. In 1983, however, Marty Lipton of Wachtell, Lipton, one of the nation's leading corporate lawyers, created an ingenious device for strengthening the directors' hand: the poison pill. A poison pill gives each shareholder of the company the right to purchase stock of the company, stock of the bidder, or both, in the event that any bidder acquires more than a specified percentage (usually 10% or 15%) of the company's stock. Often the pill is structured as a half-price sale: if the pill is triggered, shareholders (except the bidder, who is excluded) would have the right to buy, say, $200 worth of stock for $100. Since the poison pill would massively dilute the bidder's interest, bidders never permit the poison pill to be triggered. Unless the bidder can get the pill removed, the hostile bid does not go forward.

With the advent of the poison pill, together with a variety of other antitakeover devices, the battle was fully joined. Raiders made their bids, the target company resisted, and then everyone packed up their bags and went to Delaware, where many of the target companies were incorporated, to see if the defenses would be permitted.

Delaware's Choice

In three hugely important 1985 decisions, Delaware gave its answer. One question was whether poison pills should ever be allowed. After all, the effect of a poison pill is almost too good to be true for the besieged managers. The pill promises a lavish payout to every shareholder except the bad guy—the bidder, who often holds a large block of stock—a form of discrimination that you can't usually get away with in corporate law. In a case involving Household International, the Delaware Supreme Court said that poison pills were indeed permissible. But the court also established tough new standards for directors when they respond to a takeover offer. Poison pills would be permitted, but the directors would be required to demonstrate that the pill was an appropriate response in the event of an unwanted bid.[14]

The directors' responsibilities in the heat of a takeover battle fall into two categories, each named for the case that gave rise to the duties. Under the *Unocal* case, the directors can only respond to a takeover threat by stiff-arming the raider with a poison pill or other takeover defense if the raider's bid represents a threat (such as an inadequate price) and the directors' response is reasonable in relation to the magnitude of the threat involved. If the directors decide they do want to sell the company—perhaps to a "white knight" bidder who seems less threatening than the raider—their much more stringent *Revlon* duties come into play. Once it's clear that the company will be sold, *Revlon* requires the directors to try to get the highest price possible.[15]

The cases themselves were a snapshot of the 1980s boom at its peak. *Unocal* arose when, fueled by Drexel's money machine, T. Boone Pickens and Mesa Oil went after the vastly larger company Unocal. After Pickens made a tender offer that would have given him 50% of Unocal's stock, Unocal responded by making its own tender offer to the Unocal shareholders at a much higher price (Pickens's offer was $54 a share, whereas Unocal promised $72). Like a poison pill, Unocal's self-tender was discriminatory—it was available to everybody *except* Pickens; as a result, it dissuaded Unocal's shareholders from accepting the Pickens offer. Pickens cried foul, but the Delaware Supreme Court upheld the discriminatory self-tender because it agreed with the Unocal directors that the Pickens offer was coercive. Pickens had made clear that shareholders who didn't tender would be forced out at a lower price once Pickens had control, which put pressure on the shareholders to accede to his $54 offer even if they didn't think it was fair, for fear that they would be treated even worse if they didn't agree to the offer but enough of their fellow shareholders did. (A much repeated joke in the 1980s was that the only clear rule in Delaware corporate law is that T. Boone Pickens, who was viewed as a greenmailer—an investor who buys stock and then threatens to make life miserable for the company's managers unless they buy his stock back at a premium—always loses.)

Revlon was a classic battle between the old and new orders. After failing in his effort to negotiate a consensual buyout with Revlon's elegant French CEO Michel Bergerac, the not-so-elegant, cigar-chomping—and, some noted, Jewish—Ronald Perelman launched a hostile bid. Bergerac responded by turning to the buyout firm Forstmann & Little, whose Ted Forstmann was a fervent critic of junk bonds. Bergerac and the Revlon board tilted the contest to Forstmann by, among other things, signing a merger agreement with Forstmann and agreeing as part of the deal to sell Revlon's most valuable assets to Forstmann even if the Revlon shareholders rejected the proposed merger. But it was all for naught. Perelman sued to prevent Revlon from going forward with the merger or honoring the asset agreement. The Delaware Supreme Court held that, once Revlon's directors had decided to sell the company, they had an obligation to get the highest possible price. "The directors' role changed," the court concluded, in terms that reflected the medieval battle terminology of the era, "from defenders of the corporate bastion to auctioneers charged with getting the best price for the stockholders in a sale of the company." Once the dust settled, Perelman, the Drexel-financed upstart, had acquired his prize.[16]

The Lure of Consulting for Accountants and Investment Banks

In the decades after the New Deal, auditors and securities analysts had been the principal outside watchers of corporate law; their scrutiny could identify Icaran executives who were manipulating the company's balance sheet or taking inappropriate risks. As the takeover boom got going, auditors and the investment banks for whom many securities analysts work were soon enlisted as participants, as insiders to the revolution. The takeover of Trans Union by takeover maven Jay Pritzker—which gave rise to the other great 1985 Delaware Supreme Court case—shows what happened and hints at the implications that this development would have a decade later.

Although best known for his hostile bids, Pritzker was an invited guest at the Trans Union party. Trans Union had enormous tax deductions (mostly from investment tax credits and accelerated depreciation) that it couldn't fully use, because the profits from the company's railroad leasing business were much smaller than the deductions. Trans Union's directors knew that the best way to take advantage of the deductions would be to merge with or acquire a company that was making large profits. Trans Union's deductions could then be used to shelter its merger partner's profits, and both would live happily ever after. The Trans Union board was more talk than action, however, so CEO Jerome Van Gorkom, who was ready to retire, finally took matters into his own hands, suggesting to Pritzker, a "social acquaintance" of his, that Pritzker make a bid for the company. Pritzker did just that. He offered $55 per share at a time when Trans Union's stock was trading at $38 and insisted that the Trans Union board accept or reject his offer in less than three days.

Pritzker obviously couldn't have sized this deal up without a great deal of expert tax advice. After all, the value of Trans Union was tied to its tax deductions and whether they would survive a merger with his existing business. Nor was this an unusual takeover in that regard. Many of the takeovers of the 1980s were driven in large part by a quest to take advantage of unused tax benefits. The takeover career of Ronald Perelman, for instance, the hero of the Revlon battle, got under way when he acquired a $300 million tax-loss benefit along with the struggling Pantry Pride grocery store chain.[17]

Later on, a make-or-break issue for many takeovers was whether the combined company would be able to take advantage of "pooled" accounting. (Under the pooling technique, which was eliminated in 2000, the financials of the two companies were simply combined, and the acquiring company was not required to treat the difference between the purchase price and the prior market value of the target company's assets as a loss for accounting purposes.)

When I teach the basic Corporations class in law school, I often emphasize to my students how crucial a role that tax considerations play in these transactions, and then sheepishly admit how little I know about corporate tax. Takeover bidders like Jay Pritzker don't have this luxury. They need to know the tax and accounting implications. The best way to acquire this informa-

tion is to hire one of the Big Four accounting firms as a consultant. More takeovers, in other words, meant more consulting
work for accounting firms.

The 1980s takeover market created an equally pressing need
for investment-banking advice. Takeover bidders like Jay Pritzker
obviously needed to figure out how much a target company
was worth before they made a bid, and they often turned to investment banks for a sophisticated assessment of value. Until
1985, most observers assumed that a target company's directors
weren't really required to contribute to this consulting market.
Although target directors might consult with a Wall Street bank,
they also could rely on an internal valuation—that is, a valuation
by the company's own CFO—when they decided whether to accept a takeover bid.

The Trans Union case shattered this comfortable assumption.
When a group of Trans Union shareholders challenged the
Pritzker merger, the Delaware Supreme Court stunned the corporate world by concluding that, because they failed to adequately assess the Pritzker offer before accepting it, the directors
had indeed violated their fiduciary duties. Key to this conclusion—the court emphasized it several times—was the fact that
the directors hadn't bothered to obtain an independent assessment of Trans Union's value; they had simply relied on internal
calculations. (It also didn't help that the directors met for only
two hours, that none of them read the merger agreement, and
that Van Gorkom signed it during a festive outing at the Chicago
Lyric Opera.)

The court stopped short of explicitly requiring an outside
valuation. "We do not imply," Justice Moore said, "that an outside
valuation study is essential to support an informed business
judgment . . . or required as a matter of law." But the necessity
of an outside valuation was of course precisely what the court
did imply. After the Trans Union case, it was taken for granted
that the target company's board of directors had better get an

outside investment banker involved. The so-called fairness opinion soon became a staple of investment-banking life.[18]

The surge in new consulting opportunities would have dramatic consequences for the accounting and investment-banking industries. Most important of all, as we shall see, would be a rapid erosion of the effectiveness of accountants and securities analysts as curbs on the perverse effects of managerial hubris.

Icarus or the New J. P. Morgan?

As the 1980s wore on, Drexel took to calling itself a merchant bank. By "merchant," Milken and his partners meant that they were more than simply underwriters of junk bonds. They also owned a piece of the action themselves. And indeed they did. When Milken and his partners sold junk bonds for a client, they often threw in warrants—that is, the right to acquire stock—along with the bonds. Milken might keep some of the bonds and warrants, either as part of his fee or by buying them for his own account. Much like Jay Cooke after the Civil War or J. P. Morgan in the Money Trust days, Milken and Drexel wound up with a significant ownership stake in many (over 150 as of 1986) of their clients.

There were other similarities to Morgan as well. Milken ran an intensely secretive operation that included a vast network of clients and dominated access to a crucial form of financing. One prominent investor, echoing the kinds of statements once made about Pierpont Morgan himself, enthused that "Drexel is like a god in [the junk-bond and takeover] business. . . . They are awesome. You hate to do business against them." "I'm not much given to hero worship," Drexel's Leon Black gushed to a reporter in 1986, "but I . . . never thought there would be a Michael Milken. . . . He knows the balance sheets of companies better than many of our clients do. And he is so aggressive. . . . He wants one hundred percent market share."[19]

At its 1986 peak, Drexel came close, garnering nearly 70% of the junk-bond business. Drexel's clients—takeover raiders like Icahn and Perelman and the emerging takeover firms like KKR—were, in Black's view, "the modern version of robber barons. These are the guys shaking up management," he explained, "these are the guys who are building empires."

But even in the midst of these giddy days of triumph, cracks were beginning to appear in the Drexel facade. Drexel's competitors couldn't get the same mileage out of a highly confident letter as Drexel did. They didn't have the same track record in selling junk bonds to finance takeovers, so their statement that they were "highly confident" that they could arrange financing didn't have nearly the same ring as this statement had when it came from Drexel. But in the late 1980s, Drexel's competitors devised an alternative: the "bridge loan." Bridge loans were a commitment by an investment bank that it would personally finance the takeover if the bank failed to sell enough junk bonds to investors. The investment bank promised to put its money where its mouth was, providing interim financing—the "bridge"—if necessary until more permanent financing was finally raised. Bridge loans were more than simply an alternative to Drexel's highly confident letter. They were superior. Whereas Drexel's highly confident letter said only that Drexel believed it could raise the funds for a takeover, the bridge loan was a firm commitment. A takeover bidder that signed up one of the competitors, such as Salomon Brothers, to arrange its takeover financing never had to wonder whether the funds would be available when it was time to complete the deal.[20]

As the competition stiffened, complaints about Milken's and Drexel's vaunted network of clients and bond buyers grew louder. It had always been incestuous. Milken built his network by making money for everyone ("I'll make it up to you," was his standard refrain when a deal did not turn out as well as expected) and by pressuring his underwriting clients to double as buyers when he sold junk bonds for other clients. Critics grumbled that Milken flouted the securities disclosure rules in his quest to maintain secrecy and that he kept some of his important clients happy by handing out inside information.

To make matters worse, one of Milken's most important classes of clients would soon be taken away.

The S&L Collapse

The play within the play of the 1980s takeover story was the S&L debacle at the end of the decade—the end of the subplot that started with S&L deregulation at the outset of the decade. We already seem to have forgotten just how devastating the crisis was—it cost American taxpayers between $150 and $200 billion—and what a ham-handed role that Congress and regulators played throughout the predicament. This is unfortunate. The S&L crisis foreshadowed not only the fall of Milken and Drexel, but also the more recent corporate scandals.

For one golden year, the deregulation of the S&Ls in the early 1980s seemed to have saved the day. After losing over $6 billion in 1981 and nearly as much the following year, the S&Ls pulled in more than $2.5 billion in 1983. "The sun shone brightly on home buyers in 1983," according to an industry publication. "Savings institutions emerged from the interest rate storms of the preceding years and the disruption of deregulation flush with cash and a renewed dedication to housing financing."[21]

In reality, alas, the new beginning was simply a mirage. A large slice of that $2.5 billion came from a sharp dip in interest rates, which made the S&Ls' existing portfolio of loans more valuable, since the loans had been made when rates were higher. Although the interest rate drop was merely fortuitous, the other major reason for the big profits was downright ominous. Desperate to prop up the failing thrift industry, Congress and S&L regulators had invited the S&Ls to use several very misleading accounting tricks. To encourage healthy S&Ls to acquire their ailing siblings, regulators created "purchase accounting," which permitted the acquiring thrift to postpone recognition of the difference between the purchase price and the (significantly lower) value of the assets. Even worse was the way that S&Ls accounted for construction loans. Regulators permitted them to treat the loan fees they received when a loan closed as immediate profits. As a result, even the most unprofitable loans—the disastrous projects to build condos or apartments in Texas that no one wanted—showed up on the S&Ls' balance sheets as pure profit in the beginning, because of the loan fees.

The deregulation wasn't entirely misguided, but it encouraged the managers of troubled S&Ls to take outrageous risks. To attract money, so that they could grow out of their doldrums, S&Ls offered eye-popping interest rates on their deposits and hired deposit brokers to market these rates across the country. Because they were paying such high rates, the S&Ls had an incentive to gamble on risky investments. "Hot money—money bought by paying high interest rates," as one expert puts it, "leads to hot investments."[22] Especially in the Southwest, struggling S&Ls threw themselves into construction lending—something they had little prior experience with—and booked their loan-fee profits as they went. Many S&Ls turned to Milken's junk bonds for the same reason.

It wasn't immediately obvious that the S&L industry had taken on the quality of a giant Ponzi scheme. But the bottom fell out of the Texas real-estate market in 1986, thanks to a sudden drop in oil prices (which made the nouveau riche a bit less riche) and the 1986 tax reforms (which reversed several real-estate tax benefits that had been created five years earlier). From then on, the S&Ls started running out of places to hide their losses.

Most of the S&L managers were essentially honest men and women who were encouraged by the warped regulatory environment to roll the dice. But a few were crooks, attracted by the easy access to money and perks; and others were honest people who turned into crooks as time went on. Two of the most notorious—David Paul of Miami's CenTrust thrift and Charles Keating of Lincoln Savings and "Keating Five" fame—seem to fall in the last, honest-to-crook category. Their Icaran excesses were magnified by the perverse competitive landscape. Paul was a successful real-estate entrepreneur who bought CenTrust when the Miami real-estate market was booming, thinking he could parlay his real-estate know-how into big profits. After Paul bought CenTrust, saving it from the brink of collapse, "he behaved"—not to put too fine a point on it—"like a pig." Paul paid himself $16 million over the seven years from 1983 to 1990, and he "had CenTrust spend $40 million for a yacht, a sailboat, a Rubens, some impressionists, Limoges china, and Baccarat crystal." At first CenTrust seemed to be making large profits, but much of the profit came from accounting tricks such as purchase accounting and booking and upfront bank fees; and the rest came from a large portfolio of Drexel junk bonds that CenTrust started purchasing after Drexel underwrote an issuance of CenTrust bonds. By the end of the decade, the losses and Paul's extravagant use of CenTrust's funds—embezzlement, as it later turned out—would bring him crashing down.[23]

Keating was a crafty, hard-nosed but legitimate home builder when he bought Lincoln Savings and took his 1980s ride. When Lincoln started losing money, he invested in riskier and riskier projects—culminating in the Phoenician Hotel in Scottsdale, Arizona, a "resort hotel complex of Brobdingnagian proportions and Babylonian excess" that ultimately lost over $100 million. From there, it was a short step to the fraudulent transactions that were used to loot the S&L, and to funnel money out, to Lincoln's holding company. Along the way, Keating persuaded the "Keating Five" (Senators McCain, DeConcini, Cranston, Glenn, and Riegle) to pressure the S&L regulators to leave him alone. This political influence postponed the inevitable and dramatically increased the cost to taxpayers when the gig was finally up and Congress finally stepped in, forcing the liquidation of numerous insolvent banks and S&Ls by enacting the Financial Institutions Reform, Recovery, and Enforcement Act of 1989 (FIRREA).[24]

Bringing the Decade to a Close

On November 14, 1986, the controversial stock trader Ivan Boesky, an important Drexel client, pled guilty to insider trading, agreed to pay a $100 million fine (the largest ever to this point), and pledged to cooperate with the government's investigation of Wall Street securities transactions.[25] At Drexel, the date was later referred to simply as "Boesky Day." Boesky wasn't the first Wall Street trader to cop a plea—there were several others before him, including Drexel trader Dennis Levine—but none were as closely involved in Milken's junk-bond machine. Before he was done, Boesky would point fingers at Marty Siegel, a high-level Drexel corporate-finance partner, and Milken himself.

For the next three years, Drexel had to contend with the increasing competition of other investment banks (who were finally beginning to catch up), with the deepening investigation of Wall Street (which was getting closer and closer to Milken himself), and with the maturing of the takeover market that Milken's financial wizardry had done so much to spur.

It came to a head in 1989. The year before had ended with Drexel's last major triumph, the biggest hostile takeover in history. Drexel financed the LBO firm KKR in its battle with Ross Johnson over RJR-Nabisco. As breathlessly portrayed in

Barbarians at the Gate, KKR entered the picture after Johnson, the perks-loving CEO of RJR-Nabisco, proposed a management buyout of the company. KKR finally won the bidding contest when it offered $26 billion, a then-unheard of amount. The RJR-Nabisco takeover proved that Drexel could line up the financing for almost any conceivable takeover bid, no matter how large.

For Drexel, the RJR-Nabisco battle turned out to be the last hurrah. Before 1989 was over, three stakes were driven into the heart of the Drexel operation. The first was the long-looming indictment of Milken himself. Everyone knew that Milken was the big fish, the principal target of the government's Wall Street investigations. As U.S. attorney for the southern district of New York, Rudy Giuliani first came to prominence by perfecting the "perp walk"—the arrest of prominent Wall Street figures in front of live television cameras. In March 1989—shortly after Giuliani resigned to run for mayor—the government came for Milken himself. Following in the wake of a civil complaint by the SEC, the government indicted Milken for a wide range of technical securities fraud offenses. Milken was accused of engaging in several "stock-parking" schemes—schemes to arrange temporary sales of stock in order to disguise the ownership of the stock. One count accused him of "'inducing' the Boesky organization to purchase MCA stock 'for the purpose of concealing from the market that Golden Nugget was selling its MCA common stock.'" Another count accused Milken of aiding and abetting a false securities law disclosure by Boesky in another transaction. Milken loudly protested his innocence, and Drexel waged an ongoing public relations offensive in support of Milken and the bank, but the end was drawing near. A year later, Milken threw in the towel and pled guilty, eventually receiving a ten-year sentence. In subsequent years, the significance of Milken's conviction was hotly debated: some viewed him as lawless, thinking himself above the securities regulations that prohibit others from profiting from connections and inside information; others saw Milken as a scapegoat.[26]

The second stake was Congress's response to the S&L crisis, a sweeping legislative reform known as FIRREA (pronounced *fi-REE-ah*). If you closed your eyes and listened to an abstract description of the S&L scandal and the government's response, it would all sound remarkably up to date: The scandal was perpetrated by managers who paid themselves extravagant salaries while they manipulated their companies' balance sheets to disguise the millions of dollars that were going down the drain. Their accountants and lawyers—the professionals who were in the best position to root out the fraud—were busy enabling it instead. The government made things worse and was compromised by ties to the worst offenders, but it finally stepped in, passing tough new legislation calling for higher standards of corporate accountability.

As lawmakers started debating the S&L reforms in the summer of 1989, Milken's criminal indictment was much on their minds. Representative Byron Dorgan of North Dakota introduced an amendment that would prohibit S&Ls from holding junk bonds. "Junk bond investments," he argued, "are a foolish and dangerous game"—an investment that conflicted with the S&Ls' mission of translating government-insured deposit accounts into mortgages for American home buyers. Opponents pointed out that junk bonds were only a small percentage of the S&Ls' assets (roughly 1%, overall) and complained that forcing the thrifts to get rid of their junk bonds would destroy the junk-bond market. But the amendment passed easily, buoyed by the rising tide of hostility against hostile takeovers and the junk bonds that financed them.[27]

The final dagger was the Delaware Supreme Court's decision in *Paramount Communications Inc. v. Time-Warner*, which seemed to signal that the hostile takeover era was truly coming to an end. During the course of the 1980s, nearly every state enacted an antitakeover statute. Delaware, surprisingly enough, had never really joined the antitakeover bandwagon. In *Time-Warner*, however, the Delaware Supreme Court changed its tune. After agreeing to merge with Warner, the directors of Time refused to even consider a last-minute bid by an unwanted bidder, Paramount Communications. Unlike its 1985 decisions, which suggested that target companies had no right to "just say no," the Delaware Supreme Court announced in *Time-Warner* that the directors have a great deal of discretion how to respond to a takeover bid, thus permitting Time to form the company that became Time-Warner and eventually, after a disastrous merger with AOL, AOL Time Warner.

Delaware's Hamlet-like response to the takeover era—first forcing corporate directors to take hostile bids seriously but then shifting directions in *Time-Warner*—was puzzling to many observers. Despite the legacy of extensive federal regulation left by the New Deal, much of corporate law is still the prerogative of the states, which made Delaware's pronouncements extremely important and lent an urgency to the quest to understand Delaware's stance. In political terms, Delaware's reluctance to clamp down on takeovers early on may reflect the fact that both bidders and targets are incorporated in Delaware, whereas stringent antitakeover legislation was enacted in states where a small number of takeover targets have significant legislative influence. Delaware also lives in constant fear that Congress will usurp its authority in corporate law. In the late 1980s, Congress was considering a variety of proposals that would have thrown cool water on the takeover market. Delaware's judges, one suspects, were well aware by the time they issued the *Time-Warner* decision that Congress might step in if Delaware didn't do anything to help douse the fire. Whatever the reason, *Time-Warner* was one more jolt to the go-go world that Milken and Drexel had helped to create.[28]

Drexel's Last Gasp

In truth, Drexel may already have been headed for a fall by the time that Milken was hauled off to jail. In the heady days of the early and mid-1980s, the raiders had focused on companies that were underpriced, poorly managed, or both. Many of the conglomerates of the 1960s were the first to go. Raiders made enormous profits by acquiring and breaking up companies whose businesses had never belonged together in the first place. But by the late 1980s, most of the low-hanging fruit had been picked. By then, the easy profits had been made.

With stiff competition from other investment banks' bridge loans and fewer attractive takeover candidates to be found, Drexel took increasingly greater risks as it tried to maintain its grip on the junk-bond market. For the first time, Drexel deals started falling through. Mimicking the bridge-loan strategy used by Salomon and others, Drexel committed $385 million to the LBO of JPS Textile group. When the bank sold barely half of the junk bonds, it was stuck with a $200 million position. Another textile takeover, West Point–Pepperell, saddled Drexel with $250 million of junk bonds it couldn't sell. The company that had pioneered the junk market was losing its grip.

Back in 1873, Jay Cooke, another financier who had created a new financial market, was tossed into bankruptcy by his creditors. On February 12, 1990, after pleading with Treasury Secretary Nicholas Brady, Federal Reserve Chairman Alan Greenspan, and others for help, Drexel head Fred Joseph was told that he had until seven o'clock the next morning to decide to file for bankruptcy or the government itself would shut the bank down. Joseph walked into bankruptcy court the next morning and officially brought the Drexel era to an end.

Icarus Lite?

The rise and fall of Michael Milken and Drexel had many of the characteristics of a classic Icarus Effect scandal. A brilliant entrepreneur created a new market, and the corporate form enabled him to raise vast amounts of money. After a meteoric rise, he faced increasing competition and engaged in increasingly risky and, at times, fraudulent behavior, all of which led to a spectacular fall.

Yet there were important differences between Milken's fall and prior Icarus Effect scandals. Although Milken and Drexel Burnham owned stock in many of the companies they financed, their implosion did not stem from Drexel Burnham's stake in corporate America. Jay Cooke's collapse offers a revealing contrast. The failure of Cooke and his bank was caused in large part by the collapse of the vast Northern Pacific railroad to which its fortunes were tethered. Milken and Drexel Burnham weren't beholden to the success of any given company to nearly the same extent. They were more like J. P. Morgan & Co. (in this respect at least) than Jay Cooke & Company.

Another striking distinction between Milken and previous Icaran heroes was the effect of his fall. Prior Icarus Effect scandals, such as Cooke's collapse and the fall of Samuel Insull and other 1920s corporate empires, weakened the hand of managers and led to laws that were designed to keep managers in check. When we look back over the 1980s and early 1990s, by contrast, the two major reforms we find are the antitakeover statutes that more than forty states enacted and the 1989 S&L reforms. Neither of these fixed the corporate landscape in anything like the way that the New Deal reforms had done.

Think about the antitakeover laws that make it harder for raiders to take over a local corporation. In some respects, they can indeed be seen as an indirect check on managerial risk-taking. By insulating managers from takeovers, antitakeover statutes diminish the pressure for managers to live on the edge, to do anything necessary to keep the company's current stock price pumped up so that vultures won't begin to circle. But unlike the responses to earlier Icarus Effect scandals, which tapped into demands by ordinary Americans for reform, the anti-takeover statutes were promoted by managers themselves. In many states, state lawmakers enacted legislation at the behest of one or a small group of local companies—Aetna in Connecticut, for instance, and Armstrong World Industries in Pennsylvania.[29] Moreover, as we shall see in chapter 5, any curb on managerial risk-taking disappeared almost before the ink on the anti-takeover statutes was dry.

FIRREA and the litigation against participants in the S&L scandals was a response more in keeping with the true Icaran collapses of the past. (Indeed, the S&L crisis itself had the same arc as a classic wave of Icarus Effect scandals, though none of the S&L villains created a new market or invented a new financing device; they were given their wings by the government itself, through regulators' willingness to let anyone take the helm of an S&L.) Lawmakers and regulators took direct aim at the problems in S&L governance. They eliminated some of the incentives that S&L managers had to take inappropriate risks with taxpayer-insured deposit money and punished both the S&L kingpins themselves and also the directors, accountants, and lawyers who had failed to intervene. But the S&L reforms were limited to that one context. They cleaned up the S&L fiasco, but they had little effect on corporate America outside of the S&Ls.

Far more important than either legislative response was the effect that the Milken era had on American corporate and financial life. Takeover bidders brought in new managers and paid them enormous amounts of money to break up the target or transform its operational performance. The same ethos soon permeated corporate America, creating a "high-velocity" managerial environment where managers regularly moved from one company to another and were expected to produce immediate results. Risk-taking was not only invited, it was all but compelled. Reagan-era attitudes toward the second Icarus Effect factor, competition, figured prominently in the developments we have seen in this chapter and will see more of in the next. The more relaxed view of regulators and courts to concentration in any given industry created numerous takeover opportunities, and deregulation inspired a gold rush among entrepreneurs who saw the prospect of huge profits in a newly deregulated industry. Finally, the new hands-off stance toward antitrust enforcement removed an indirect curb on the third factor, corporate size and complexity. Gone was the suggestion, most famously articulated by Judge Learned Hand in 1945, that one goal of antitrust law should be "to perpetuate and preserve, for its own sake and in spite of possible cost, an organization of industry in small units." The 1980s did not, however, immediately bring the kinds of manipulations of the corporate form that have characterized previous periods of American business history. If anything, takeovers tended to simplify a company's corporate structure. But any simplification was purely temporary. Just as financial innovation helped to make the takeover era possible, it also would soon lead to remarkable new sophistry with the corporate entity.[30]

There were legitimate business justifications for this new world where regulators retreated and the market was given a freer reign, as we have seen. But together, these developments diminished many of the post–New Deal constraints on Icaran excesses. And the 1980s were just the beginning. The real excitement was yet to come.

Five Enron, WorldCom, and the Transformation of Icarus

For many of us, there was a moment in the late 1990s when we first fully realized the scope of the dot-com bubble and the pervasiveness of the "irrational exuberance" that Alan Greenspan had tsk-tsked about in 1996. My bubble moment came in Thirtieth Street Station, Philadelphia's main train station. As I walked past a pub in the station, as I do every day when I arrive on the commuter train, I noticed that all three of the pub's overhead televisions were tuned to CNBC, with talking heads chattering about business developments and a stock-market ticker streaming across the bottom of the screen. One and sometimes two of the TVs stuck with the market even in the evening, rather than shifting to ESPN or a Philadelphia 76ers or Phillies game. The market was obviously the most popular sporting event of all.

The market collapse that followed is often described as a single episode—the bursting of the Internet bubble. But this isn't quite right. The collapse really was two intertwined but separate events, the dot-com collapse in 2000 and the Icarus Effect failures of Enron and WorldCom in late 2001 and 2002. As devastating as the dot-com bust was to Silicon Valley and to the people and publications that the bubble had spawned, there were no calls for dramatic reform of American business. There had always been a surreal quality to the high-tech craze. (Legendary investor Warren Buffett refused to invest in Silicon Valley companies because he said he didn't understand them.) The companies that failed had relatively few employees and only a brief history. Now it was simply over. These were not Icarus Effect failures.

Contrast the collapse of Enron and WorldCom, of Adelphia and Global Crossing. Almost as soon as Enron imploded, stories with titles like "Washington Wants Wall St. Changes" and "The Race Is On for Tougher Regulation" sprouted in newspapers across the country.[1] It wasn't just the whiff of fraud that surrounded these collapses. It was the magnitude of Enron and WorldCom and the fact that Ken Lay and Bernie Ebbers had so recently been hailed as businesses geniuses whose companies had revolutionized their markets. It was also the fact that the collapse of confidence triggered by Enron and WorldCom affected more ordinary American investors, in a more direct way, than any previous Icarus Effect failure in American business history.

Enron's Rise from Humble Pipeline to "World's Greatest Company"

The company that most personified the corporate meltdown started out as a natural-gas company called Houston Natural Gas (and before that, prior to a series of mergers during the course of the twentieth century, as Kirby Oil).[2] Ken Lay came aboard as CEO in 1984, shortly after HNG had fended off a takeover bid from Coastal Corporation. The son of a Missouri farmer who went bankrupt after a truck of his chickens crashed and who later became a Baptist minister, Lay spent his childhood plotting his escape to a life of business success. After a starry career at the University of Missouri, he joined Humble Oil (the predecessor of Exxon) as a senior economist. Lay volunteered for the Navy during the Vietnam War, then followed his Missouri economics professor and mentor Pinkney Walker to Washington in 1971. Working under Walker at the Federal Energy Regulatory Commission, Lay gave "impassioned speeches in favor of deregulation and the benefits of the free market." Armed with his free-market credo, Lay reentered the private sector, working as a gas executive in Florida and then Houston. When he took the mantle at Houston Natural Gas, the diminutive, sandy-haired Lay had arrived.

Lay had correctly predicted that deregulation would transform the natural-gas industry from its traditional status as the poor cousin of oil (natural gas, after all, was simply an accident of the oil drilling process, the waste gas that one finds along with the black gold) to a lucrative business in its own right. Lay pushed the deregulatory envelope from the beginning, buying and selling gas on a spot-market basis, for instance, before the spot market was officially created by the deregulation of gas prices. He also launched an acquisition spree, buying gas pipelines and bidding on utility projects all over the world. When Enron bid for, won, and successfully built an enormous $1 billion natural-gas plant in Teesside, England, the business world stood up and took notice.

But Enron's stroke of genius, its great innovation, was the project it called a "Gas Bank." Lay didn't dream up the idea himself; it came from Jeff Skilling, a hotshot McKinsey & Co. consultant who was advising Enron and brainstorming with its executives about business opportunities. The volatility of natural-gas prices under deregulation had made it hard for gas companies to obtain credit (their income was too unstable) and was similarly worrisome to gas buyers (a spike in gas prices could wreak havoc on their costs). Under Skilling's plan, Enron would create a "bank" of gas by contracting with a large group of gas suppliers; it would then sell the gas to buyers. The plan was extremely risky, since it would work only if Enron placed most of the gas industry under contract, and thus had a dependable supply of gas for its buyers, so that it didn't have to worry about price competition when the time came to deliver.[3]

When Skilling presented the idea to twenty-five Enron executives, his proposal was met by blank, skeptical silence. But one of the executives was sold; fortunately for Skilling, the enthusiast was Ken Lay. Lay hired Skilling to run the Gas Bank division, and in 1989 the scheme was underway. After a rocky start, the bank took off, almost single-handedly invigorating the natural-gas industry in Texas. Before the Gas Bank, Enron's vision had been to become the "premier natural-gas pipeline in America." Once the bank took off, Lay reconsidered. Enron's new mission was to become the "world's first natural-gas major"—that is, the first natural-gas company with global standing.

Lay's political connections didn't hurt, and may have helped. In 1992, he chaired the reelection campaign of Senator Phil Gramm, the free-market purist who would briefly compete for the Republican presidential nomination in 1996. Conveniently enough, shortly after the 1992 election, Gramm's wife Wendy, who was the outgoing chair of the Commodity Futures Trading Commission, rushed through an exemption from regulation for, among other things, energy derivatives (derivatives are contracts or securities whose value is determined by [or "derived" from, hence the label] changes in the price of something else, such as interest rates, currency prices, the stock market, or in this case energy prices) before Bill Clinton took over the presidency and named a new chair. Thanks to Gramm's exemption, the energy contracts that were bought and sold at Enron's trading desk (which grew out of its Gas Bank) wouldn't be subject to the disclosure requirements and other restrictions that must be met by derivative contracts that are traded on exchanges such as the Chicago Board of Trade.

Almost as soon as she left Washington, Gramm was invited to join Enron's board of directors, where she later earned hundreds of thousands of dollars in cash and stock-based compensation.

Buoyed by the stunning success of its energy trading operations, which had become Enron Capital & Trade Resources as of 1995, Enron decided to try the same strategy in other areas, branching out well beyond its original natural-gas expertise. The company would corner the market in electricity trading, mineral contracts, and even weather derivatives. Although Skilling, who was now Enron's chief operating officer, had long been an Internet skeptic, Enron took on the world of Internet services, establishing Enron Broadband Services in 1999.

"Enron is moving so fast," Lay wrote in Enron's 1999 annual report, "that sometimes others have trouble defining us. But we know who we are. We are clearly a knowledge-based company," he continued. "We are participating in a New Economy, and the rules have changed dramatically. What you own is not as important as what you know."

In 2000, as Enron's share price reached $90/share and its spectacular implosion was still safely in the future, Lay immersed himself in George W. Bush's presidential campaign. Although Lay was even closer to Bush the Elder than to George W., he and George W. often rubbed shoulders at charity events and in Lay's box seats at Enron Field, the home of the Houston Astros baseball team. Their friendship was genuine—George W. penned affectionate Christmas cards to "Kenny Boy," replete with good-natured jokes about their wives' superiority to the two men.

There were striking similarities between Lay's relationship with George W. Bush and Jay Cooke's friendship with Ulysses S. Grant a century and a half earlier. Like Cooke, Lay was widely hailed as a business genius. Washington had been very good to Lay and Enron, as it was to Cooke and Jay Cooke and Company.

So when Bush emerged from the 2000 election imbroglio as president, he and some commentators assumed, as they had with Cooke, that the head of "the World's Coolest Company" might well be named secretary of the Treasury. What better way to cap off a stunningly successful career than to serve in his pal's cabinet.

WorldCom's Never-Ending Acquisition Spree

If anything, WorldCom owed even more to deregulation than Enron. WorldCom got its start in 1983, shortly before Judge Harold Green splintered the AT&T phone monopoly, limiting AT&T to long distance and divvying up local service among the newly created regional Bells. In early 1984, several friends of Bernie Ebbers launched LDDS with an eye to reselling long-distance service in small southern cities that were outside the reach of MCI and Sprint, the two principal competitors to AT&T.

The founders brought Ebbers into the picture because of his success raising money for a small chain of hotels he had acquired after a brief career as a high school basketball coach in Mississippi. Ebbers was a six foot four former basketball player whose college career had been sidetracked by a glass bottle that a local tough threw at him, severing his Achilles tendon, after Ebbers ran out of gas on a trip home to Canada before his senior year at Mississippi College.

At first, Ebbers stayed in the background. But as the company floundered, he stepped forward. "Look," he told his partners, "if we're going to go under, I at least want to pilot the ship." Ebbers's business strategy was quite simple. He spent like crazy, leading LDDS into one acquisition after another. LDDS acquired Re Tel Communications in Franklin, Tennessee, and the Phone Company in Jackson, Mississippi, in 1985. In 1987, Ebbers added Southland Systems, another Mississippi phone company, and it went on from there. After its acquisition of IDB WorldCom in 1994, which launched it into the overseas market, LDDS formally changed its name to WorldCom.[4]

Throughout WorldCom's acquisition spree, federal regulators lent a hand by prohibiting AT&T from lowering its long-distance rates and by subsidizing the new long-distance companies' access to local networks. WorldCom's business plan was quite simple. Much like the railroads in the nineteenth century, WorldCom wanted to expand as quickly and widely as possible, so that it could be one of the small group of companies that survived the gold rush and became a dominant player in the telecom industry.

Ebbers, the former gym instructor, proved to be an extraordinarily charismatic leader. WorldCom became one of the darlings of Wall Street, and the leading telecom analyst in the country— Jack Grubman of Salomon Smith Barney—became WorldCom's biggest cheerleader. By 2001 Grubman and Ebbers were so close that Grubman felt comfortable offering advice to Ebbers on how to handle analysts prior to a potentially contentious WorldCom conference call.

WorldCom's biggest acquisition of all was its $37 billion merger with MCI in 1997. The MCI merger made WorldCom the nation's third largest supplier of long-distance phone service, as well as a leading supplier of Internet services. And WorldCom still wasn't ready to stop. In 1999, Ebbers announced that World-Com intended to swallow an even bigger competitor, by acquiring Sprint in a $115 billion merger. At this point, however, the U.S. and European antitrust regulators finally balked. WorldCom and Sprint were forced to abandon their merger the following year.

Analysts, the Financial Media, and the Charismatic CEO

Ebbers and Lay, together with CEOs like Gary Winnick (a former Drexel Burnham banker who'd left before Drexel's collapse but would engineer a collapse of his own in 2002) of the telecom behemoth Global Crossing and Dennis Kozlowski of Tyco, represented the new 1990s corporate superstars, the winners in the new market-based corporate world ushered in by the takeover era. With each, a key ingredient of their success was the sheer force of their charisma.

It wasn't simply an accident that most high-flying executives of the 1990s banked on their charisma. The Wall Street of the 1990s demanded it. With trillions of dollars being thrown around in the rising market, the companies that attracted analysts' attention—the companies that stayed hot—were the ones that seemed to be thriving in the new economy. If you were trying to wow a superstar analyst, it helped a great deal to have a smooth, charismatic CEO.

The financial media reinforced the emphasis on charisma. The rise of cable television, with its hundreds of channels, created a new niche for business media, and the boom in stock ownership assured a large and growing audience. Business oriented channels like CNBC and MSNBC could quickly turn a telegenic CEO into a celebrity, much as they did with star analysts and other pundits. "The rise of the business media and analysts," according to Rakesh Khurana, a Harvard business professor and author of *Searching for a Corporate Savior*, "introduced a new set of informal ground rules to CEO succession: a critical consideration in evaluating a potential CEO today is his or her ability to command attention from the media and stock-market analysts in a way that will establish credibility for the firm and inspire confidence in both investors and others."[5]

By these standards, Global Crossing's Gary Winnick had what

it took. Winnick's "dizzying rise to become the richest person in Los Angeles," the *Los Angeles Business Journal* enthused in 1999, "started just three years ago with a big idea and a relatively small investment. He's the $6.2 billion man." "What genius did Winnick bring to the table?" *Fortune* asked. "Nothing remotely technical. . . . Before putting up $15 million to place a $750 million bet on his first undersea cable, Winnick watched a video to educate himself on how they were laid. . . . Winnick did have a telecom expertise: an ability to make a good cold call [to sell the deal to equally naive investors]."[6]

Ken Lay and Bernie Ebbers cut similar figures. Lay was held in awe for his unflappable calm, his free-market fervor, and his A-list Washington and Texas contacts. Ebbers sported a closely trimmed white beard and portrayed himself as a folksy, down-home hero who was taking on the stodgy telecom giants—AT&T and the regional Bells—and holding his own.

In a short article in *Corporate Board Member,* a publication available only to corporate directors, Tyler Mathieson, the host of CNBC's *Marketwatch,* offered a few words of wisdom on how media-savvy CEOs can make an impression:

> Remember that television tends to "bland out" even the most energetic speaker. So be animated; wave your hands if that is your wont. Never forget that your voice is a musical instrument. It is meant to be played, loud as well as slow. Your tone matters. It is no coincidence that many of the CEOs who come across best are the ones whose companies are in the communications business. . . . These men not only know their businesses cold, they also know the value of a compelling performance.

Some celebrity CEOs took the media emphasis even further and lined up a ghostwriter to pen a flattering celebrity biography. During the 1990s, the autobiographies of Jack Welch, Al Dunlap, and other superstar CEOs regularly graced the *New York Times* best seller list (as did new biographies of predecessors such as John Rockefeller and Pierpont Morgan).

It is hard to overstate how dramatically this emphasis on charisma altered the job description of the CEOs of America's largest corporations. By the late 1990s, the emphasis on charisma meant that being able to play a corporate genius on TV was almost more important than actually being one. Enron's Lay oversaw the "World's Coolest Company," and WorldCom's Ebbers carefully cultivated his image as a good ole boy financial wizard in cowboy boots and a flannel shirt. But there is a great deal of evidence that neither fully understood the company he was overseeing.

The Trouble with Stock Options

If CEOs were required to act like celebrities, they would of course expect to be paid like celebrities as well. They did, and they were. In the past thirty years, ordinary Americans have seen their annual salary increase by roughly 10%, from $32,522 to $35,864 in inflation-adjusted, 1998 dollars. For the CEOs of America's one hundred largest corporations, the increase has been a tad larger. In 1970, they averaged $1.3 million, or thirty-nine times the salary of the average worker. In 1999, CEOs were pulling in an average of $37.5 million a year—well over one thousand times what ordinary Americans take home.[7]

Of even more importance than the magnitude of CEO pay was the form it increasingly took. One of the messages of the 1980s takeover boom had been that managers who owned a lot of stock were likely to pay much more attention to shareholders' interests than those who didn't. Even the companies that were busy fending off takeovers took the message to heart in at least one respect—they started making stock and stock options an increasingly large portion of managerial pay. A dollop of stock, everyone said, and the Berle-Means problem of the separation of ownership and control starts to go away.

Congress stoked this trend in 1993. When George Bush the Elder took a group of auto executives with him to Japan to talk about trade issues in 1991, the dramatic contrast between the U.S. automakers' outrageous salaries and the more modest compensation of Japanese CEOs ignited a firestorm of criticism about overpaid U.S. managers. Bill Clinton picked up on the theme, making CEO pay an issue in the 1992 election. Shortly after Clinton became president, Congress amended the Internal Revenue Code to prohibit companies from treating an executive's salary as a business expense to the extent it exceeded $1 million per year. Because stock options didn't count toward the $1 million limitation, companies juiced up their managers' pay with options. It also didn't hurt that options don't require the company to fork over any cash. In 1980, less than half of the country's CEOs were given stock options; by 1994, this figure had climbed to 70%.[8]

As they watched merger and acquisition activity surge in the 1990s, most scholars viewed stock and stock options as if they were manna from heaven. Load up your managers and directors with stock options, and traditional worries about what the managers are up to will disappear. Harvard Business School's Michael Jensen, one of the country's most prominent business scholars, speculated that stock options and takeovers were transforming American business. In the brave new world of American industry, LBO firms would run the show in many of nation's traditional industries, and their managers would be "incentivized" by stock options and other flavors of performance-based pay.

Let me be the first to admit that I joined the chorus too. A decade of students listened to me sing the praises of stock options, and this enthusiasm spilled over into my scholarly writing as well. What's the best way to counteract the Berle-Means bugaboo, I asked at the outset of my Corporations class each year, to solve the intractable separation between ownership and control? To give managers stock options, of course, so that they'll be shareholders too.

This wasn't entirely wrong—stock options do tend to concentrate managers' attention on the company's stock—but we now realize that options also have a pernicious flaw. They're all upside and no downside for the managers. If the company's stock price goes up, the managers win and they take home their money. But if the price goes down, there's no pain. The managers don't lose anything; they simply let the options expire without exercising them. (Or better yet, they persuade the company to "reset" the options—that is, to lower the exercise price so that the managers can try again.) With everything to gain from rolling the dice, and nothing to lose, managers had an enormous incentive to take big risks with the company's business and to pump up the stock price in any way possible.

The rewards could be unbelievably large. Bernie Ebbers was making an hefty $9.8 million a year in 1995, but this was a mere pittance compared to the $100 million he pulled in at the end of the decade, thanks to his WorldCom options. Gary Winnick of Global Crossing, the other high-flying telecom company, took home just as much.

The two trends I have just described, the emphasis on executive charisma and the heavy use of option-based pay, strongly reinforced one another when it came to corporate performance. Both the success of a media-savvy CEO and the pay that he or she took home depended on his or her ability to make sure that the company's earnings kept climbing. This, in turn, would translate into a constantly increasing stock price and regular visits from the financial media.

Enron, WorldCom, and many of their peers responded in

much the same way to these pressures: they kept moving. Enron prided itself on moving so fast that its competitors "have trouble defining who we are." WorldCom's approach to acquisitions was similar to a shark's relationship to water. Just as sharks never stop swimming, lest they drown, WorldCom started looking for its next acquisition target as soon as it finished swallowing the last.

Notice how far we have come from the CEOs of the 1950s, the era when "what's good for GM is good for America." Unlike their predecessors, the new CEOs were expected to continuously push the edge of the envelope, to act like entrepreneurs. Icaran risk-taking wasn't just permitted, it was all but compelled.

The Surge in Technological and Financial Innovation

The 1990s also saw extraordinary technological and financial innovation. Before the mid-1990s, most Americans had little exposure to the Internet; by the end of the decade, it was ubiquitous. (Netscape's IPO in 1995 is often seen as the birth both of the Internet phenomenon and of the stock-market bubble.) There is still a great deal of debate over how much, and how, the Internet will alter business in the long term. What is indisputable, however, is that companies can shift their resources into Internet-related businesses much more quickly than with traditional bricks-and-mortar businesses.

Enron was a vivid illustration. Within months of Jeff Skilling's decision to invest in broadband in 1999, Enron seemed to be well on its way to becoming a major player. During the winter and spring of 2000, Enron announced that it would be delivering financial Web content to Roadshow.com, broadcasting an international cricket tournament, and joining forces with Compaq "to provide capacity for one million simultaneous broadband streams of Windows Media Player." In July, Enron capped off the flurry of investment by signing a major deal with Blockbuster to jointly market online movies, an innovation that Lay touted as "the killer app for the entertainment industry" and Blockbuster's CEO called the "ultimate bricks-chicks-and-flicks strategy."[9]

Innovations in financial technology were proceeding at the same breakneck pace. In Milken's era, Wall Street had not yet entered the computer age. "At Citibank in the early 1980s," securities law scholar Frank Partnoy recalls, "only one trader on the trading floor even had a computer, a clunky Radio Shack TRS-80, which was primitive even for its time." Within a decade, every bank would have a stable of rocket scientist economists applying sophisticated models to Wall Street finance.[10]

The two most important innovations were derivative securities and structured finance. As noted earlier, derivatives are simply securities whose value is derived from some other value. A stock option can be seen as a derivative, for instance, because the value of the right to buy a share of stock at a specified price is based on the value of the underlying stock. An option to buy a share of IBM stock for $50 two months from now is quite valuable if IBM stock is selling for $75 per share, but less valuable if the stock is wallowing at $25 or $30 per share. Futures contracts are another simple derivative contract with a long pedigree in American financial life. The value of a futures contract that gives a farmer the right to sell a bushel of corn for $30 in six months falls if the price of corn—the asset from which the contract is "derived"—rises, but rises if corn prices decline.

As the term futures *contract* suggests, derivatives are generally designed as a contract between two parties. In the late 1980s, Wall Street bankers began to recognize the potential versatility of derivatives. Derivative contracts could be based on any imaginable asset or event that an investor or corporation was concerned about. Under its visionary CEO Charles Sanford, Bankers Trust, the biggest player in the early derivatives game, had started selling long-term stock-index options, a derivative whose value rose or fell depending on the overall performance of all the stocks in a given stock market. Bankers Trust also began marketing custom-made derivatives to companies like Procter & Gamble, which purchased complicated interest-rate derivatives, pursuant to which Procter & Gamble paid Bankers Trust if interest rates increased, while Bankers Trust profited if the rates declined. Bankers Trust also profited from the fees it charged for arranging the contracts.[11]

The beauty of derivatives is that they can be used to protect against almost any conceivable risk. Suppose a company has a large customer base in Thailand and will be hurt if the Thai baht falls vis-à-vis the dollar, because this makes its products more expensive for Thai citizens. To counteract or "hedge" against this risk, the company can simply go to Citigroup or another bank and buy a currency option. If the baht falls as feared, the company would receive a payment that offset its lost business. If the baht rises, the contract would be worthless, but the only cost would be the cost that the company paid to purchase the currency option.

The problem is that derivatives also can be used to take enormous gambles, as the nation learned when Procter & Gamble lost millions of dollars on its Bankers Trust derivatives in 1994 and Orange County treasurer Robert Citron's derivatives activity landed the home of Beverly Hills 90210 in bankruptcy court. Only a few months later, Long-Term Capital Management, a hedge fund masterminded by John Merriweather and whose economist-traders included Nobel laureate Merton Miller, was brought down by failed currency bets and might have triggered a worldwide liquidity crisis if the U.S. Treasury hadn't stepped in and engineered a bailout. (Hedge funds are investment entities that are permitted to operate largely in secrecy because they have a small number of investors, all of whom are institutions or wealthy individuals.)

The disastrous bets made by Citron, Long-Term Capital and Joseph Jett, a rogue trader at Kidder Peabody who lost $350 million trading Treasury bond derivatives in the early 1990s, graphically illustrated the dangers of derivatives. Although these traders were not themselves Icaran executives—Citron was a public official, Long-Term a private fund, and Jett a midlevel trader—very little prevents corporate managers from gambling corporate assets in the same way. In Icaran terms, derivatives have magnified the first Icaran tendency, the pressure to take excessive risks, by providing a complex and radically new way for corporate decision makers to take enormous risks if they are inclined to do so.

Structured finance, the second financial innovation, has also dramatically increased the ability for firms to take risks, and it has done so through a remarkable new manipulation of the boundaries of the corporate entity. In a structured-finance transaction, the corporation sells home mortgages, credit card loans, or other assets to a newly created entity, which raises money for the purchase by selling bonds or other securities to investors. The new entity, which is referred to as a special purpose entity (SPE) or special purchase vehicle (SPV), is often a corporation, though it may also be a partnership or trust. The SPE, which is designed to be completely separate from the company that set it up, collects the payments due under the mortgages or accounts receivable that it purchased, then uses some of this money to pay its investors. By packaging large numbers of mortgages or other assets together, structured finance makes it possible to create public markets for assets that would be too risky for investors if they were sold separately. It started with the government-sponsored companies Fannie Mae and Sallie Mae, which securitized mortgages and student loans, and spread from there.

Like derivatives, structured finance also has a darker, more morally ambiguous side. During the 1990s, the raison d'être of many structured-finance transactions was to evade regulatory restrictions, a strategy often referred to as "regulatory arbitrage." When regulators started requiring S&Ls to maintain financial reserves for every dollar they held in junk bonds, for instance, First Executive's Fred Carr, one of Michael Milken's most enthusiastic clients, sidestepped the new stricture with a structured-finance innovation known as "collateralized bond obligations" (CBOs). By selling bonds to an SPE, which then created three securities of differing priorities, and buying the securities back itself, First Executive was able to claim that the top two classes of securities were safe and should not require reserves.[12]

Enron took the strategy even further, setting up an enormously complicated web of SPEs, the most famous of which were given Star Wars names like Jedi and Chewco. Enron used the structured-finance "sales" to move underperforming assets and the debt that was associated with them off its balance sheet, relying on an accounting rule that permitted Enron to treat the SPE as a separate entity so long as at least 3% of its value had been contributed by outside investors. It was a strategy that had an awful lot in common with Samuel Insull's holding-company manipulations in the 1930s. The only difference was that Enron's strategy was far more sophisticated, and the biggest losers were the shareholders of the principal corporation, Enron, not the individuals and institutions who invested in the separate entities. But the overall result was quite similar: Enron's corporate structure was so sprawling and vast—in the end, Enron had well over two thousand SPEs, subsidiaries, and other related entities—that almost no one understood the gambles that Enron's executives were taking and the financial precariousness of the enterprise.[13]

The New Icarus: A Brief Summary

If American corporate and financial life discouraged the creation of Icaran heroes in the 1950s by domesticating the leaders who ran America's largest corporations, the developments we have just considered had precisely the opposite effect. Congress's continuing deregulation of major industries like energy and tele-com created the possibility of large profits for the companies, the Enrons and WorldComs, that could stake out the market first. Takeovers had ushered in a new breed of CEO, and the star-making machinery of the financial media placed a premium on bringing in star-quality managers. The managers who rose to the top were much more willing to take risks than were their coun-terparts from forty years earlier. At the same time, the technolog-ical and financial innovations of the 1990s made it easier for Icaran executives both to take risks and to manipulate the corpo-ration's boundaries to hide these risks than ever before.

In retrospect, it doesn't take a genius to realize that mass pro-ducing new Icaran heroes du jour and at the same time giving them the ability to take huge risks almost instantly is a lethal mix. The new Icaran executives, whose status depended in no small part on the image they portrayed to the public, faced al-most irresistible pressure to disguise their company's travails or bet the ranch, or both, to keep the dream alive if the company's performance failed to keep pace with its image. The new innova-tions made it oh-so-easy to do so.

Enron epitomized each of these dangers. In the face of com-petition in its energy-trading market, and pressured by the need to keep expanding its earnings, Enron created its broadband di-vision from scratch in a matter of months and used structured finance—the infamous "raptor" entities with Star Wars names—to shed debt from its financial statements and to generate fake profits by selling dubious assets to the new entities at artificially inflated prices. (WorldCom's misbehavior was much more pedestrian; CFO Scott Sullivan manipulated its accounting through one of the oldest tricks in the book, treating current op-erating expenses as if they were long-term costs, in order to push them into the future.)

None of the developments we have seen was occurring in a vacuum, of course. Institutional shareholders, the board of directors, auditors, securities analysts, and even the company's own employees were each, at least in theory, in a position to alert investors to the possibility of a catastrophe. But they didn't. Their silence was, as we shall see, due to the corporate and financial version of a perfect storm: the same developments that were magnifying the Icaran tendencies in corporate America also discouraged each of the would-be sentries from standing guard.

What Were the Institutional Shareholders Doing?

When the bull market of the 1990s took hold, the shareholders of America's leading corporations looked quite different than they had in the Berle-Means era. The key difference was the dramatic growth of stock ownership by institutions such as pension funds, mutual funds, banks, and insurance companies. (The ultimate owners of the pension and mutual-funds' assets were ordinary Americans, a fact that will figure prominently in our discussion below.) Collectively, these institutions now owned a whopping 57% of the stock in the thousand largest American companies by the mid 1990s.[14] In many of the nation's leading corporations, fifteen or twenty institutional shareholders held, as they still do, close to half of the company's stock.

On paper, the enormous ownership stake held by institutional shareholders looks like the seeds of a shareholder revolution. If the institutional shareholders flexed their muscles, surely they could reign in the managers of America's corporations. Institutional shareholders have indeed become a major force in American corporate governance, but they haven't thrown their weight around as much as their stockholdings might suggest. Because mutual funds try to keep their costs as low as possible (especially index funds, which take one of everything, holding stock in every company in a market or index rather than trying to pick and choose) and because policing the corridors of American corporate life is costly, mutual-fund managers usually stay on the sidelines. The investment advisors who manage private pension funds stay quiet for a more unseemly reason: a good, old-fashioned conflict of interest. The investment advisor for a company's pension fund is either a company officer or an advisor picked by the company's managers. Either way, the investment advisor is well aware that the managers won't look kindly at an advisor who has developed a reputation for making corporate managers' lives difficult. Far better, if the investment advisor wishes to develop a thriving client base, to keep quiet and mind her own business.

The one group of institutions that has taken a substantially more active role is public pension funds such as CalPERS (the California state employees' pension fund) and SWIB (Wisconsin's state pension fund). State pension funds aren't beholden to corporate managers like their private siblings are, and they aren't forced by market pressures to keep costs down as much as mutual funds, so they have much more flexibility to put their mouth where their money is. For the past decade or so, CalPERS has done just this. It publishes a list of corporate-governance principles on its website, and each year the fund selects a group of underperforming companies to focus its energies on in the coming year.[15]

So why didn't CalPERS and other institutional investors take aim at Enron, WorldCom, or Global Crossing as they spiraled out of control? Why was no one complaining about their deceptive accounting and unjustified business risk? One reason is that these companies were making money for their shareholders, or seemed to be, as the bubble market inflated. CalPERS and its peers tended to save their ammo for companies whose stock was declining and whose board of directors was stacked with insiders or had loaded up with antitakeover protections. CalPERS, in fact, was one of Enron's favored investors. CalPERS invested in several of Enron's SPEs, earning enviable 20% and 30% rates of return for its trouble. CalPERS eventually got cold feet about the investments, but Enron made sure CalPERS was paid in full, and CalPERS didn't whisper a word about any concerns it had about what Enron was up to. Another explanation for the funds' relative silence is that they are subject to enormous political pressures, and many of their trustees are themselves political appointees. Bob Monks and Nell Minow note, for example, that "When the Wisconsin state pension fund wanted to object to General Motors' $742.8 million forced greenmail payment to Ross Perot, it was stopped by the governor, who was trying to get General Motors to build some plants in his state."[16]

What Were the Outside Directors Thinking?

What about the board of directors? What were the outside directors doing while Enron and WorldCom hurtled toward destruction, "imploding" as Enron whistle-blower Sherron Watkins had warned, "in a wave of accounting scandals"?[17]

The directors claimed that they were duped, that they didn't know what the managers were up to because it was well hidden and the outside accountants signed off on everything. Enron's SPE transactions were indeed stunningly complex. But there was precious little evidence that the directors paid much attention as the tide turned at each of these companies. At Enron, the company's Code of Ethics prohibited Enron managers from standing on both sides of a transaction with the company. No problem—the Enron directors voted not once, but twice, to waive off the Code of Ethics so that Andy Fastow could run Chewco, the most notorious of the SPEs, and make millions of dollars at Enron's expense. Nor do any of the directors seem to have asked any serious questions about Enron's increasingly grandiose plans to create markets in everything under the sun.

The WorldCom directors were little better. Not only did the directors accede to each of Ebbers's acquisitions, but they continually threw money at him, paying him tens of millions of dollars a year in overall compensation and, when that wasn't enough, making an eye-popping $400 million loan to him. "Rule No. 1" at WorldCom was "Always do what Bernie says." And "Rule No. 2: See rule No. 1."[18]

Now, the first place to look when the directors aren't doing much directing is the composition of the board. If the board is dominated by managers or if the supposedly outside directors are really just cronies of the CEO, this may be the source of the problem. Cronyism may have been part of the reason that WorldCom's board let Bernie Ebbers do whatever he wanted. The inner circle on the board consisted of the managerial directors (Ebbers, Scott Sullivan) and several of Bernie's childhood friends. But WorldCom also had several truly independent directors, and Enron seemed to have even more. In some respects, the Enron directors look like a board straight out of central casting. Nearly all of the directors were outsiders, rather than managers. And the outside directors weren't simply lightweights. Included on the board were the CEOs of several major corporations and investment companies, the former dean of the Stanford business school, and of course Wendy Gramm, the former chair of the Commodity Futures Trading Commission.

Once we scratch beneath the surface a bit more, the Enron directors don't look quite so robustly independent. Several of the directors had direct financial ties to Enron—Robert Belfer is CEO of Belcom Oil & Gas, for instance, which had contracted with Enron for several years. Several others worked for non-profits (Anderson Cancer Center, the University of Texas School of Law) that received six-figure donations from Enron during their tenures on the board. It doesn't take a conspiracy theorist to suspect that directors with these kinds of ties might be reluctant to ask hard questions about the company that has been so kind to their institution.

But these subtle conflicts of interest only begin to explain the complete passivity of the Enron and WorldCom boards. Two other factors made things much worse. The first was the directors' option-based compensation. By 2001, the directors of Enron were making nearly $300,000 a year, much of it in stock options, all for simply showing up at eight or nine meetings a year. High pay has a way of silencing dissent; and the use of options exacerbated this problem, since it gave the directors the same upside without a corresponding downside, as was true for Ebbers and Lay.

The other problem was the messianic zeal of the CEOs themselves. If Bernie Ebbers hadn't cast a spell on Wall Street, WorldCom would never have reached the upper echelons of corporate America, and the same could be said of Enron and Global Crossing. The companies that really took off were the ones with a charismatic CEO. But the same qualities that made these companies winners also discouraged dissent. Who was a WorldCom director—even an accomplished director—to challenge the man who had transformed WorldCom from a struggling peddler of long-distance service to one of the world's great companies? Quite simply, the outside directors of each of these companies were cowed by the magnificence of the CEO.

What Were the Auditors Doing?

Even if they had been watching more than their fees, the directors of the country's high-flying corporate juggernauts couldn't have rooted out every problem, every subtle manipulation of the financial statements. That was the accountants' job. They were the ones who were supposed to understand the pyrotechnics of Enron's SPEs and to ask CFO Scott Sullivan what he was doing when he treated billions of dollars of WorldCom's expenses as long-term rather than current costs, then flag the problems for the benefit of everyone else.

Once upon a time, Arthur Andersen, who did the accounting honors for both companies, wouldn't have put up with any of the financial sleight-of-hand. The Arthur Andersen who sorted through the wreckage of Samuel Insull's empire prided himself on unflinching, uncompromising investigation of the companies he audited. The Arthur Andersen auditors who held their noses and signed off on the Enron and WorldCom financial statements were another breed altogether.

What happened? What changed was the consulting opportunities created by the Wall Street boom of the 1980s and 1990s. In 1976, more than 70% of the major accounting firms' revenue came from auditing. By 1998, this number had plummeted to 38%. Accounting firms that had achieved prominence by developing an international reputation for their audits of large corporations started to look like consulting companies that did a little auditing on the side. (Andersen spun off its consulting business in the late 1990s—launching Accenture—but quickly went right back into the consulting fray.) Consulting tasks like advising on mergers and acquisitions, designing a company's internal compliance system, or dreaming up tax dodges like the strategies used by Enron and other high-flying corporations were far more profitable than grinding through the books—not to mention sexier and more fun.

Even before consulting took over, accounting firms faced pressure to keep their clients happy. There is a simple reason for this: if the auditors continually question a company's financial statements and make themselves a thorn in the managers' side, there is a risk that the company will fire the auditors and move on to someone else. But the managers' temptation to fire an aggressive auditor is offset by the fact that, if the company suddenly dumps its auditor, everyone will assume that something funny is going on with its financial statements. In the old days, that meant that auditors wanted to keep their clients happy, but the cost to the company of firing them gave the auditors enough cover so that they could carefully scrutinize the company's books.

The rise of consulting rewrote all these old rules. In 2000 and 2001, Arthur Andersen pulled in roughly $25 million a year from Enron for consulting services and another $25 million for audits. With other clients, consulting revenues dwarfed the auditing fees. As legal scholar John Coffee points out, if Enron was unhappy with Andersen's auditors, it could simply take its consulting business elsewhere. Unlike firing the auditor, doling out consulting work to other Big Five firms wasn't a red flag to the market. America's largest companies spread their consulting work around, so a drop in Andersen's business at Enron wouldn't necessarily signal that there's a problem. So long as Andersen was desperate to keep the consulting business, and they were, Enron held all the cards.[19]

By the mid-1990s, the Big Five were more profitable than ever before, but they were beholden to their corporate clients to an extent that would have seemed unimaginable to the real Arthur Andersen. The same developments that magnified the Icaran tendencies in American business—such as deregulation and the advent of junk bonds, which fueled the huge rise in takeovers— also discouraged auditor oversight, since these developments created lucrative new consulting opportunities (as did cases like *Smith v. Van Gorkom*, as we saw in chapter 4) at the same time.

The Analyst as Cheerleader

The story with Wall Street's securities analysts, the sophisticated experts who were supposed to keep a watchful eye on corporate America, has an all-too-similar plot: the same awkward balance as with the accounting firms, the same sudden pressures knocking it completely out of whack—another phase of the perfect storm.

The traditional role of a securities analyst was to carefully investigate a group of companies in the industry he or she covered and to provide reports for his or her own bank and the bank's clients. (Some securities analysts are independent and provide reports for institutional investors, but most work for investment banks.) Securities analysts usually weren't (and aren't) paid directly for their reports; instead, clients reward the analyst through the commissions they pay to the analyst's firm when they buy or sell stock based on the recommendation. Andy Kessler, who worked as a securities analyst for Paine Webber and then Morgan Stanley, recounts an experience that illustrates the analyst's traditional responsibilities. Kessler was ordered to fly to Kansas City to meet with Hank Hermann, a Paine Webber client who wanted to hear more about a critical report Kessler had issued on the computer-chip industry. Jack Grubman, after hearing that Kessler was headed for Kansas City, "strolled [into Kessler's office] laughing his head off and chimed in 'Hank is known as the Piranha. He chews up and spits out every analyst who comes into his office, the Piranha tank. You're toast.'" As it turned out, the client was impressed with Kessler's willingness to criticize a trendy industry, which meant that he was likely to continue using Paine Webber brokers for his stock transactions.[20]

As with auditors, there's a built-in tension with securities analysis, which makes it harder than we'd like for analysts to actively sleuth out Icarus Effect failures in the making. The analyst receives much of her information from meetings and conference calls with the companies she's investigating. If she writes negative reports and advises clients to sell (or hold) a company's stock, the company's managers may stop answering the phone. Information is harder to acquire from people you've criticized. As a result, analysts have always had a subtle incentive to err on the side of niceness. But analysts also have a reputation to protect. If they're consistently praising skanky companies, no one will pay any attention to them.

Until the late 1980s and 1990s, when the takeover market and then the dot-com boom kicked in, this uneasy balance prevailed. Integrity was the norm, and if you read a report, you could generally assume that it reflected the analyst's true beliefs about the quality of the company. An important jolt came in 1975, when the SEC forced Wall Street to abandon the fixed rates that all of the firms charged as commissions. The SEC dictate—now referred to as the "Big Bang"—unleashed fierce competition on commission prices, which dramatically lowered both the cost to investors and the profitability of commissions for brokers. As a result, analysts increasingly marketed their research to institutional clients (such as the money managers who pick stocks for mutual funds) rather than ordinary investors.

But the tidal wave came with the enormous increase in IPOs and merger and acquisition activity in the 1990s. A key distinction among publicly held companies is whether they are followed by analysts. Analysts can't be everywhere, so they pick and choose which companies to study, based on prominence, apparent quality, or other factors. To be a player and generate real interest on Wall Street, a company needs to attract analysts' attention. In the 1990s companies that were selecting an investment banker to handle their IPO or merger business started insisting that the investment-bank guarantee that its analysts would cover the stock thereafter. In theory, there was a wall of separation between the investment bankers and analysts—a so-called Chinese Wall—that prohibited the bankers from passing information about a company to the securities analysts (who could then tip off their clients). But the wall steadily eroded, and securities analysts increasingly turned into adjuncts of the investment-banking operation.

As early as 1990, a memo from Morgan Stanley's corporate-finance department to its securities analysts announced that "our objective is . . . to adopt a policy, fully understood by the entire Firm, including the Research Department [that is, the analysts], that we do not make negative or controversial statements about our clients as a matter of sound business practice." At Credit Suisse First Boston, Frank Quattrone instructed the analysts who followed the tech industry to report directly to him, so that he could use them to drum up investment-banking business in Silicon Valley. By the end of the 1990s, it was routine for securities analysts to participate with their investment banking colleagues in the "beauty contests" (also known as "bake-offs") staged by client companies that were selecting an investment bank. "What used to be a conflict," Jack Grubman famously smirked, reveling in his relationship with his investment-banking partners at Salomon Smith Barney, "is now a synergy. Someone like me who is banking intensive would have been looked at disdainfully by [our clients] 15 years ago. Now they know I'm in the flow of what's going on."[21]

Securities analysts were well paid for their contributions to the firm's investment-banking success. (Indeed, analysts' bonuses were closely and sometimes explicitly tied to the amount of investment-banking business they brought in.) In 1980, a top analyst earned about $100,000 a year. By the turn of the century, some made $10 or $15 million by the time all of their salary and bonuses were tallied up. In this environment, it's hardly surprising that twelve of the thirteen analysts who followed Enron were still touting the World's Coolest Company as it prepared to file for bankruptcy, and that there were ninety-two buy recommendations for every suggestion that investors should sell at the height of the market bubble.[22]

The Pressures Within: Internal Culture and the Risk-taking CEO

The last potential check on Icaran tendencies was the internal culture of the corporation itself. Even in an earlier era, when CEOs were invariably chosen from within the company, the promotional practices of corporate America tended to encourage at least some risk-taking. Managers, as Robert Jackall puts it in his fascinating 1988 book *Moral Mazes*, "must prove themselves again and again to each other. Work becomes an endless round of what might be called probationary crucibles. Together with the uncertainty and sense of contingency that mark managerial work, this constant state of probation produces a profound anxiety in managers, perhaps the key experience of managerial work. It also breeds, selects, or elicits traits in ambitious managers that are crucial to getting ahead." The probationary crucible, to use Jackall's term, favors executives who are self-confident and do not subject themselves to agonizing reappraisal, who are good at winning the short-term contest of proving themselves at each step up the ladder.[23]

In the 1950s and 1960s, the incentives to take risks were counteracted by the internal culture of the company. The employees of Americas largest corporations were often unionized, and many spent their entire careers with the same company. This gave them a strong stake in the long-term stability of their company, rather than in risk-taking. The CEOs were also products of this culture. This meant that at each step in his or her rise, a budding CEO needed to win the confidence of fellow employees who would look askance at notably risky behavior, at decisions that jettisoned the corporation's traditional norms.

By the 1990s, this internal culture had been replaced by a much more "high-velocity" corporate environment, to borrow a term from corporate-law scholar Don Langevoort. Sherron Watkins, the Enron whistle-blower, describes how Enron's bonus system—which was coupled with a "rank and yank" rule that the employees who fell in the bottom 20 percent of Enron's performance scale be "demoted, passed-over, or fired" each year—created enormous pressure to come up with blockbuster deals. When Watkins finally succeeded, lining up a joint venture with a large

South Korean corporation, she pocketed a cool $175,000 bonus—not bad for a midlevel manager.[24]

Enron was an exaggerated example of a tournament-style, winner-take-all corporate culture, but the fluidity of American corporate life transformed the internal culture even at less trendy companies. Both ordinary employees and executives regularly moved from firm to firm. The fact that the rising star of the 1990s was likely to end up running a different firm than the one he or she was currently working for gave executives an even shorter term perspective than the promotional crucibles would have encouraged in another era. And the fact that most ordinary employees also didn't expect to finish their career at their current company gave them much less incentive to push back against the risky decision making of their superiors. There were benefits to the new, high-velocity corporate culture, of course. Successful employees had more employment options, and were much more highly compensated, than their 1950s predecessors. But, by the late 1990s, the internal culture of America's largest companies magnified an Icaran executive's incentive to take risks; it no longer served as a serious check on the Icaran excesses in American corporate and financial life.

What Ordinary Investors Have to Do with It

When Enron and WorldCom collapsed, thousands of employees lost their jobs, and the ripples were felt throughout communities in Texas, Alabama, and elsewhere. WorldCom laid off nearly 13,000 of its 75,000 workers even before it filed for bankruptcy and subsequently slashed its payrolls still further. By the time that Enron prepared to emerge from bankruptcy in 2004, the company was a mere shell of its former self. The energy trading desk was long gone, and tens of thousands of employees had been given their pink slips.

Much worse than the layoffs alone was the fact that large numbers of employees saw their retirement savings go up in smoke also. Until the 1980s, most large American corporations offered their employees so-called defined-benefit pensions. Under a defined-benefit plan, retirees are promised a specified yearly income after the retirement. After the advent of the first 401(k) in 1981, and a thumbs up from the IRS shortly thereafter, companies began switching to the "defined-contribution" approach. In a defined-contribution plan such as a 401(k), the company's promise extends only to the initial contribution, and the employee makes the choice how to invest the money. Under the companies' 401(k) plans, employees have a variety of investment options, ranging from stock funds to bonds and other fixed-income investments. But most, having been repeatedly reminded that stocks have outperformed bonds and other investments for over a century, put much or all of their funds in the stock market.[25]

The new retirement regime was a recipe for disaster when the market collapsed. To make matters worse, many Enron and WorldCom employees had loaded up on their employer's stock, due to ignorance, loyalty, or subtle (and sometimes not so subtle) company pressure.[26] Employee contributions had helped to fuel the market euphoria, and employees fell the hardest when the bubble burst.

Notice how far we have come since America's first great corporations emerged in the nineteenth century. Before Jay Cooke, most Americans' savings were tied up entirely in hard assets. Cooke's door-to-door sales introduced ordinary Americans to government debt and then railroad bonds, but Americans with excess savings were still most likely to invest in real estate. In the Gilded Age, corporate stock and debt replaced real estate as the investment of choice for Americans with savings to spare.

The stock run-up in the 1920s reinforced this trend, with ordinary investors gravitating toward the apparent stability of corporate bonds. After World War II stock replaced bonds as the investment of choice, and during the 1990s, millions of ordinary investors acquired a stake in the stock market.

These ordinary investors are the ones who demanded that Congress respond to the Icarus Effect scandals at the outset of the new century. The irony, as we shall see, is that American investors are more vulnerable now—not less—than they were before the scandals.

Six "The Most Sweeping Securities Law Reforms since the New Deal"

If it weren't for WorldCom, Congress might not have responded to the corporate scandals. Early 2002 saw a parade of hearings. Enron's Ken Lay and Andy Fastow raised their right hands, then invoked their Fifth Amendment rights, and refused to answer any questions; only Jeff Skilling, Enron's "Darth Vader," confronted the Congressional critics head on. Several major reforms were introduced, including a bill by Senator Paul Sarbanes and another by Senator Richard Durban and Congressman William Delahunt. But by the early summer, the media seemed to be losing interest. Most days, the scandals were no longer on the front page, and some days the corporate breakdown didn't even make the front page of the business section. It was becoming old news.

The WorldCom collapse changed everything. On June 25, WorldCom stunned Wall Street by admitting that the company had inflated its earnings by $3.8 billion, a number that was later adjusted upward to $11 billion. It was Enron all over again, and on an even larger scale. When WorldCom staggered into bankruptcy less than a month later, it claimed $110 billion in assets, making it the largest bankruptcy in American history. The message of WorldCom was clear: corporate America still hadn't hit bottom yet.

If WorldCom set the stage for reform, a much-touted speech by President Bush clinched it. On July 9, Bush came to Wall Street in order to calm the markets in the wake of the WorldCom bombshell and to start rebuilding confidence in corporate America. With an elegant, soothing blue background behind him and the words *corporate responsibility* printed over and over in white, President Bush portrayed the corporate crisis as the nefarious work of a few bad apples. The solution, he argued, was long prison sentences and aggressive enforcement against the corporate executives who had misbehaved. For the rest of corporate America, the answer was a new commitment to business ethics, to "capitalism with conscience."

The speech was a disaster. On CNBC, the stock-market ticker streamed along the bottom of the screen; viewers could watch the market falling even as the president spoke. The general perception was that the administration's proposals were designed to fend off the more sweeping proposals that had begun gaining traction in Washington since the WorldCom collapse.

With both the markets and ordinary Americans now demanding a more significant package of reforms, the Bush administration had little choice but to jump on the reform bandwagon. After spending much of the year trying to fend off the Sarbanes bill, the administration started sending signals that the president would sign the legislation when it reached his desk. The bill was rushed through Congress with very little debate; and on July 30, President Bush signed the Sarbanes-Oxley Act into law. By the end of the year, New York attorney general Eliot Spitzer had engineered a series of additional reforms, as part of a global settlement between regulators and the leading investment banks.

The goal of the reforms was to increase CEO accountability and to root out the conflicts that undermined accounting and securities-analyst oversight. As we shall see, the new reforms are, as journalists regularly proclaimed in articles about Sarbanes-Oxley, "the most sweeping changes to the securities law in a generation." The question is just what this means and whether the postscandal reforms will bridle the Icaran tendencies that underlay the recent corporate scandals.

Reforming the Corporate Board

CEOs don't like the Sarbanes-Oxley Act at all. A CEO of a major national company who came to speak to my Corporations class in spring 2003 repeatedly referred to the legislation (with a chuckle, I should add) as the new "Oxley Moronic" laws. Every time he uses the company credit card, he complained, he could be running afoul of the new restrictions.

So what are these restrictions? The most widely discussed of the rules is a new certification requirement and a new obligation that companies establish and regularly review an internal control system. Every time the company files one of its regular financial reports with the SEC, its CEO and CFO are required to personally vouch that they reviewed the report; that to the best of their knowledge the report doesn't contain any untrue statement concerning a "material" fact ("material facts" have been defined by courts to mean facts that a reasonable investor would care about); and that the report as a whole fairly presents the financial condition and performance of the company. The CEO and CFO are also required to vouch that they have reviewed the "internal control" system that the company has in place to make sure that it is producing accurate financial data and policing for internal misbehavior.[1]

The two other most dramatic restrictions on corporate managers prohibit companies from making any personal loans to their managers and require the CEO and CFO to give back any profits they make from selling company stock, as well as any bonuses they receive, during the year leading up to any restatement of the company's accounting numbers due to "material noncompliance" with generally accepted accounting principles. (The sweeping language of the loan restrictions can be read to prohibit the use of a company credit card for personal items, even if the manager later reimburses the company—hence, the ire of the CEO who spoke to my class.)

The new law also ratchets up the criminal penalties for violating the certification requirements or any other provision of the securities laws. There's a new crime for any CEO or CFO who makes a false certification. If she does so "willingly," she faces a $1 million fine and up to ten years in jail; for "knowing" falsifications, the penalties go up to $5 million and up to twenty years of jail time. The maximum prison term for other forms of securities fraud jumps up to twenty-five years, and there are a variety of other new criminal penalties as well.

Each of the provisions is, of course, aimed directly at the behavior of CEOs like Ken Lay and Bernie Ebbers. Lay and Ebbers both claimed to be focusing so intently on the big picture that they had no idea about the deceptions taking place within their company—hence, the requirement that CEOs sign off on the numbers percolating up from within the corporate structure. Both Lay and Ebbers were also the recipients of massive loans from their companies (over $100 million for Lay and a whopping $400 million for Ebbers), and Lay sold millions of dollars of stock ($220 million, by some accounts) on the eve of Enron's collapse.[2]

As part of the effort to make CEOs and CFOs more accountable, lawmakers and regulators also attempted to shift decision-making authority over several ticklish issues from insiders to independent outside directors on the board. The most important example of this shift is the choice of an outside accounting firm to audit the company's books. This choice has traditionally been the prerogative of the CFO. It's not hard to see the problem with this arrangement. If the CFO holds the keys to the company's auditing work, the auditor has an obvious incentive to keep the CFO happy. The simplest way to do this is for the auditors to bring back good news each time they make a foray into the company's books, as Arthur Andersen's Carl Bass quickly learned when he tried to question Enron's Star Wars–inspired, off-balance-sheet entities.

Under Sarbanes-Oxley, the company's auditors must be selected by an audit committee consisting entirely of outside independent directors. The directors who serve on the committee cannot have any significant financial ties to the company and thus will not have nearly so great a stake in the outcome of the audit. The audit committee thus takes the place of the CFO as the auditors' principal point of contact with the company. The audit committee requirements are supplemented by new stock-exchange rules that have the same effect when it comes to compensation decisions. Both the New York Stock Exchange and NASDAQ, where nearly all of the nation's largest companies are listed, now require that disinterested directors be the ones who decide how much Ken Lay or Bernie Ebbers will be paid.[3] In theory, at least, this means that charismatic CEOs won't be in a position to write their own tickets in the future.

Ditto when it comes to nominating directors each year and to the board as a whole. The two major stock exchanges now require that the company's slate of directors be chosen by a nominating committee consisting of independent directors. They also require that a majority of the company's board of directors must be independent and that the independent directors meet regularly without any insiders in attendance.

Mending or Ending Auditor and
Securities-Analyst Conflicts

In addition to the CEO, CFO, and board of directors, the other principal magnets for regulatory attention were auditors and securities analysts (recall the conflicts from our discussion in chapter 5). If Arthur Andersen had subjected Enron's off-balance-sheet science fiction to serious critical scrutiny, it would have put more than $25 million in annual consulting business at risk; a securities analyst who asked whether there was really any "there there" in Enron's broadband operations, to paraphrase Gertrude Stein, might be hanging her investment-banking colleagues out to dry.

Having listened to investors' outcry over auditors' conflict of interest, lawmakers loaded up Sarbanes-Oxley with provisions that drive a wedge between the auditing and consulting services that accounting firms provide. Many commentators had argued that accounting firms should be forced to make a choice to either audit or consult, but should be prohibited from doing both. The new reforms didn't go this far. Accounting firms can still perform both functions; they just can't do both for the same client. To reduce the likelihood that individual auditors will become too cozy with the companies they audit (think of Andersen's David Duncan and his regular golf outings and family get-togethers with his buddies at Enron), the Sarbanes-Oxley Act also requires that the lead auditing partner be rotated every five years.

Concerns about the conflicts that bedevil securities analysis were addressed on a very different playing field. Eliot Spitzer had seized the initiative as the scandals gathered steam by suing Merrill Lynch under the Martin Act, a venerable New York state law that authorizes the attorney general to bring civil or criminal charges against any individual or firm that participates in a fraudulent sale of securities in New York. In May 2002, two months before the Sarbanes-Oxley Act was passed, Spitzer reached a settlement with Merrill Lynch, whose star analyst Henry Blodget had left a trail of e-mails that made it clear he had his eyes on Merrill's investment-banking business. (In the midst of a squabble with his investment-banking colleagues in late 2000, for example, Blodget had threatened to stop flacking dubious stocks for the benefit of the investment bankers and "just start calling the stocks . . . like we see them, no matter what the ancillary business consequences are.") From there, Spitzer, along with the SEC and other state and federal regulators, took on the investment-banking industry as a whole. By the end of the year, the parties had hammered out the basic terms of a global settlement. The investment banks agreed to pay over $1.4 billion as part of a three-part package that included $900 million in fines (Salomon Smith Barney topped the chart at $300 million, and Merrill Lynch and Credit Suisse agreed to $200 million each), $450 million for independent research, and $85 million for investor education.[4]

As with the accounting reforms, the settlement doesn't require securities analysts to pack their bags and go looking for a new employer. Investment banks can still include both securities analysts and bankers, but the reforms try to create a stronger wall of separation. The settlement forbids banks from tying any portion of securities analysts' paychecks to the investment-banking business they help to bring in, and it also prohibits analysts from coming along on the "road shows" where investment banks compete to be selected as the underwriter for a securities offering. Spitzer's goal was to completely sever the links between securities analysts and their investment-banking colleagues, so that the analysts will focus solely on the quality of the companies they cover, not on the possibility that the companies may direct investment-banking business to the analyst's bank. To supplement these restrictions, the banks agreed to subsidize research by independent research firms (this is the $450 million for independent research) for the next five years. In effect, the banks are paying for a second opinion from firms that offer research but not investment-banking services and are therefore are more fully independent than Salomon, Merrill Lynch, and their peers.

The Benefits of the Postscandal Reforms

What should we make of the recent reforms? What implications do they have for the Icaran tendencies in American corporate and financial life?

Start with the new do's and don'ts for corporate executives and the board. The most important benefit of these restrictions came at the moment that President Bush signed the Sarbanes-Oxley Act. It had very little to do with content and a lot to do with the signal that the new legislation sent. Whatever else the legislation did, it shook up America's boardrooms and forced corporate executives to rethink the way they had been doing things. One corporate scholar likes to refer to this as the "cognitive disruption" caused by the corporate-responsibility legislation.[5]

The virtues of the particular provisions themselves are less clear. Once the shock of being required to certify the company's financial numbers wears off, the new requirements won't alter a CEO's or CFO's job description a great deal. Even a well-intentioned CEO can't realistically keep tabs on what's going on at every level of a large company. The certification requirements won't change this, since they start with a very important caveat, "based on the officer's knowledge." To be sure, it isn't quite so easy to get off the hook by saying, like Sergeant Schultz on the old *Hogan's Heroes* sitcom, "I know nothing!" Large companies are now required to institute internal procedures that "ensure that material information relating to the [company] and its consolidated subsidiaries . . . is made known" to the CEO and CFO.[6] But it would be a mistake to assume that corporate executives will now take a more hands-on approach than ever before.

The next Bernie Ebbers can still claim that he was so intent on the big picture that he wasn't aware of what his underlings were up to. It also is not clear that the obligation to establish internal controls will make the internal culture of America's largest corporations kinder, gentler and more ethical. Delaware's judges had been exhorting corporations to establish internal compliance programs since the mid 1990s, first in a much-discussed judicial opinion involving Caremark Industries and then in a series of speeches by Delaware chief justice Norman Veasey. The corporate responsibility legislation has taken internal compliance out of Delaware's hands, and made it a federal obligation. But there is a danger that large companies will simply hire a new executive, the "corporate compliance officer," to satisfy the SEC, but that little else will change.

Indeed, this is essentially the way many corporations have responded to recent efforts to curb sex discrimination in the workplace. In the 1990s, the Supreme Court made clear that it will usually reject Title VII discrimination suits if the employer has a formal complaint procedure in place. Big companies have done a great job setting up formal procedures, but many observers worry that the procedures simply mask discrimination that continues to occur.

As for the new emphasis on independent directors, this sounds more impressive than it is. Most large corporations already have a majority of disinterested directors on their boards. The Business Roundtable, a group of executives from the nation's leading companies, has been promoting this strategy since 1990, and institutional investors such as CalPERS have made disinterestedness a major focus of their corporate-governance initiatives. It also isn't entirely clear whether the move to disinterested directors actually helps. One well-known study found, in fact, that the companies with the most outside directors performed worse overall, not better. These findings may simply reflect systematic differences between companies that tend to rely on inside and interested directors. The board of high-tech Silicon Valley companies often include mostly interested directors such as managers, lenders, and consultants, for instance, and high-tech firms tended to outperform the market throughout the 1990s. It is also possible that companies tend to bring in outside directors when they are performing badly in an effort to get the business back on track. But it is just as plausible that outside directors simply do not have a significant effect on corporate performance. Whatever one concludes, the evidence does underscore that outside directors aren't a cure-all for Icaran risk-taking or fraud. Indeed, Enron itself vividly illustrated the limitations of disinterested directors. All but two of Enron's directors were disinterested, and Enron had disinterested audit and compensation committees, yet the directors simply nodded their heads as Lay and Jeff Skilling spun their web of magnificent promises and prophecies.[7]

Most experts believe that the accounting and securities-analyst reforms will make more of a difference in the long run. Off the record, even accountants admit that the huge increase in consulting revenues influenced the way that the auditors looked at their audit clients. The new reforms don't sever these links altogether; and there will be a great deal of quibbling over what is and isn't on the list of prohibited consulting services. But there is now a much sharper line between the Big Four's auditing and consulting operations.

With securities analysts, it isn't even necessary to go off the record for admissions that celebrity analysts like Jack Grubman and Henry Blodget were valued more for the investment-banking business that they brought in than for their stock-picking prowess. By the late 1990s, as a prominent former analyst recalls, "it was clear to everyone on Wall Street that research was a facade to support deals." The Spitzer settlement will eliminate the most obvious manifestations of the bubble-era ethos. No more bonuses based on the investment-banking business the analyst's bank receives from companies he or she follows; no more doling out stakes in hot IPOs to executives like Bernie Ebbers who have lots of investment-banking business to spread around.[8]

The good news, then, is that investors no longer need to worry quite so much that a company's financial statements, or the pronouncements of securities analysts featured on CNBC, are really just advertisements for somebody's consulting or investment-banking services. But this doesn't mean that the problems that bedevil accounting and investment-banking oversight have been truly solved. They haven't. Although some of the conflicts have been addressed, others remain. They're simply less visible, like crabgrass that seems to be gone when a lawn has been mowed, but soon returns, as virulent as ever.

With accounting firms, the most obvious problem is that the company itself still chooses and pays its own auditor, as they always have. Even if disinterested directors do the choosing and the auditing partner is rotated, there will never be truly independent oversight so long as the company itself decides who its auditor will be. Even disinterested directors, for instance, will be hesitant to choose an auditor that is likely to rock the boat.

In the Wall Street banks, investment banking is still the straw that stirs the drink, and there is a risk that securities analysts will remain beholden to their jet-setting investment-banking colleagues. True, the banks can no longer base their analysts fees' directly on the investment-banking business they bring in. But there are subtle ways to achieve the same effect. Indeed, even before the bubble burst, many banks had already begun to cover their tracks. "Analysts didn't get paid directly for deals at Morgan Stanley," according to Andy Kessler, who worked there under Frank Quattrone. "They didn't want a paper trail back to the formula, so compensation remained a loose concept. Bankers had input into my year-end bonus. A good or bad word from bankers could add or subtract 25% of my pay in a heartbeat. Obviously, when bankers called you listened."[9]

Better Ways to Slice the Gordian Knot of Conflicts

Even when the reforms were first put in place, many commentators worried that they wouldn't do enough to keep executives honest and to clean up the conflicts in accounting and securities analysis. The most striking omission was the lack of a provision requiring that the stock options granted to executives be treated as an expense in a company's financial statements. Stock options were "crucial," a prominent financial reporter noted, "to both the misrepresentation and the enrichment that have caused a crisis of confidence in business and financial markets." Yet one searches the sprawling Sarbanes-Oxley legislation in vain for any requirement that companies at least deduct the value of these options from their earnings. Accountants, according to a skeptical postmortem in the *Economist*, "showed that they had not lost all their political clout by persuading legislators to dilute a clause in the original bill that would have forced companies to rotate their auditors every five years." Instead, only the lead partner must be rotated, a "ludicrous proposal," according to a Harvard Business School professor quoted in the story.[10]

It is tempting to think that if lawmakers simply finished the job they started, the Icarus Effect tendencies could be held in check for another generation. Let's imagine for a moment what the corporate landscape might look like if lawmakers were willing to truly slice through the Gordian knot of conflicts that interfere with director, auditor, and securities-analyst oversight.

The first adjustment is easy (and is finally nearing implementaton by the Financial Accounting Standards Board [FASB] as this book goes to press): regulators would add the missing stock option reform, no matter how loudly the Silicon Valley high-tech firms (who derailed it the first time around, with help from allies like Senators Joe Lieberman and Dianne Feinstein) protest. Stock options should be treated as an expense on a company's financial statements, rather than buried in footnotes where even the most intrepid stock analyst is likely to miss them. Throughout the 1990s, the ability of companies like WorldCom to ignore the cost of options when they tallied up their earnings helped them to dramatically overstate their earnings, which stoked the speculative frenzy in two closely related ways. The options themselves gave Ebbers and other executives an incentive to take risks— since the options were a one-way racket with all upside and no downsides—and the too-good-to-be-true accounting treatment made it hard to resisting doling them out as compensation.

With the board of directors, the alternatives are limited. It's unlikely that outside directors will rein in wayward CEOs as effectively as advocates of director independence would like to imagine. Nevertheless, in early 2003, the SEC began toying with a strategy that would at least shake things up a bit. Under one version that was initially considered, a company would be required to include directorial candidates nominated by shareholders in the company's proxy materials if at least 5% of the shareholders were on record as supporting the nominations. The proposal was subsequently weakened, but may be implemented in some form. In effect, for the first time, the company would be required to subsidize shareholder nominations, which would sharply increase the number of contested elections. Contested elections could actually alter directors' perception of what is expected of them. One thing that became clear during the 1990s is that outside directors will often respond if the spotlight shines on them. In 1991, after a futile effort to secure a seat on the board of Sears, which was performing miserably, shareholder activist Robert Monks purchased a full page ad in the *Wall Street Journal*. The ad consisted of a large, attention-grabbing silhouettelike outline of the nine Sears directors, with the name and position of each listed below. In enormous black letters, a headline beneath the picture referred to the directors as "Non-Performing assets." The ad clearly attracted the directors' attention: within five months they had announced plans to divest Sears' financial services operation, as Monks and others had called for.[11] Competitive elections would have a similar effect. At the least, directors would think twice about skipping three out of every four meetings, as one of Enron's directors did, or serving on dozens of different boards, if these details were likely to come up at the next directorial election.

With auditors and securities analysts, truly severing the Gordian knot would require a more dramatic innovation. The most glaring flaw in the current framework—a flaw which is so long-standing that it is almost invariably ignored in proposals for change—is the fact that the *company itself* decides who its watchers will be. The problem with letting companies choose their own auditor is that the auditor's judgment will inevitably be distorted due to what psychologists call "self-serving bias" if she thinks of the company as her client. The phenomenon is graphically illustrated by an experiment conducted by several experimental psychologists. As described in the *Economist*, "139 auditors were given five ambiguous auditing vignettes and asked to judge the accounting in each. Half were told to suppose that they had been hired by the company they were auditing; half that they had been hired by another company that was doing business with it. For all five vignettes, the subjects were, on average, 30% more likely to find that the accounting behind the numbers complied with GAAP if they were playing the role of auditor to the firm." If this much distortion occurs in a carefully controlled, hypothetical environment, the effect when actual money is at stake is likely to be far greater.[12]

Drawing a sharper line between accountants' auditing and consulting services obviously won't solve this problem. The only way to fully address the bias would be to take the choice of auditor out of the company's hands. If lawmakers were looking for someone else to make the choice, their first thought would probably be the SEC. The SEC already oversees the nation's widely held companies, and auditors would be much less forgiving if they viewed the SEC rather than the company as their client. But the SEC is chronically overtaxed and underfunded. Adding yet another responsibility of this magnitude to the SEC's plate would be a recipe for disaster. As one commentator pointed out at the height of the Enron scandal, another regulator would be much better positioned to handle this kind of task, however: the stock exchanges. Investors often don't think of the New York Stock Exchange and NASDAQ as regulators, but in reality, the exchanges are the first line of defense for investors. If a company wants to sell stock or bonds widely and generally to attract investors' attention, it needs to be listed on a major exchange. And nearly every significant company is. Because the exchanges compete to attract these companies, they have a powerful incentive to police the companies that they list and to establish a reputation for quality. This is one reason that the exchanges "delist" companies that are on the verge of bankruptcy. Before the SEC was created in 1934, the New York Stock Exchange served, in effect, as the nation's leading securities regulator; and it had started developing its own disclosure rules shortly before the securities laws were enacted.

The mechanics of assigning auditors would be quite simple. Each stock exchange would keep a list of approved auditors, and it would assign an auditor to each of its listed companies each year. Each exchange could develop a process for including auditors on its list and for kicking out auditors that misbehaved or performed poorly. Earnings restatements would serve as a red flag in this respect. If a company were forced to restate its earnings due to an accounting inaccuracy, the exchanges would open an investigation to determine whether the auditor had performed an adequate audit. If the restatement reflected an accounting breakdown, the auditor could be suspended or its list of assignments cut back for the next year. With the stock exchanges at the helm, it is impossible to imagine the repeated accounting scandals that Arthur Andersen got itself into even before Enron or the stunning increase from three accounting restatements in 1981 to seven hundred in the period from 1997 to 2000.[13]

The same strategy could also be used for securities analysis.

One of the most vexing problems for a midsized or newly public company is getting analysts to "follow" the company. (A friend of mine who serves on the board of such a company complains that the directors do cartwheels and wear funny hats, but they still can't get anyone to notice.) Analysts focus on big or trendy companies, a pattern that was exacerbated by the quest for investment-banking business in the 1990s, since big or trendy companies tend to be the ones that are busy issuing new securities or launching merger and acquisition campaigns. If the securities exchanges were required to assign a securities analyst to every listed company—and to pay the analysts from companies' listing fees—investors would know that there was at least one analyst covering every listed company. Here, too, the exchanges could develop rules for implementing the scheme. The analyst assigned to any given company should be forbidden from performing any investment-banking services for the company, for instance. The exchanges could also rate their analysts' performance and give more assignments to the superior performers. The independent research requirement of the Spitzer settlement is designed with somewhat similar objectives in mind. The investment banks are required to pump $450 million into research by independent analysts, thus subsidizing a class of independent competitors. But the independent research may begin to shrivel up once all of the money has been doled out, and listing fees are a more logical source of funds for research than are investment banks—who compete with the independent analysts, after all.

The Icaran Tendencies Left Untouched

As a forty-something investor with both an academic interest and most of his retirement funds at stake, it is fair to say that I feel slightly more comfortable now when I watch the financial gurus on CNBC, knowing that the ugliest of the conflicts of interest have been partially addressed. Better yet would be an investors' "bill of rights" that added further reforms of the sort just described. Better boards, more vigorous auditor and analyst oversight.

But would this be enough to keep the Icaran tendencies at bay for another generation? Think back to the series of related developments (discussed in chapters 4–5) that lay at the heart of the spectacular Icarus Effect collapses that inaugurated the new century. The first was the general pattern of deregulation and a more flexible approach to antitrust scrutiny. These developments fueled the rise of takeovers and market-based corporate governance, which ushered in the era of the celebrity CEO. Internal corporate culture changed at the same time, eliminating an important brake on corporate risk-taking. The principal watchers, who might otherwise have served as a check on the new Icaran leaders, were coopted by the very same forces that had magnified the risk of Icarus Effect failures. Finally, technological and financial innovations made it easier than ever before both to manipulate the boundaries of the corporation and to take huge bets with corporate assets.

From this broader perspective, what is striking is not that the postscandal reforms were "the most sweeping securities law reforms in a generation." They were, though this says more about the scarcity of significant, post–New Deal securities legislation than it does about the recent reforms. Most striking is how narrowly focused the reforms were. Of the four developments just described, only the conflicts that undermined board, auditor, and securities-analyst oversight received sustained attention.

In Icaran terms, the corporate-responsibility reforms discussed thus far focused entirely on the first of the three Icarus Effect tendencies, the danger that corporate executives will take excessive or fraudulent risks. Lawmakers and regulators pushed back after the corporate scandals, but they left the second and third Icaran factors, competition and the misuse of corporate size and complexity almost entirely untouched. With a few minor exceptions (see chapter 7 for specifics), there has been little serious discussion about rethinking the deregulation of industries like telecom and energy or otherwise reforming the competitive structure of the markets. Similarly, the widespread manipulation of corporate boundaries through structured finance and other maneuvers has been largely ignored.

One recent initiative that many people don't associate with the corporate scandals at all, but which is designed to curb corporate influence over the lawmakers and regulators who are supposed to keep them in check, is the recent campaign-finance legislation. Under the McCain-Feingold Act—as the reform is widely known, in honor of two of its principal proponents—corporations can no longer make so-called soft money contributions to political parties (the money is called "soft" because it falls outside the explicit restrictions of federal election law), and they are prohibited from running "issue" advertisements (which often are disguised contributions to a particular candidate) within sixty days of an election. Although the new restrictions tighten up the restrictions that were first put in place under Teddy Roosevelt in 1907, they are unlikely to have more than a modest effect on the ability of corporations to stymie regulatory efforts. The reforms apply only to political campaigns, and even then corporate managers and their employees can still make individual contributions to candidates and parties.

After all the sound and fury over the postscandal reforms, then, we do not yet have a regulatory response that has even begun to catch up to the remarkable changes in corporate America. Nearly all of the conditions that produced the most recent Icarus Effect scandals are still in place. The television cameras are still rolling at CNBC. The only thing missing is the next charismatic CEO.

Seven "We Have Met the Corporation and It Is Us"

It has now been more than two years since the corporate-responsibility reforms were first enacted. The trials of many of the executives whose names are associated with the excesses of the late 1990s are under way or have been completed. Martha Stewart, whose conviction for lying about her access to inside information was only loosely related to the corporate scandals, has been sentenced. Bernie Ebbers of WorldCom and Jeff Skilling of Enron have been indicted, and Tyco's Dennis Kozlowski will soon be tried for the second time, after his first trial for looting corporate assets ended in a mistrial.

We now are far enough away from the scandals to begin to take stock both of the transformation of American corporate and financial life in the 1990s and of the regulatory response to these developments. The pressure for corporate executives to take risks and the rewards for risk-taking were greater than ever before in the 1990s, as we have seen. Deregulation ushered in competition in markets that previously had been dominated by a small number of heavily regulated companies. And the corporate structure of many companies mutated as businesses took advantage of new strategies for creating value such as the structured-finance transactions described in chapter 5. The question we must answer in this chapter is whether regulators have caught up to these changes in the marketplace. In the ongoing cat-and-mouse game between regulators and America's corporate leaders, the regulators have had their move.

It is not enough simply to assess where things stand with each of the three Icaran factors, however. As we consider the current landscape, we also will need to make sense of an even more dramatic change, a development with complex and at times surprising implications: after a century in which the stock market was identified far more with the wealthy than with the middle class, more Americans now hold corporate stock than ever before. As the *New York Times* recently put it, "in the spirit of Pogo, the Walt Kelly cartoon character, we must increasingly say that we have met the corporation and it is us."[1]

The Risk-Taking Machinery of the Large-Scale Corporation

As we saw in chapter 6, the corporate-responsibility reforms focused almost entirely on the first of the three Icaran factors, the danger that corporate executives will take excessive or even fraudulent risks. Starting from the view that, as one commentator puts it, "It's the Gatekeepers, Stupid," the reforms are designed to root out the conflicts of interest that interfered with auditor, securities analyst, and directorial oversight in the 1990s.[2]

Even if these gatekeepers do start to exercise dramatically more vigilance in their oversight, however, there is no reason to believe that the underlying pressures that encouraged executives to take risks have been altered in any significant way. The most fundamental change within the corporation has been the transformation of the employment relationship. The mobility of both executives and ordinary employees has created an entirely new internal corporate culture. The promotional crucibles that determine which employees will rise to the top of the corporate hierarchy are now more likely to lead to another company than to the helm of the executive's current employer. Influences that once promoted stability—such as unionization and executives' recognition that their success depended upon the support of the employees they passed on their ascent to the upper floors—disappeared in the 1990s, and they have not reemerged.

To be sure, the corporate-responsibility reforms have provided new protections for employees who act as whistleblowers—the principal protection is often referred to as Sarbanes-Oxley's Sherron Watkins provision—and they now require that every publicly held company put a compliance program in place. But none of these changes will alter the fundamental economics of the twenty-first-century corporation. The reality is that the tournament-style, winner-take-all atmosphere makes perfect sense from a purely economic perspective. Because it spurs a company's most ambitious employees to continuously push the performance envelope, the internal pressure cooker can directly enhance a company's bottom line.[3]

External factors like the financial media, which poured oil on the fire throughout the 1990s, also are still in place. During the 1990s, the media's breathless portrayal of charismatic CEOs like Bernie Ebbers was central to the companies' success, particularly as reflected in the value of their stock. The fragility of this media halo, and the perceived need to preserve it, magnified the executives' incentives to take risks and to cook the books as the company's fortunes declined. More recently, in the aftermath of the scandals, the media has offered a more sober look at the nation's most prominent corporations. Lou Dobbs has focused particular attention on the outsourcing of jobs by American companies to cheaper workers in India and other countries. But it is hard to imagine that this more critical perspective will do much to dampen corporate risk-taking in the long run. The rags-to-riches tale of an executive who rose from nothing to the upper reaches of corporate America is an irresistible storyline, and it is a safe bet that the financial media will continue to lavish attention on charismatic executives.

Nor have the new opportunities to take risks disappeared. As the growing debate over outsourcing suggests, the shift in American business to more service- and technology-oriented operations has continued. A major corporation can still start up a new high-tech venture almost instantly, as Enron did with the broadband initiative that figured so prominently in its collapse. Similarly, executives who, due either to desperation or overconfidence, are inclined to go for broke can still turn to derivative contracts and other sophisticated new financial innovations. The SEC has tinkered with the requirements for disclosing derivatives in the past several years, but regulators do not yet have a compelling strategy for ensuring that companies use derivatives to hedge against currency-rate changes and other risks, rather than to gamble with the company's assets.

Each of the developments I have described has a more optimistic side, of course. The transformation of internal corporate culture has provided rich rewards for successful employees, and the shift to a high-tech economy has led to stunning productivity gains in the past several decades. But as we look over the history of American corporate and financial life, it is hard not to conclude that regulators don't yet have the risk-taking of the 1990s under control. The scandals galvanized public attention, but demand for reform has never guaranteed that the reforms will be effective.

Competitive Confusion: The Electricity and Telecom Crises

If we turn to the second Icaran factor, competition, the picture is, if anything, even bleaker. In an article surveying the recent history of American antitrust law, legal scholars Thomas Sullivan and Robert Thompson point out that the Supreme Court seems to have lost interest in antitrust regulation in the past several decades. No clear theme can be detected in the recent decisions, and there is no reason to think this will soon change. Antitrust enforcement by regulators has been similarly inconsistent. Current regulators have occasionally taken tough stands, but they also largely abandoned the campaign to weaken Microsoft's monopoly.[4]

Even more telling is the continuing fallout of deregulation. The turmoil is graphically illustrated by regulatory breakdowns in the utilities and telecom industries—the very industries that spawned the biggest Icarus Effect collapses of 2001 and 2002. The electricity industry saw two crippling crises at the outset of the current decade alone. In the months before 9/11, California was roiled by a series of rolling blackouts that were precipitated by a flawed state-deregulation plan. California's scheme put a ceiling on the price that electricity companies could charge consumers, but deregulated the wholesale cost of electricity; retail prices were thus capped, but wholesale costs were not. To make matters worse, the electricity companies were prohibited from signing long-term contracts with suppliers to lock in the price of the wholesale electricity.

So long as wholesale energy prices stayed low, the regulation wasn't a problem. But suppliers like Enron manipulated the framework, clogging up transmission lines or selling energy to out-of-state suppliers who sold it back to California companies at inflated prices. Enron energy traders referred to its strategies with "colorful nicknames such as 'Get Shorty,' 'Ricochet,' and 'Death Star,'" and joked about bilking poor grandmothers during the energy crisis. "We always knew we were getting screwed," a California regulator later remarked. "We just didn't know they had names for it." It wasn't long before the wholesale cost was too high for California's energy companies to make a profit. When California lawmakers rejected their requests to raise the price to consumers, the energy companies started cutting back on the electricity they supplied.[5]

August 2003 brought a second crisis, the largest blackout in American history. The blackout was caused by a power disruption in the Midwest that transmission system operators failed to identify until it had already begun to disrupt power supplies throughout the Northeast and Midwest. The transmission grid has been atrophying for decades, a trend that was magnified by the deregulation of electricity generation starting in 1992. Because they can charge market prices for the electricity they generate, but receive only a small, fixed return for any money they put into improving the transmission grid, electricity companies have directed vastly more capital to generation than to the grid.[6]

The crisis in telecom regulation hasn't been quite so dramatic—the phones of millions of Americans haven't suddenly been cut off—but the industry is similarly unstable. The Telecommunications Act of 1996 left the long-distance market almost entirely deregulated, after regulators stoked the entry of upstart companies like WorldCom by prohibiting AT&T from cutting its long-distance prices in the 1980s. Local telephone service, by contrast, is still tightly regulated and dominated by the Baby Bells.[7]

In each of these markets, as with the railroads in the nineteenth century, there are huge economies of scale and scope that make it all but inevitable that the industry will be dominated by a small number of very large companies. A decision by regulators to simply back off, or even to spur entry by new competitors, predictably triggers a gold rush by companies attempting to secure a dominant position in the industry. This was true when railroad robber barons like Jay Gould emerged in the nineteenth century—and equally true with Enron and WorldCom at the end of the twentieth. This doesn't mean that deregulation is always a mistake. Private companies generally provide goods and services much more efficiently than the government, since the prospect of profits gives them a powerful carrot that government bureaucrats don't have. But the competitive process can backfire after sudden deregulation. This danger, particularly in industries that have traditionally been seen as natural monopolies, suggests that when lawmakers introduce competition into an industry that previously was heavily regulated or state owned there may actually be a need for more supervision by regulators, rather than less—re-regulation, in a sense, not simply deregulation. But this isn't what we see at all. Regulatory oversight has been softened, not ratcheted up, and there is little evidence of a coordinated strategy of regulating competition.

Twenty-First-Century Strategies for Taking Advantage of Corporate Size and Complexity

If we turn to the final piece of the American corporate and financial puzzle, the picture is somewhat more mixed. Like the planets in *The Little Prince* that spawned new planets, which then spawned more new planets, Enron and other major corporations divided their operations into hundreds or even thousands of separate entities, many of them SPEs. At Enron, Andy Fastow's principal expertise was his "genius at creating off-balance-sheet vehicles" that, in the words of a fawning article in *CFO* magazine, "transformed finance into a capital-raising machine." Many of these transactions were used, as we now know, to disguise Enron's financial condition from investors. Enron and other companies also used separate entities to shift profits into sub-sidiaries that were incorporated in states like Delaware that of-fered favorable tax treatment. Tyco went even further. Although its principal operations are all in the United States, Tyco reincor-porated in Bermuda. Tyco didn't change anything about its un-derlying business. It simply filled out the documents necessary to make it a Bermuda corporation in order to avoid paying taxes at the U.S. rate.[8]

Some of these manipulations of the corporate structure are being addressed by the SEC and other regulators. Enron's most notorious off-balance-sheet entity—the SPE known as Chewco—seems to have violated even existing accounting rules, since it did not have the 3% of outside equity investment that is required if a company wishes to treat an SPE as separate from its main operations. But the vast majority of the entities in Enron's menagerie were perfectly legal under these remarkably permissive rules. In response, the SEC and the Financial Accounting Stan-dards Board are tightening the standards for removing SPEs from a company's balance sheets. The SEC was also instructed by Congress to conduct a study comparing American accounting standards to the International Accounting Standards used in Eu-rope. Under IAS, regulators rely less on simple, rigid rules like the 3% requirement and have more discretion to recharacterize a transaction that is being used to manipulate a company's balance sheet.

Even if regulators are given much broader oversight powers, there will still be a great deal of room for manipulation by com-panies that are bent on gaming the system. The problem is valua-tion. The assets that Enron sold to its "raptor" entities consisted of so-called dark fiber—optical fiber that was not yet in use and for which there was no readily ascertainable market value. Enron took advantage of the valuation uncertainty by attaching eye-poppingly generous valuations to the fiber. When the value of an SPE is anybody's guess, it is extraordinarily difficult for regulators to sleuth out problems. Auditors and securities analysts provide two more sets of eyes, but there are simply too many opportunities for taking advantage of valuation uncertainties to be confident that the gatekeepers will catch even glaring manipulations of the corporate entity.

The ease of crossing national borders multiplies the opportunities for deception and makes oversight still more difficult. Another of Enron's tricks, which involved offshore SPEs, is illustrative. As Enron examiner Neal Batson documented in Enron's bankruptcy case, Enron and Chase Manhattan used a Jersey Isle entity called Mahonia to effect loanlike transactions known as "prepaid swaps." In a prepaid swap, Chase paid money to Enron by way of the Mahonia entity, and Enron then repaid it later. Enron then took the position that the swap wasn't technically a loan and therefore did not need to be accounted for as debt on its balance sheet.[9]

These structural manipulations are the twenty-first-century equivalent of Samuel Insull's elaborate holding-company structure, and their effect is quite similar: by manipulating the corporate structure, corporate executives can raise much more capital that they would have had access to if investors had any inkling of the company's true financial condition. Thus far, no one has stepped in to sweep out the temple in anything like the way that the New Dealers did when they enacted the Public Utilities Holding Company Act of 1935.

The Limits of Shareholder Democracy

From the perspective of the three factors we have considered throughout the book, the picture looks quite unsettling. Although the 1990s seem like an increasingly distant memory, the legacy of the decade is still very much with us. If I am right in my diagnosis, the Icaran tendencies in American corporate and financial life went into remission after the shock of the corporate scandals. But the remission is already over.

For some readers, my assessment will sound much too bleak. After all, there seem to be at least a few major changes in the business of American business. The most dramatic evidence that a happier day is dawning is the sudden upsurge in shareholder activism. "Shareholder activism has now gone mainstream," James Surowiecki wrote in an evenhanded assessment in the *New Yorker* in June 2003: "More than a thousand shareholder resolutions have been filed this year . . . , most of them attempts to reform the way executives get paid or the way a company is run. In the past, such resolutions were voted down, but this year dozens have been approved."[10]

The biggest shareholder initiative was a vote of no confidence at Disney. With Roy Disney, Walt's nephew, and former board chairman Stanley Gold leading the charge, a stunning 43% of Disney's shareholders withheld their votes from CEO Michael Eisner at Disney's 2004 annual meeting in Philadelphia. Almost as soon as the three thousand attendees who had packed a convention center meeting room filed out past Cinderella and Mickey Mouse, Disney's directors responded by making former Senator George Mitchell chairman of the board in place of Eisner, while leaving Eisner as CEO. The SEC has also become an advocate for more shareholder democracy. As shareholders have begun flexing their muscle, the SEC has proposed a new rule that would permit shareholders to include their own directorial nominations in a company's proxy materials in some circumstances, as we saw in Chapter 6. For the first time in decades, American corporate governance seems to be taking on the flavor of a New England town meeting.[11]

But how much difference will shareholder democracy really make? One of the most telling examples of the limits of the new shareholder activism came as the first trial of Tyco tycoon Dennis Kozlowski and his CFO Mark Swarz neared its climax. Th same day that the papers were filled with the startling news that the Tyco jury was in turmoil and a mistrial might be imminent, a tiny story buried in the business section of the *New York Times* noted that Tyco's shareholders had rejected a proposal to move the company's incorporation from Bermuda back to the United States. Tyco's move offshore had been exhibit A in numerous stories by the *Times*' David Cay Johnston and others about the manipulations used by American corporations to escape U.S. taxes. Yet Tyco's shareholders took a pass when the opportunity to protest arose. How close was the vote? Seven percent of the shareholders cast their votes in favor of the proposal to return to the United States, while the other 93% were happy to leave things just the way they are.[12]

It isn't hard to explain this distinct lack of activism. Staying in Bermuda and taking a permanent vacation from a large portion of the taxes it would otherwise owe provides a direct benefit to Tyco's shareholders. Unlike the citizens at a New England town meeting, who look at the community from a variety of perspectives, most shareholders are concerned solely about the corporation's bottom line. Although there are important benefits to this perspective, it means that shareholder activism often won't curb problematic behavior if the behavior in question is profitable to the corporation. Economists refer to shareholders' tendency to ignore the costs of corporate behavior—pollution is the usual example—that doesn't harm the shareholders themselves (or harms them much less than the benefit the shareholders receive) as an "externality" problem.

There's a second, more subtle limitation to shareholder activism as well. Suppose a shareholder proposed to limit the CEO's pay to $1 million per year or to some multiple of the salary of the company's ordinary employees. This proposal would save money for the corporation and thus for its shareholders. But shareholders of any given company might be reluctant to approve such a provision. If one company limited the pay of its top executives, but none of its competitors followed suit, the company that unilaterally decided to scale back compensation would find it extremely difficult to attract top executives, who could make much more working for one of the competitors. Even if the shareholders of every company would be better off if managerial pay were curbed, the shareholders of any given company would, in effect, be punished if their company was the first to take the plunge. Ben & Jerry's learned this lesson the hard way in the 1990s, when it tried to find a new CEO who would join the company at a salary that couldn't exceed seven times the salary of Ben & Jerry's lowest paid employees. Ben & Jerry's finally abandoned the restriction, after they couldn't find any qualified executives who were willing to give up the much higher salaries they could earn elsewhere.

Vigorous shareholder involvement is certainly better than the quiescence that we generally associate with the shareholders of the nation's largest corporations. The prodding of leading shareholder activists like Nell Minow, who now runs the Corporate Library, had helped to spur institutional shareholder activism even before the recent scandals, and the activism has subsequently spread well beyond the giant mutual funds and pensions. But the focus of contemporary shareholders is too limited for them to counteract the developments we have seen by themselves.

Can Anything Else Be Done?

The fact that the shareholder revolution has been oversold does not mean that nothing could be done to rein in the Icaran tendencies in American corporate life. With each of the three factors, lawmakers could take direct aim at the dangers that have come with the remarkable technological and financial innovations of the past two decades. What might a more effective package of reforms look like?

The most difficult of the three factors to control is Icaran risk-taking. Risk-taking is, after all, central to the American imagination, and it is important not to discourage corporate executives from pursuing bold innovations and new business strategies. Nothing ventured, as the old cliché puts it, nothing gained. Since shareholders can diversify their interests, there is nothing wrong with companies taking well thought out, strategic risks. The problems come when Icaran executives cross the line to excessive risk-taking, manipulation, or fraud.

A repeated theme in the past several chapters has been the transformation in internal corporate culture and the managerial labor market starting in the 1980s. Companies competed, and still compete, for charismatic CEOs, and these CEOs are expected to deliver immediate miracles. It would be both futile and misguided to attempt to reverse these developments altogether, but there is a simple way that lawmakers could begin to cool down the market: by curbing executive compensation. In 1992, Congress imposed a substantial tax penalty on companies that paid an executive more than $1 million, prohibiting the company from deducting these amounts as a business expense. But performance-based pay was excluded from the calculation, which (as we saw in chapter 5) inspired firms to load up on option-based compensation. By revisiting this provision, raising the ceiling to $4 million, and including compensation of every kind in the calculation (for options, this would mean valuing the options at the time they were granted), lawmakers could cool down the bidding war for corporate executives to some extent. Since the bidding war has contributed mightily to the expectation that the CEO serve as corporate savior, curbing executive compensation would help to dampen the incentive to take risks.[13]

Simply cooling off the bidding war for executives isn't enough.

This still leaves the ease with which Icaran executives can gamble with the company's assets. The new financial instruments are so versatile that it is almost impossible for regulators to keep up with the innovations. The SEC has been trying to respond. The commission has finally beefed up its disclosure requirements— companies must now give more information about their derivatives use, and give it more quickly, than in the past—and the newly enhanced disclosure certainly can't hurt. But this alone won't rein in derivatives bets. A more complete regulatory response must rethink how derivatives fit into the overall financial picture.

Financial institutions like banks and insurance companies are required to meet strict capital requirements in order to maximize the likelihood that they will remain financially stable. A company that has significant derivatives exposure has a great deal in common with these financial institutions—much more, at times, than with a traditional bricks-and-mortar corporation. "Enron," as Frank Partnoy has written, "reinvented the U.S. corporation, trading every commodity imaginable, not just natural gas, but also electric power, plastics, metals, bandwidth, pollution, and even complex bets on the weather."[14] Yet the regulatory framework ignores this financial reality. As my student Raffaele Scalcione argues in a new work-in-process, regulators should tailor derivatives regulation to the profile of each corporation, rather than relying on categorical labels that distinguish banks from insurance companies from industrial corporations. If a corporation wishes to take on significant derivatives exposure, they should be required to hold reserve capital (as banks do) to protect against the downside risk. A corporation that wishes to act like a financial institution—as Enron did— should be regulated like a financial institution, rather than regulated as if it were an old-fashioned industrial corporation or utility.[15]

With competition, the principal solution is both obvious and devilishly difficult to implement. The excesses of the 1990s underscore the need for consistent antitrust enforcement and show the risks of deregulation, particularly in the energy and telecom industries. The obvious implication is that we need to rethink the deregulatory impulses of the past two decades—particularly the role that public investment and regulatory oversight should play in deregulated industries.

One possible strategy for future deregulation would be to make use of regulatory funding mandates. Given that deregulation often creates a need for more policing, lawmakers should be required to earmark new funding for the relevant regulator—FERC for energy, the FCC for telecom—in connection with any legislation that would relax regulation or introduce additional competition into an industry. The environmental laws provide a useful analogy for how regulatory earmarking could work. When developers propose a project that may affect the environment, they are required to submit an environmental impact statement exploring the potential impact and the developer's plans for minimizing the potential harm. A regulatory earmarking strategy would call for an analogous process, with lawmakers making legislative findings as to the likely effect of deregulation and earmarking new or additional funds to ensure that a regulatory cop will be walking the beat.

Curbing Misuse of Corporate Size and Complexity

The most serious new abuse of corporate size and complexity has been the multiplication of SPEs in order to disguise the company's true financial condition, as most vividly illustrated by

Enron's vast web of connected entities. In response to other misuses of the parent-subsidiary structure in the past, corporate scholars have sometimes argued for an approach known as "enterprise liability." Under this rule, which was forcefully defended by Adolph Berle in the post–New Deal era, courts would ignore the boundaries between SPEs if the SPEs were clearly part of a larger corporate enterprise. The entire business would be responsible for the liabilities of any of the related entities, rather than treating the various outposts of the empire as separate.[16]

The problem with this approach is that there often are good reasons for establishing separate entities. If a company wishes to launch a new venture, but wants to protect the rest of the enterprise from its risks, it may make perfect sense to set up a separate entity. So long as the creditors of the separate entity are aware that they are dealing only with the new entity, they can adjust accordingly and no one is the worse for the separation.

The discussion earlier hinted at a more fine-grained solution for the SPE problem. The accounting treatment of SPEs should give regulators the authority to focus on whether the spirit of the SPE status is being violated. SPEs that are not truly separate from the overall company should be denied separate treatment for accounting purposes. A similar approach should be used in other contexts. Although SPEs should not automatically be lumped together with the larger enterprise, courts should ignore the SPE boundaries if the separation is a sham—if it is being used to mislead investors or if the company has itself ignored the boundaries between the SPE and the larger business.

The solution to the other major recent abuse of corporate size and complexity—the migration offshore of companies like Tyco to avoid U.S. taxes—is quite simple: the loophole should be closed. Lawmakers should impose the same tax burden on U.S.-based corporations that incorporate in Bermuda that is borne by corporations that are incorporated in the United States.

The Implications of the New Stockholding Class

Although some of these reforms are novel, others aren't new at all. The issue of executive compensation, for instance, has long been a topic of conversation, as has the expatriation of companies like Tyco that are trying to avoid U.S. taxes. Why has there been so little pressure to take action on these kinds of reforms? Why, after the enactment of the Sarbanes-Oxley legislation, did the clamor for more pervasive reforms quickly fade away?

One obvious explanation is directly political. The Republican party has long been more sympathetic to corporate America than the Democrats. With Republican control of the presidency and both houses of Congress after Enron and WorldCom collapsed, there may have been less enthusiasm for corporate reform than under a Democrat administration. The Bush administration's resistance to the Sarbanes-Oxley legislation until it could not be ignored adds some credence to this straightforward political explanation.

But it seems very unlikely that party affiliation is a complete explanation for the absence of more sweeping reform. On other issues, the simple political calculus often hasn't added up. It was a Democratic president, Bill Clinton, who ended "welfare as we know it" and promoted legislation that required welfare recipients to move into the workforce. President Nixon, a Republican, reopened relations with communist China, not President Johnson before him or President Carter after. And in an earlier era, George Bush's Republican hero Teddy Roosevelt was the one who launched the early-twentieth-century campaign against the "malefactors of great wealth." Moreover, if party politics were the only thing that distinguished the tepid corporate-responsibility reforms from a more pervasive response, we would expect to see evidence of a widespread, unsatisfied public demand for real reform. Yet we don't. And the fact that the Republican party actually increased its hold on the House and Senate in the 2002 midterm elections—a striking contrast to the stunning political reversal after Jay Cooke's fall in 1873 and to the Democrats' landslide in 1932, when they emerged with a 311 to 116 advantage in the House and 60 to 35 in the Senate—suggests that the demand for additional reform was limited even while the shock of the corporate scandals was still fresh.[17]

Perhaps ordinary Americans didn't appreciate the limitations of the 2002 corporate-responsibility reforms. The recent scandals also were not quite as economically devastating as the 1873 and 1930s failures. But another explanation is more revealing. In our era, ordinary Americans no longer see corporations as "other." For the first time ever, more than half of all Americans now own stock. This development has profoundly affected Americans' perspective on the nation's large-scale corporations.

The dramatic shift in stock ownership is due principally to the change in American retirement holdings. In 1980, 83% of workers who had pension benefits were part of a defined-benefit plan. By 1998, the percentages were almost exactly reversed, with only 33% of workers with pension coverage being included in a defined-benefit plan, while the rest had 401(k) or other defined-contribution pension arrangements. Participating in a defined-contribution plan means that the worker invests her own assets, and for most this means investing part or all of their retirement funds in a stock-based mutual fund.[18]

The fact that most of us are now stockholders has muddied the nation's response to the breakdown in American corporate life. The scandals galvanized public attention, but there were far fewer calls for a complete rethinking of the policies of the past twenty years—such as the scope of deregulation—than one might have expected. An important new study by Dallas Federal Reserve Economists John Duca and Jason Saving offers tantalizing evidence of the shift that seems to be taking place. Duca and Saving find a direct correlation between stock ownership and the

Republican vote in recent Congressional elections. As stock ownership goes up, so does the Republicans' share of the Congressional vote. It stands to reason, although Duca and Saving do not draw such a conclusion, that the perceived kinship between ordinary Americans and corporate America has gone up at the same time. No longer is there nearly so sharp a distinction between "the struggling masses" and "the idle holders of idle capital," as William Jennings Bryan put it in his famous 1896 "Cross of Gold" speech. It is this revolution in corporate ownership that best explains our willingness to settle for such limited change.[19]

The Extraordinary Risk of the New Icaran Tendencies for Ordinary Americans

The increasing identification between ordinary Americans and corporate America is perfectly understandable, but beneath it lurks a terrible irony: at the same time as our passion for real reform has declined, the risks have radically increased. These dangers stem in part from the stunning changes that we have considered at length in the past three chapters. Never before have corporate executives faced so much pressure to roll the dice, and never before has it been so easy for charismatic executives to do so.

But the dangers also stem from the nature of Americans' stake in the market. In the past, when Americans invested money in the stock market, the money they were investing was savings at risk. Even in times of market euphoria like the 1920s, investors were well aware that stock-market investments aren't guaranteed. With the advent of defined-contribution pension plans and the tax-favored treatment of personal IRAs and the like, this distinction between ordinary savings and savings at risk has broken down. Much of the money that is now directed into the stock market is ordinary savings—it is investors' retirement nest egg—rather than savings they have knowingly putting at risk.

Let me repeat this for emphasis: for the first time in history, the stock market is the investment of choice for a portion of many Americans' ordinary, "safe" savings, not just their savings at risk.

Nor is this likely to change in the coming years. If anything, Americans' exposure to the market could substantially increase. During the 2000 election campaign, then-governor Bush proposed that the social security system be partially privatized. This proposal, which would give Americans "private accounts" for investing part of their social security money, hasn't yet made it to the floor of Congress. But President Bush and his advisors have made clear that establishing private accounts would be a major legislative objective—possibly, the single biggest objective—in a second Bush term. If enacted, these accounts would hitch the fortunes of ordinary markets to the performance of the stock market even more.

A New Vision for Corporate Reform: Investor Insurance

The shift in Americans' exposure to the market means that it is no longer enough to focus solely on legal and regulatory efforts to reign in the three Icaran factors. As important as that goal is, it is also essential to directly protect investors against the potential consequences of another corporate collapse.

The first step is to make sure that Americans' pension investments are properly diversified. One of the most disturbing images of the corporate collapse was the picture of hundreds of Enron and WorldCom employees who had all of their retirement money in their company's stock—and lost everything when the bottom fell out. Mandatory portfolio diversification requirements are a simple solution to this problem. If Congress prohibited workers from putting more than 10% of their retirement funds into any single stock, employees would no longer face the risk of losing everything in the event that their company later imploded. After the corporate scandals, a somewhat similar reform proposal made the rounds in Washington, but it was never actually enacted.

Mandatory diversification alone isn't enough, however. Diversification can eliminate the risks that are unique to any given company (economists call this "idiosyncratic risk"), but it doesn't protect investors from a jolt to the entire market, like the jolt from the recent corporate scandals. The potential consequences of a market-wide crash are most severe for an employee who is well into her career and can't look forward to twenty more years of work to recover some of the lost pension value before it is time to retire. Another wave of corporate scandals could devastate the retirement savings of these employees. As we have seen, another wave of scandals is hardly out of the question.

How should these savings be protected? Recall from chapter 3 how Roosevelt and his New Deal allies responded in the 1930s when Americans not only suffered huge losses on utility bonds, but also watched bank runs jeopardize bank accounts they had thought of as completely secure. The New Deal reformers enacted deposit insurance, which guarantees that bank accounts will be completely secure; not a cent of our savings in insured accounts will ever be at risk.

Now, it obviously wouldn't make sense to simply transplant this absolute guaranty into the 401(k) context and to promise that every portfolio gain will be protected against any subsequent decline. But this doesn't mean that Americans' ordinary savings can't or shouldn't be protected. They should. One possible solution is to adopt an insurance scheme that guarantees a minimum payout over time. Once a worker's 401(k) plan has been in place for a specified period of time—say, five years—the worker could be promised an overall return of at least 3% on the money she put in the plan. Stock-market enthusiasts remind us that the stock market has rarely suffered multiple-year declines and that it averages double-digit returns over the long run. This suggests that a minimum guarantee wouldn't be a major cash drain on the Treasury. Only in the wake of a corporate crisis, when workers' retirement funds were decimated, would Uncle Sam need to step in to protect Americans' savings.

Another alternative, modeled on the federal deposit insurance financing scheme, is to adopt a self-financing, general-investor protection scheme. If a company's executives misstated the company's financials and its stock price later plummeted, the insurance fund could be used to pay shareholders' losses. This doesn't mean every investor who loses money in the stock market is paid—only the ones who lost money because of improper accounting or corporate fraud of the sort alleged in WorldCom and Enron.

Companies that wanted to join the federal investor insurance scheme would make payments to the fund each year, just like banks do with federal deposit insurance. The federal investor insurance corporation—or FIIC—would determine how much they should pay. And FIIC would also provide a lot more oversight of big companies and their auditors than regulators did in the 1990s. The corporate responsibility reforms already include a provision with a similar spirit. As noted in chapter 6, the CEO and CFO of a company that misstates its earnings are required to disgorge any bonuses or profits from stock sales they received in the twelve months following the misstatement. The threat of disgorgement may make executives think twice about the integrity of their company's accounting, but it will not provide much compensation for the investors who are misled. If the CEO of a company whose shareholders hold 20 million shares is forced to return a $1 million bonus, for instance, the disgorgement would amount to only 5 cents for each share. A federal investor protection scheme would supplement and complete the protection provided by the 2002 reforms.[20]

Is There Any Hope for Genuine Reform?

As we survey the nation's corporate and financial landscape, it is hard to be optimistic that lawmakers will consider any of the changes described in this chapter. The risk to ordinary Americans has never been greater, but ordinary Americans also have never been so likely as now to identify their interests with those of the nation's large-scale corporations. And the initial outrage at the corporate chicanery of the 1990s seems to have largely faded away.

Hidden in this irony, however, is a fact that offers at least a hint of hope for change. Although more Americans have a stake in the stock market than ever before, the stake of most is still much smaller than our identification with corporate America might suggest. Although the vast majority of Americans who have pension coverage now have 401(k)s, for instance, only about half of all American workers are covered by any plan. These figures are consistent with the more general evidence of stock ownership, which suggests that slightly more than a majority of Americans own stock. This means that a large number of Americans do not directly or indirectly own stock. Moreover, many Americans who do have stock through their pension plan own only a small amount. The identification that so many Americans feel with the corporate sector may thus be based as much on perception as on reality.[21]

Perhaps this means there is hope that Americans will seriously rethink the way that corporations are now regulated and demand a more complete response to the developments that have transformed the Icaran tendencies in American corporate and financial life.

In a commercial that aired many years ago, a wizened auto mechanic looked up from a four-figure engine-repair job and said, "You can pay me now, or you can pay me later." If customers didn't buy a Fram oil filter to keep their engine running smoothly now, he suggested, they would be confronted with expensive engine repairs later. We face something like the same choice in American and business financial life today. I have suggested several ways that the threat of Icarus Effect failures could be reduced and, more importantly, that ordinary Americans could be protected from the fallout of the next unexpected collapse. As a society, we have a very clear decision in front of us: we can pay now, or we can simply wait until the next corporate and financial crisis, and watch millions of ordinary Americans pay later.

Notes

Introduction

1. Alexis de Tocqueville, *Democracy in America,* book 3, chap. 18.

2. Although Gould is often credited with having invented the mousetrap, the actual inventor was his grandfather. Maury Klein, *Jay Gould* (Baltimore: Johns Hopkins University Press, 1988), 29.

3. Thomas L. Friedman, "Dear Dr. Greenspan," *New York Times,* Feb. 9, 1997, sec. 4.

4. The poem, an old Anglo-Saxon account of Icarus, is quoted in H. A. Guerber, *The Myths of Greece and Rome* (repr. New York: Dover, 1993), 222.

5. W. H. Auden, "Musée des Beaux Arts," in *The Norton Anthology of Modern Poetry* (2d ed.; New York: Norton, 1988), 740–41.

6. Quoted in Ted Nace, *Gangs of America* (San Francisco: Berrett-Koehler, 2003), 49.

7. Larry Ribstein makes a similar point about the political effect of market crashes, but he is much more skeptical about the implications, arguing that unnecessary regulation is often enacted after a market

bubble bursts. Larry E. Ribstein, "Bubble Laws," *Houston Law Review* 40 (2003): 77. This book suggests, to the contrary, that the regulation is often quite necessary.

8. Mark West argues that reform is usually triggered by exogenous changes such as scandals in nations that do not have jurisdictional competition; Mark D. West, "The Puzzling Divergence of Corporate Law: Evidence and Explanations from Japan and the United States," *University of Pennsylvania Law Review* 150 (2001): 527. West's argument is complementary, though different in some details, to the theme of this book, which is that certain scandals have galvanized American business and financial reform, most of which has come at the federal level (where interjurisdictional, state competition is absent).

9. Mark West explores the structure of Japanese corporate scandals, and contrasts them to the United States, in detail in a new book manuscript. Mark West, "Scandal Nations: Japan and America" (unpublished manuscript, 2004).

Chapter 1

1. Robert J. Shiller, *Irrational Exuberance* (New York: Broadway, 2001 [paperback edition]).

2. Zbigniew Herbert, *Still Life with a Bridle* (New York: Ecco Press, 1991), 48.

3. Henry A. Boardman, *The Bible in the Counting House: A Course of Lectures to Merchants* (Philadelphia: Lippincott, Grambo, 1853), 132.

4. Stuart Banner, *Anglo-American Securities Regulation: Cultural and Political Roots, 1690–1860* (Cambridge: Cambridge University Press, 1998), 76.

5. The discussion in this paragraph and the next is drawn from David A. Skeel Jr., "Rethinking the Line between Corporate Law and Corporate Bankruptcy," *Texas Law Review* 72 (1994): 471, 482–85.

6. Cited in Margaret M. Blair, "Locking in Capital: What Corporate Law Achieved for Business Organizers in the Nineteenth Century," *UCLA Law Review* 51 (2003): 387, 389n.3.

7. Henry Hansmann and Reinier Kraakman, "The Essential Role of Organization Law," *Yale Law Journal* 110 (2000): 387.

8. The Schuylkill Coal Company pamphlet is quoted in Blair, "Locking in Capital," 437–38.

9. If stock sold for $10 a share, for instance, a shareholder could be asked to contribute another $10 (for a total of $20) if the corporation failed and could not pay its debts. Double liability was particularly popular for banking corporations, and several states still had double liability provisions in place for other kinds of corporations late in the nineteenth century. The Massachusetts provisions are described in ibid., 54.

10. Alfred D. Chandler, *The Visible Hand: The Managerial Revolution in American Business* (Cambridge, Mass.: Belknap, 1977 [repr. 2002]); the initial quote is on 3, the discussion of the Western Railroad from 96–98, and the discussion of McCallum and the Erie Railroad from 100–101, 103–4.

11. The history of par value and preemptive rights is summarized in Adolf Berle and Gardiner Means, *The Modern Corporation and Private Property* (New York: Macmillan, 1932)(revised edition 1968), 143-45 (par value), 226-30 (preemptive rights). The best treatment of current par value rules is Bayless Manning and James J. Hanks, Jr., *Legal Capital* (Westbury: Foundation, 3d ed. 1990).

12. Chandler, *The Visible Hand*, 146; Frederick A. Cleveland and Fred W. Powell, *Railroad Finance*, reprinted in Alfred D. Chandler's *The Railroads: The Nation's First Big Business: Sources and Readings* (New York: Harcourt, Brace & World, 1965), 50 (local share subscriptions).

13. Frederick and Powell, *Railroad Finance*, reprinted in Chandler, *Railroads*, 49 (Congressional subsidies). For discussion of state and local subsidies, see, for example, David E. Pinsky, "State Constitutional Limitations on Public Industrial Financing: An Historical and Economic Approach," *University of Pennsylvania Law Review* 111 (1963): 265, 277–78.

14. Chandler, *The Visible Hand*, 146.

15. Ellis Paxson Oberholtzer, *Jay Cooke: Financer of the Civil War* (2 vols.; New York: Burt Franklin, 1907 [repr. 1970]), 1.103.

16. Ibid., 1.107. Cooke's efforts to sell the loan are detailed on 1.103ff.

17. The newspaper account is quoted in ibid., 1.173–74 (quoting a report from the secretary of the Treasury about the success of the campaign).

18. Quoted in Matthew Josephson, *The Robber Barons: The Great American Capitalists* (New York: Harcourt, Brace, 1934), 78–79.

19. Ibid., 92.

20. The initial quote is from ibid., 92. Ames is quoted on 93.

21. For the mileage quotes, see ibid., 92; the celebration is quoted on 91.

22. A colorful, comparatively brief account of the Erie battle is given in ibid., 127–34. The classic historical account is Charles Francis Adams Jr. and Henry Adams, *Chapters of Erie and Other Essays* (New York, 1871). The classic contemporary treatment is John Steele Gordon, *The Scarlet Woman of Wall Street: Jay Gould, Jim Fisk, Cornelius Vanderbilt, the Erie Railway Wars, and the Birth of Wall Street* (New York: Weidenfeld & Nicolson, 1988).

23. Josephson, *Robber Barons*, 66.

24. Ibid., 129–30.

25. Adams's description comes from *Chapters of Erie*, the most famous early account of the Erie battle, and is quoted in Maury Klein, *The Life and Legend of Jay Gould* (Baltimore: Johns Hopkins, 1988), 11.

26. The description of Fisk is quoted in ibid., 135.

27. Oberholtzer, *Jay Cooke*, 1.113.

28. Ibid., 2.389.

29. For details, see, for example, ibid., 2.189–92; Josephson, *Robber Barons*, 167.

30. Quoted in Oberholtzer, *Jay Cooke*, 2.381, 383.

31. Josephson, *Robber Barons*, 64.

32. Oberholtzer, *Jay Cooke*, 2.420.

33. Ibid., 2.423–24.

34. "Your own good sense," Cooke wrote to a sixty-four-year-old man in a letter penned by his secretary, "will show you that a [Northern Pacific] bond thus secured [by land] and thus receivable cannot be a bad investment even though the skies should fall." Quoted in ibid., 2.412. The letter on behalf of Eliza is quoted on 2.516.

35. "The American Panic—Nelaton's Death," *New York Times*, Oct. 6, 1873 (article by unnamed Paris correspondent).

36. "The Approaching State Election," *New York Times*, July 18, 1875 (article by unnamed correspondent).

37. The insight that concentrated interest groups often benefit at the expense of more diffuse interests is often associated with Mancur Olson, *The Logic of Collective Action* (Cambridge: Harvard University

Press, 1971). For a survey of the literature, see David A. Skeel Jr., "Public Choice and the Future of Public-Choice-Influenced Legal Scholarship," *Vanderbilt Law Review* 50 (1997): 647.

38. See, for example, Pinsky, "State Constitutional Limitations." The quotation in this paragraph appears on 279.

39. Harold Marsh Jr., "Are Directors Trustees? Conflict of Interest and Corporate Morality," *Business Lawyer* 22 (1966): 35, 36–37 (quoting *Wardell v. Union Pacific Railroad Co.*, 103 U.S. 651, 658 [1880]).

40. Quoted in Oberholtzer, *Jay Cooke*, 2.44.

41. William Jennings Bryan, "Cross of Gold" (July 9, 1896) (available at http://douglassarchives.org/brya_a26.htm).

42. "Resolutions of the Second National Agricultural Congress," May 1873, quoted in Chandler, *Railroads*, 188.

Chapter 2

1. The Massachusetts statute is discussed in E. Merrick Dodd Jr., "Statutory Developments in Business Corporation Law, 1886–1936," *Harvard Law Review* 50 (1936): 27, 32.

2. Alfred D. Chandler, *The Visible Hand: The Managerial Revolution in American Business* (Cambridge, Mass.: Belknap, 1977 [repr. 2002]), pp. 148, 149.

3. For discussion, see Morton J. Horwitz, *The Transformation of American Law, 1870–1960: The Crisis of Legal Orthodoxy* (Oxford: Oxford University Press, 1992), 86.

4. Quoted in ibid., 82.

5. Jean Strouse, *Morgan: American Financier* (New York: HarperCollins, 2000), 3, xii.

6. Alfred D. Chandler, *The Railroads: The Nation's First Big Business: Sources and Readings* (New York: Harcourt, Brace & World, 1965), 88 (Morgan's turn to the railroads).

7. Maury Klein, *Jay Gould* (Baltimore: Johns Hopkins Press, 1988), 285.

8. Strouse, *Morgan*, 240–41 (Northern Pacific), 248–49 (Pennsylvania-New York Central), 260 (attempt at truce).

9. The quote is from Matthew Josephson, *The Robber Barons: The Great American Capitalists* (New York: Harcourt, Brace, 1934), 48.

10. Ibid., 381.

11. Sherman Antitrust Act of 1890, 15 U.S.C.A. secs. 1–7.

12. *United States v. E. C. Knight Co.*, 156 U.S. 1, 13, 17 (1895) (overruled in 1948).

13. Josephson, *Robber Barons*, 381–82.

14. Charles W. McCurdy, "The *Knight* Sugar Case of 1895 and the Modernization of American Corporation Law, 1869–1903," *Business History Review* 53 (1979): 304.

15. Brian R. Cheffins, *Investor Sentiment and Antitrust Law as Determinants of Corporate Ownership Structure: The Great Merger Wave of 1897 to 1903* (unpublished manuscript, 2002), 17 (citing *United States v. Trans-Missouri Freight Association,* 166 U.S. 290 [1896]; *United States v. Joint Traffic Association,* 171 U.S. 505 [1898]).

16. Edward Q. Keasbey, "New Jersey and the Great Corporations," *Harvard Law Review* 13 (1899): 198, 210.

17. Lawrence M. Friedman, *A History of American Law* (2d ed.; New York: Simon & Schuster, 1985), 524 (quoting William W. Cook, *A Treatise on Stock and Stockholders, Bonds, Mortgages, and General Corporation Law* [3d ed., 1894], 2.1603–5).

18. Cheffins, *Investor Sentiment,* 8 (citing Naomi R. Lamoreaux, *The Great Merger Movement in American Business, 1895–1904* [1985]).

19. Thomas R. Navin and Marian V. Sears, "The Rise of a Market for Industrial Securities, 1887-1902," *Business History Review* 29 (1955): 105, 106, 115.

20. The quote is from Josephson, *Robber Barons,* 445.

21. These statements are quoted in ibid., 448.

22. Ibid., 448–49. The quote by Morgan in the next paragraph comes from 451 n. 5.

23. *Cong. Rec. H.* 41 (Jan. 21, 1907) 1452 (Representative Robinson). For discussion and an argument that many corporations were strong-armed by politicians into making contributions, see Robert H. Sitkoff, "Corporate Political Speech, Political Extortion, and the Competition for Corporate Charters," *University of Chicago Law Review* 69 (2002): 1103, 1129, 1134.

24. Sitkoff, "Corporate Political Speech," 1134.

25. Theodore Roosevelt, "Sixth Annual Message," in *Theodore Roosevelt, 1858–1919: Chronology, Documents, Bibliographical Aids* (ed. Gilbert J. Black; Dobbs Ferry, N.Y.: Oceana, 1969), 78.

26. Ibid., 84.

27. The proposed federal incorporation statute is discussed in Lamoreaux, *The Great Merger Movement*, 169-72.

28. Josephson, *Robber Barons*, 445.

29. Mark Roe points to the Pujo hearings as powerful evidence of the long-standing American hostility to concentrated economic power in his influential work emphasizing the political determinants of American corporate governance. Mark J. Roe, *Strong Managers, Weak Owners* (Princeton: Princeton University Press, 1996).

Chapter 3

1. The principal biography of Insull is Forrest McDonald, *Insull* (Chicago: University of Chicago Press, 1962). Insull's bond sales are discussed on 185, and his work on the Chicago Civic Opera Company building on 243.

2. "The legal assumption that directors serve gratuitously," according to a leading 1950s management treatise, "was a natural concomitant of director-stockholder concurrence in the small local enterprise, in which directors had the incentives of stockholders to serve the common interest." Actually, it isn't quite accurate to say the directors weren't paid at all. When they arrived at a directors meeting, they often found a single gold coin—a "double eagle"—on their seat; this coin was a little gesture of thanks to the director for coming to the meeting. Percival E. Jackson, *Corporate Management* (Charlottesville, Va.: Michie, 1955), 158–59. For a helpful historical overview of directorial compensation, see Charles M. Elson, "Director Compensation and the Management-Captured Board—The History of a Symptom and a Cure," *SMU Law Review* 50 (1996): 127.

3. The AT&T figures can be found in Adolf Berle and Gardiner Means, *The Modern Corporation and Private Property* (New York: Macmillan, 1940), 47, 52; the quote in the text comes from 81–82. A later study concludes that Berle and Means overstated the extent of the shift to managerial control to some extent. Philip H. Burch, *The Managerial Revolution Revisited: Family Control in America's Large Corporations* (Lexington: D. C. Heath and Company, 1972), 103.

4. Brian R. Cheffins, "Investor Sentiment and Antitrust Law as Determinants of Corporate Ownership Structure: The Great Merger

Wave of 1897 to 1903" (unpublished manuscript, 2002), 12 (payment in stock), 15 (unwinding holdings after a merger).

5. Berle and Means, *Modern Corporation,* 18.

6. Ibid., 109 (summarizing data).

7. Archibald MacLeish, "The Times Were Right for Ivar Kreuger," *Fortune,* May–July 1933, 58 (repr. Feb. 11, 1980); John Picton, "The Death of the World's Greatest Swindler," *Toronto Star,* Aug. 21, 1988.

8. Franklin D. Roosevelt, "New Conditions Impose New Requirements upon Government and Those Who Conduct Government," in *The Public Papers and Addresses of Franklin D. Roosevelt* (ed. Samuel I. Rosenman; New York: Random House, 1938), 742, 755.

9. McDonald, *Insull,* 14 (article in *Scribner's Monthly*), 16 (interview with Edison representative).

10. Ibid., 97–98.

11. Ibid., 104 (utility rates), 105 (quotation).

12. Ibid., 35 (moustache conceals sneering).

13. Ibid., 147–48 (Gladys's withholding of sex).

14. Ibid., 261.

15. Most of the details in this paragraph come from ibid., 148–61; the quote is on 154. The tally of twenty utilities is in "Emergence of Electrical Utilities in America," available online at http://www.american history.si.edu/csr/powering/past/h1main.htm.

16. The trusts are described in McDonald, *Insull,* 281–82.

17. *Hearings Before Committee on Interstate and Foreign Commerce on H.R. 5423,* 74th Cong., 1st Sess. 343 (1935) (hereafter, *PUHCA Hearings* (*House*)).

18. The quote is from "Emergence of Electrical Utilities in America." The benefits of setting up separate corporate subsidiaries are discussed in detail in several important recent articles. See, for example, Henry Hansmann and Reinier Kraakman, "The Essential Role of Organizational Law," *Yale Law Journal* 110 (2000): 387; George C. Triantis, "Organizations as Internal Capital Markets: The Legal Boundaries of Firms, Collateral, and Trusts in Commercial and Charitable Enterprises," *Harvard Law Review* 117 (2004).

19. McDonald, *Insull,* 281.

20. Ibid., 250 (capitalization of United in the previous paragraph), 252 (Napoleon quote), 19 (inability to imagine failure). The *New Re-*

public quote is from Marquis W. Childs, "Samuel Insull, III: The Collapse," *New Republic*, Oct. 5, 1932, 201–2.

21. The Andersen quote comes from Arthur Andersen, "The Accountant and His Clientele," in *Behind the Figures: Addresses and Articles by Arthur Andersen, 1913-1941* (Chicago: Arthur Andersen, 1970), 165, 172. The characterization of Andersen's findings comes from McDonald, *Insull*, 298.

22. McDonald, *Insull*, 324 (indictment), 329–30 (defense).

23. The quote is from *House Report No. 1318*, 74th Cong., 1st Sess. 48 (1935).

24. B. E. Sunny, "Utility Securities as an Investment" (June 14, 1923, address before Bond Men's Club of Chicago).

25. *PUHCA Hearings (House)*, 60 (statement of Walter Splawn, ICC Commissioner), 288 (statement of Robert Healy, SEC Commissioner).

26. McDonald, *Insull*, 95.

27. Berle's role as Roosevelt speech writer is described in ibid., 310 n. 8. The Brain Trust debate can be traced back to the 1912 presidential campaign between Theodore Roosevelt's New Nationalism, which called for muscular federal control, and Woodrow Wilson's small business and competition-oriented New Freedom.

28. The debate and the legislation are described in detail in Ralph F. De Bedts, *The New Deal's SEC: The Formative Years* (New York: Columbia University Press, 1964), 112–43.

29. *PUHCA Hearings (House)*, 780 (statement of John Zimmerman, president of United Gas Improvement Co.), 727 (statement of Agnes Jenks).

30. Temporary National Economic Committee, *Final Report and Recommendations of the Temporary National Economic Committee*, Sen. No. N. 35, 77th Cong. 1st Sess. (1941), 9.

31. The federal incorporation proposal is discussed in Joel Seligman's classic history of the SEC. Joel Seligman, *The Transformation of Wall Street: A History of the Securities and Exchange Commission and Modern Corporate Finance* (Boston: Houston Mifflin, 1982), 208–10.

32. Contrary to the contention that companies will voluntarily disclose, there are a variety of reasons why companies, if left to their own devices, would disclose less information than investors would like to see. Some of them are understandable—a concern that disclosure will

reveal too much to the company's competitors, for instance—others less so. The classic theoretical defense of mandatory disclosure is John C. Coffee Jr., "Market Failure and the Economic Case for a Mandatory Disclosure System," *Virginia Law Review* 70 (1984): 717. A few scholars have attempted to devise empirical tests to determine whether the mandatory disclosures are reflected in the value of a company's stock. Although the earliest studies were mixed, the most recent evidence suggests that compliance with SEC disclosure requirements is costly for small firms, but produces important benefits (such as an increase in stock price and a more active market for shares). Brian J. Bushee and Christian Leuz, "Economic Consequences of SEC Disclosure Regulation: Evidence from the OTC Bulletin Board" (April 2004) AFA 2004 San Diego Meetings (available at http://ssrn.com/abstract=307821).

Chapter 4

1. David Halberstam, *The Fifties* (New York: Villard, 1993), 119.

2. Ron Chernow, *The House of Morgan: An American Banking Dynasty and the Rise of Modern Finance* (New York: Simon & Schuster, 1991), 599–600.

3. Ibid., 597.

4. W. Braddock Hickman, *Corporate Bond Quality and Investor Experience* (Princeton: Princeton University Press, 1958).

5. The "leper" quote comes from Connie Bruck, *The Predators' Ball: The Inside Story of Drexel Burnham and the Rise of the Junk Bond Raiders* (New York: Penguin, 1989), 29. A description of Milken's early career at Drexel can be found on 26–33.

6. Ibid., 84.

7. Ibid., 100.

8. Frank H. Easterbrook and Daniel R. Fischel, "The Proper Role of a Target's Management in Responding to a Tender Offer," *Harvard Law Review* 94 (1981): 1161; Lucian R. Bebchuk, "The Case for Facilitating Competing Tender Offers: A Reply and Extension," *Stanford Law Review* 35 (1982): 23; Ronald J. Gilson, "Seeking Competitive Bids Versus Pure Passivity in Tender Offer Defense," *Stanford Law Review* 35 (1982): 51. The debate is described in more detail in David A. Skeel Jr.,

"A Reliance Damages Approach to Corporate Lockups," *Northwestern University Law Review* 90 (1996): 564, 581–83.

9. This is quoted in Bruck, *Predators' Ball*, but it's a common point.

10. For a recent account of these developments, see Fred S. McChesney, "Talking 'bout My Antitrust Generation: Competition for and in the Field of Competition Law," *Emory Law Journal* 52 (2003): 1401.

11. The events in this paragraph are described in Mimi Swartz and Sherron Watkins, *Power Failure: The Inside Story of the Collapse of Enron* (New York: Doubleday, 2003), 28–29.

12. The details of S&L regulation can be found in Daniel Fischel, *Payback: The Conspiracy to Destroy Michael Milken and His Financial Revolution* (New York: HarperBusiness, 1995), 190–97; Martin Lowy, *High Rollers: Inside the Savings and Loan Debacle* (New York: Praeger, 1991).

13. Melvin A. Eisenberg, *The Structure of the Corporation* (Boston: Little, Brown, 1976).

14. *Moran v. Household International Inc.*, 500 A.2d 1346 (Delaware 1985).

15. *Unocal Corp. v. Mesa Petroleum Co.*, 493 A.2d 946 (Delaware 1985); *Revlon Inc. v. MacAndrews & Forbes Holdings Inc.*, 506 A.2d 173 (Delaware 1985).

16. The battle is described in detail in Bruck, *Predators' Ball*, 193–240.

17. Perelman's $300 million tax benefit is described in ibid., 18.

18. *Smith v. Van Gorkom*, 488 A.2d 858 (Delaware 1985).

19. The quotes in this paragraph and the next come from Bruck, *Predators' Ball*, 244–45; the market share figure comes from 48.

20. The emergence of bridge loans as competition for Drexel's highly confident letter is discussed in Fischel, *Payback*, 142–43.

21. The quotation and details come from Lowy, *High Rollers*, 59–60.

22. Ibid., 100.

23. Ibid., 152. The other details in the paragraph come from 152–53 and Fischel, *Payback*, 263–70.

24. Lowy, *High Rollers*, 147.

25. See Bruck, *Predators' Ball*, 317ff.

26. The Milken charges are described in Fischel, *Payback*, 158–67. The quote is at 163.

27. The Dorgan quote can be found in ibid., 202.

28. There is a long history of debate about Delaware's role in the regulation of American corporate law. In its current incarnation, the debate dates back to an article by William Cary (criticizing Delaware corporate law) and a response by Ralph Winter (critiquing Cary's "race to the bottom" view). William L. Cary, "Federalism and Corporate Law: Reflections upon Delaware," *Yale Law Journal* 83 (1974): 663; Ralph K. Winter Jr., "State Law, Shareholder Protection, and the Theory of the Corporation," *Journal of Legal Studies* 6 (1977): 251. Many commentators have noted the threat to Delaware of federal intervention. For an extensive recent treatment, which suggests that Delaware's stance toward hostile takeovers (including its mid 1980s decisions facilitating them) has been shaped by the prevailing views of federal authorities, see Mark J. Roe, "Delaware's Competition," *Harvard Law Review* 117 (2003): 588. Marcel Rahan and Ed Rock argue that Delaware law, with its emphasis on judicial decision making, is designed to minimize the likelihood of federal intrusion. Marcel Kahan and Edward Rock, "Our Corporate Federalism and the Shape of Delaware Corporate Law" (unpublished manuscript, 2004).

29. The politics of the antitakeover statutes are discussed in Roberta Romano, "The Political Economy of Takeover Statutes," *Virginia Law Review* 73 (1987): 111.

30. The reference to "high-velocity" managerial environments is borrowed from Don Langevoort. The Learned Hand quote comes from *United States v. Aluminum Co. of America*, 148 F.2d 416 (2d Cir. 1945), and is discussed in McChesney, "Talking 'bout My Antitrust Generation," 1407 n. 27.

Chapter 5

1. See, for example, David Leonhardt, "How Will Washington Read the Signs? The Race Is On for Tougher Regulation of Business," *New York Times*, Feb. 10, 2002, Money and Business section; Alex Berenson, "Washington Wants Wall St. Changes. But How?" *New York Times*, Feb. 28, 2002, sec. C.

2. A brief history of Lay's career can be found in Mimi Swartz and Sherron Watkins, *Power Failure: The Inside Story of the Collapse of*

Enron (New York: Doubleday, 2003), 16–32. The quote in this paragraph is on 24.

3. Ibid., 45–46.

4. Lynne W. Jeter, *Disconnected: Deceit and Betrayal at WorldCom* (Hoboken, N.J.: Wiley, 2003), 28 ("pilot the ship" quote); 53 (IDB WorldCom).

5. Rakesh Khurana, *Search for a Corporate Savior: The Irrational Quest for Charismatic CEOs* (Princeton: Princeton University Press, 2002), 78. The quote in the next paragraph is on 78, and the Mathieson article described below is quoted on 78–79.

6. Jason Booth, "The Fiber-Optics Fortune: Billionaire Gary Winnick Generates Success from Fiber Optics Business," *Los Angeles Business Journal*, May 24, 1999, 26; Thomas Easton and Scott Woolley, "The $20 Billion," *Fortune*, April 19, 1999, 243.

7. The figures come from Paul Krugman, "For Richer: How the Permissive Capitalism of the Boom Destroyed American Equality," *New York Times Magazine*, Oct. 20, 2002, 62, 64.

8. John Cassidy, "The Greed Cycle: How the Financial System Encouraged Corporations to Go Crazy," *New Yorker*, Sept. 23, 2002, 64, 68.

9. The quotes and Enron details come from Swartz and Watkins, *Power Failure*, 202.

10. Frank Partnoy, *Infectious Greed: How Deceit and Risk Corrupted the Financial Markets* (New York: Times Books, 2003), 11.

11. Ibid., 36–39 (Sanford and Bankers Trust), 54–57 (P&G derivatives).

12. Ibid., 78–79.

13. Enron's use of SPEs is described in detail in Rebecca Smith and John Emshwiller, *24 Days: How Two Wall Street Journal Reporters Uncover the Lies That Destroyed Faith in Corporate America* (New York: HarperCollins, 2003).

14. Melvin A. Eisenberg, *Corporations and Other Business Associations: Cases and Materials* (8th ed.; New York: Foundation Press, 2000), 160 (citing *The Brancato Report on Institutional Investment* [Jan. 1996]).

15. The details of this paragraph, and some of the text, come from David A. Skeel Jr., "Shaming in Corporate Law," *University of Pennsylvania Law Review* 149 (2001): 1811, 1837–38.

16. Robert A. G. Monks and Nell Minow, *Watching the Watchers: Corporate Governance for the 21st Century* (Cambridge: Blackwell Publishers, 1996), 125.

17. Watkins' whistle-blowing efforts are described in Bethany McLean and Peter Elkind, *The Smartest Guys in the Room: The Amazing Rise and Scandalous Fall of Enron* (New York: Portfolio, 2003), 354-61. The warning that Enron could "implode" is quoted at 355.

18. Jared Sandberg, "Six Directors Quit as WorldCom Breaks with Past," *Wall Street Journal*, Dec. 18, 2002 (quoting Mike Lewis).

19. John C. Coffee Jr., "Understanding Enron: 'It's About the Gatekeepers, Stupid,'" *Business Lawyer* 57 (2002): 1403.

20. Andy Kessler, *Wall Street Meat: Jack Grubman, Frank Quattrone, Mary Meeker, Henry Blodget and Me* (N.P.: Escape Velocity Press, 2003), 25–26. The role of securities analysts is also described in Arthur Levitt, *Take on the Street: What Wall Street and Corporate America Don't Want You to Know/What You Can Do to Fight Back* (New York: Pantheon, 2002), 69–71.

21. Levitt, *Take on the Street*, 74 (analyst salaries), discusses the participation in beauty contests. Grubman is quoted in Kessler, *Wall Street Meat*, 193.

22. Levitt, *Take on the Street*, 74; the 92:1 buy ratio comes from 73.

23. Robert Jackall, *Moral Mazes: The World of Corporate Managers* (New York: Oxford University Press, 1988), 40. My thanks to Don Langevoort for pointing me to Jackall's book and for his own important work on these organizational issues. See, for example, Donald C. Langevoort, "Resetting the Corporate Thermostat: Lessons from the Recent Financial Scandals About Agency Costs, Self-Deception and Deceiving Others" (unpublished manuscript, 2004).

24. Chris Seay, *The Tao of Enron: Spiritual Lessons from a Fortune 500 Fallout* (Colorado Springs: Nav Press, 2002), 67 (rank and yank policy); Swartz and Watkins, *Power Failure*, 148 (Watkins bonus). The literature on tournament-style promotion schemes is discussed in David Wilkins and Mitu Gulati, "Reconceiving the Tournament of Lawyers," *Virginia Law Review* 84 (1998): 1581. The discussion in this paragraph and the next is similar in spirit to Kim Krawiec's fascinating analysis of rogue traders in Kimberly D. Krawiec, "Accounting for Greed: Unraveling the Rogue Trader Mystery," *Oregon Law Review* 79 (2000) 301.

25. The advent of 401(k)s, and their effect, is discussed in Robert J. Shiller, *Irrational Exuberance* (New York: Broadway, 2001 [paperback edition]), 32.

26. When a WorldCom employee sold a chunk of WorldCom stock, he was invited to lunch with Bernie Ebbers at a favorite Ebbers dive. After the two enjoyed a pleasant lunch, the employee returned to find all of his office belongings packed up in several large boxes outside his office. There was nothing left for him to do but walk out. The Ebbers story is recounted in Jeter, *Disconnected,* 1–2.

Chapter 6

1. The Sarbanes-Oxley reforms have already generated an enormous academic literature. Useful discussions include Lawrence A. Cunningham, "The Sarbanes-Oxley Yawn: Heavy Rhetoric, Light Reform (and It Just Might Work)," *University of Connecticut Law Review* 36 (2003); Charles M. Elson and Christopher J. Gyves, "The Enron Failure and Corporate Governance Reform," *Wake Forest Law Review* 38 (2003): 855. A good, highly critical assessment is Larry E. Ribstein, "Market vs. Regulatory Responses to Corporate Fraud: A Critique of the Sarbanes-Oxley Act of 2002," *Journal of Corporate Law* 28 (2002): 1.

2. Andrew Hill, "The Barons of Bankruptcy: Part III," *Financial Times,* Aug. 2, 2002, 10 (Gary Winnick of Global Crossing sold even more stock than Lay, an estimated $500 million); "Corporate America's Woes, Continued," *Economist,* Nov. 26, 2002, 60.

3. Under the New York Stock Exchange rule (NYSE Listed Company Manual, sec. 303A), the decision must be made by a compensation committee consisting entirely of independent directors. Both with compensation and with directorial nominations, which are discussed below, NASDAQ (rules 4200 and 4350) gives the company the option either to use a separate committee with only independent directors or to rely on approval by a majority of directors overall.

4. John Cassidy, "The Investigation: How Eliot Spitzer Humbled Wall Street," *New Yorker,* April 7, 2003, 55, 61 (Blodget quote). On the investment-bank settlement, see, for example, Randall Smith, "Regulators Set Accord with Securities Firms, But Some Issues Persist," *Wall Street Journal,* Dec. 23, 2003, sec. C; Susanne Craig, "Independent Re-

search May Not Necessarily Mean Better Analysis," *Wall Street Journal*, Dec. 23, 2003, sec. C.

5. I have borrowed this characterization from corporate-law scholar Donald Langevoort.

6. Sarbanes-Oxley Act, sec. 404.

7. The finding that outside directors don't seem to improve performance comes from a prominent study by Professors Sanjay Bhagat of the University of Colorado and Bernie Black of Stanford University. For a review of the studies on directorial performance, and studies on accounting as well, together with a scathing critique of Sarbanes-Oxley, see Roberta Romano "The Sarbanes-Oxley Act and the Making of Quack Corporate Governance" (unpublished manuscript, 2004).

8. The quote is from Kessler, *Wall Street Meat*, 180.

9. Ibid., 122–23.

10. Gretchen Morgenson, "Bush Failed to Stress Need to Rein in Stock Options," *New York Times*, July 11, 2002, sec. C (writing after President Bush's corporate-responsibility speech); "Corporate America's Woes, Continued," *Economist*, Nov. 30, 2002, 59, 60 (quoting Max Bazerman).

11. The Monks campaign is discussed in David A. Skeel Jr., "Shaming in Corporate Law," *University of Pennsylvania Law Review* 149 (2001): 1811, 1846–48.

12. The experiment is described in "Corporate America's Woes, Continued," 61.

13. The increase in accounting restatements is discussed in Levitt, *Take on the Street*, 117.

Chapter 7

1. Diana B. Henriques, "Putting the Corporation in the Dock," *New York Times*, Sept. 14, 2003, Business section.

2. John C. Coffee Jr., "Understanding Enron: 'It's About the Gatekeepers, Stupid,'" *Business Lawyer* 57 (2002): 1403.

3. The "Sherron Watkins" provision requires that the audit committee investigate any complaint about the company's accounting practices and that a hotline be set up to handle complaints; Sarbanes-Oxley, sec. 301. The compliance requirement is included in sec. 404.

4. E. Thomas Sullivan and Robert B. Thompson, "The Supreme Court and Private Law: A Thirty-Year Retrospective of Economic

Regulation in Securities and Antitrust" (unpublished manuscript, 2004).

5. The quotes are from Smith and Emshwiller, *24 Days*, 366. Enron's manipulations are also described in Swartz and Watkins, *Power Failure*, 240–41.

6. The problems with the grid are discussed in detail in Neela Banerjee and David Firestone, "New Kind of Electricity Market Strains Old Wires beyond Limits," *New York Times*, Aug. 24, 2003, sec. A.

7. For a discussion of these problems by an advocate of deregulation, see J. Gregory Sidak, "The Failure of Good Intentions: The Collapse of American Telecommunications after Six Years of Deregulation," 2002 Beesley Lecture on Regulation (Royal Society of Arts, Oct. 1, 2002), 7. A revised and expanded version of the lecture was published in *Yale Journal on Regulation* 20 (2003): 207.

8. The quotes are from Swartz and Watkins, *Power Failure*, 167.

9. The Mahonia transactions are discussed in Partnoy, *Infectious Greed*, 301, 338–39.

10. James Surowiecki, "To the Barricades," *New Yorker*, June 9, 2003.

11. An early version of the SEC proposal is discussed in Stephen Labaton, "S.E.C. May Ease Voting for Outside Directors," *New York Times*, July 16, 2003, sec. C.

12. "Tyco Holders Reject Move to U.S. from Bermuda," *New York Times*, March 26, 2004, sec. C. Johnston recently published a book based on the tax-evasion concerns identified in his stories. David Cay Johnston, *Perfectly Legal* (New York: Portfolio, 2003).

13. The 1992 tax change and the effect of options-based compensation are discussed in Cassidy, "Greed Cycle," 64, 68. For an extensive analysis of performance-based pay and its abuses, see Lucian Bebchuk and Jesse Fried, *Pay without Performance: The Unfulfilled Promise of Executive Compensation* (Cambridge: Harvard University Press, 2004).

14. Partnoy, *Infectious Greed*, 347.

15. Scalcione is exploring this insight in a graduate dissertation at the University of Pennsylvania Law School. See, for example, Raffaele Scalcione, "S.J.D. Proposal: Financial Derivatives, Innovation and Corporate Governance" (Oct. 2003).

16. The classic argument for enterprise liability is Adolph A. Berle Jr.,

"The Theory of Enterprise Liability," *Columbia Law Review* 47 (1947): 343.

17. The 1932 figures are discussed in Jacob S. Hacker and Paul Pierson, "Business Power and Social Policy: Employers and the Formation of the American Welfare State," *Politics & Society* 30 (2002): 277, 296.

18. The percentages are detailed in Richard A. Ippolito, "Bankruptcy and Workers: Risks, Compensation, and Pension Contracts," *Washington University Law Quarterly* (forthcoming, 2004): 17.

19. Because detailed data on changes in stock ownership are not available, Duca and Saving use mutual-fund costs as a proxy for changes in Americans' stock ownership patterns. (Decreases in mutual-fund costs are closely correlated with increased stockholdings; when costs go down, stock ownership goes up, and vice versa.) They find that as mutual-fund costs decline, and thus stock ownership increases, the Republican share of the Congressional vote goes up. John V. Duca and Jason L. Saving, "The Political-Economy of the Mutual Fund Revolution: How Rising Stock-Ownership Rates Affect Congressional Elections" (unpublished manuscript, Dec. 2002).

20. The disgorgement provision is Sarbanes-Oxley Act, sec. 304. The federal investor protection proposal was originally developed as a commentary for Marketplace. My thanks to the commentaries editor, Liza Tucker, for suggesting many of the ideas in the proposal.

At roughly the same time as this proposal was developed, Joshua Ronen offered a proposal for a private version of financial statement insurance. See Joshua Ronen, "Post-Enron Reform: Financial Statement Insurance and GAAP Revisited," *Stanford Journal of Law & Business* 8 (2002): 39. For a modified and extended version of the Ronen proposal, see Lawrence A. Cunningham, "Choosing Gatekeepers: The Financial Statement Insurance Alternative to Auditor Liability," *UCLA Law Review* (forthcoming, 2004). Although Ronen's scheme parallels the proposal in the text in some respects, governmentally provided insurance seems more attractive, both because of the risk of significant gaps in the private insurance market (due, for instance, to the possibility of cherry-picking by insurers) and because of the governmental interest in protecting the savings of ordinary Americans.

21. The pension figures are discussed in Ippolito, "Bankruptcy and Workers," 37.

Index

Cooke, Jay. *See also* 1873 Panic; Jay
Cooke & Co.
bankruptcy of, 10, 139, 140
and Civil War bonds, 7, 13, 29–31
compared to Lay, Ken, 147–148
compared to Milken, Michael, 130
on the gold standard, 45–46
and government bonds, 173
and Grant, Ulysses S., 8, 39
history of Drexel Burnham, 113
as Icaran Executive, 43
impact on political reforms, 210
and Insull, Samuel, 87
and the Northern Pacific railroad,
36–40
political influence of, 42
and Populism, 45
"core competence," 117
Corning, Erastus, 27
CorpAmerica Inc., 16
Corporate Board Member magazine,
151
*Corporate Bond Quality and Investor
Experience*, 112
corporate bonds. *See* bonds (corporate)
corporate charters, nineteenth century, 18–19
"corporate compliance officer," 183
Corporate Library, 204
corporate size and complexity. *See
also* holding companies; Icarus
Effect; Roosevelt, Teddy; special
purpose entities
anti-trust policy, 104–105, 142
conglomerates, 109–110
derivatives, 156–158
in the nineteenth century, 5–6,
52
regulatory reforms of, 191–192
and structured finance, 8, 13,
158–159, 194
and tax policy, 208
ultra vires doctrine, 52–55, 63–64
Corporation Securities Company, 85,
88
Corporation Service Company, 16
corporations. *See also* incorporation;

managers; New Deal; regulators; takeovers
advantages of, 21, 22
after World War II, 108–111
Berle-Means, 77–78
and the Brain Trust, 92–94
and the charismatic CEO, 152, 205
conglomerates, 109–110, 139
culture of mobility, 195
1873 Panic, 44–45
English Bubble Act, 18
Gilded Age, 10, 49
"internal affairs" doctrine, 64
internal culture of, 170–172
and Internet technology, 155–156
investor insurance as reform,
212–214
limited liability, 10, 19–20, 22–26
in New Jersey state law, 63–64
in the nineteenth century, 5–6, 10,
21–22
outside directors of, 122–125,
183–184
Public Utilities Holding Company
Act, 99–100
pyramid structure, 85
retirement holdings in, 210–211
and Roosevelt, Teddy, 10–11, 71–72
and Sarbanes-Oxley, 177–178,
182–183
shareholders (institutional),
161–163
shareholder activism, 202–204
stock options, 152–154
ultra vires doctrine, 52–53, 55
Cortelyou, George, 70–71
Cranston, Alan, 135
Crédit Mobilier, 32–33, 38–39, 42,
43–44
Credit Suisse First Boston, 170, 181
"Cross of Gold," 46, 211
CTA Advantage, 16

Daedalus, 4–5
Dallas Federal Reserve, 210–211
dark fiber, 200
"Darth Vader," 175
"death penalty," 99

regulators. *See also* Congress; deregulation; Securities and Exchange Commission (SEC); states as regulators
after deregulation, 199
derivatives, 206
1873 Panic, 44
and the Grangers, 48
holding companies, 86
Icarus Effect, 7, 9, 196
ineffectiveness of, 13, 194
and investor capitalism, 67
junk-bond era, 12
market collapse of the 1990s, 144
in the New Deal, 11–12, 93–94, 98–100, 104–105
in the nineteenth century, 7–8
and "purchase accounting," 133
in the Reagan administration, 119–120, 142
and Rockefeller, John D., 10
and Roosevelt, Teddy, 74
S&L crisis, 121–122, 141
Second National Agriculture Congress, 46–47
and special purpose entities, 158–159, 200–201, 208
stock exchanges as, 189–190
takeovers in the 1980s, 118–119
and WorldCom, 149
Republican National Committee, 70–71
Republican Party, 68, 209–210
"restraint of trade," 60–61
Reuther, Walter, 109
Revlon company, 126–127, 128
Revlon Inc. v. MacAndrews & Forbes Holding Inc., 125–127
"Ricochet," 198
Riegle, Donald, 135
risk-taking. *See also* Icarus Effect; managers
in the 1990s, 193
American admiration of, 3–4
competing views on in Franklin D. Roosevelt's presidency, 93
Congressional controls of, 205–207

and corporate reforms, 191–192, 194–196
dangers of, 211–212
and derivatives, 158
and Drexel Burnham, 139
in government owned companies, 48
and internal corporate culture, 170–172
New Deal reforms, 104–105
and regulators, 7
S&L crisis, 133
and stock options in the 1990s, 154, 187
stock ownership, 14
takeover laws, 141–142
RJR-Nabisco, 107, 117, 135–136
"road shows," 181
Roadshow.com, 155
robber barons
Drew, Daniel, 34
and the Erie Railway, 47–48
Fisk, Jim, 34
Gould, Jay, 3, 34, 199
Insull, Samuel, 84
and nineteenth-century corporations, 35
of the twentieth century, 131
Vanderbilt, Cornelius, 34–35
Rockefeller, John D.
biographical information, 59
biography of, 152
and corporate holding-company structure, 86
and the Gilded Age, 10
Northern Securities Corporation, 69
"rationalized" competition, 51
and Roosevelt, Teddy, 68
trusts, emergence of, 60
Rockefeller Family, 51
Roosevelt, Franklin D. *See also* New Deal
banking reforms, 96–98
and the Brain Trust, 92–94
corporate reforms, 104
First Hundred Days, 91–92
and Frankfurter, Felix, 101

special purpose entities, 158–159, 199–201, 207–208. *See also* Enron

special purpose vehicle (SPV), 158

Spitzer, Eliot, 176–177, 180–181, 184–185

Sprint, 148, 149

Standard Oil, 10, 59

Stanford University, 118

states as regulators. *See also* Delaware
   antitakeover statutes, 141
   and corporate trusts, 60
   1873 Panic, 43–45
   Minnesota and Northern Securities Corporation, 69
   in the nineteenth century, 52
   and the "Seven Sisters," 65
   Sherman Act, 62–64

Steel Trust, 58

Steichen, Edward, 56

Steinberg, Saul, 114

Stewart, Martha, 193

stock market, 56–57, 110

Stock Market Crash, 11, 75

stock options, 152–154, 165, 186–187, 205

stock ownership
   history of in America, 13–14, 28
   as investment of choice, 66
   investor insurance as reform, 212–214
   and par value, 26
   and preemptive rights, 26
   and retirement plans, 173–174, 210–212
   and twenty-first-century reforms, 215–216

"stock-parking," 136

Stone, Oliver, 116

structured finance, 8, 13, 158–159, 194

Sullivan, Scott, 160, 165

Sullivan, Thomas, 197

Sunny, B. E., 89–90

Supreme Court
   and Chase, Salmon, 30
   deregulation, 197
   Northern Securities Corporation, 69

and Populist legislation, 48

Sherman Act, 61–62

and *ultra vires* rulings, 55

Supreme Court of Delaware. *See also* incorporation
   Household International case, 125
   Paramount Communications Inc. v. Time-Warner, 137–138
   Revlon Inc. v. MacAndrews & Forbes Holding Inc., 127
   Smith v. Van Gorkom, 129–130
   and takeovers, 123

Surowiecki, James, 202

Swarz, Mark, 202–203

Swedish Match, 79

SWIB, 162

Taft-Hartley Act, 109

takeovers. *See also* corporate size and complexity; individual companies
   beginnings of, 107–108, 110–111
   benefits from, 116–118
   Berle-Means corporation, 117
   and charismatic CEOs, 160
   and corporate oversight, 127
   "highly confident letter," 115–116
   and Ichan, Carl, 116
   KKR, 117, 135–136
   and managers, 140–142
   "merchant" banks, 130
   and outside directors, 122–125
   Paramount Communications Inc. v. Time-Warner, 137–138
   poison pills, 124
   S&Ls, 121–122
   securities analysts' conflicts, 168–169
   stock options in the 1990s, 152–153
   tax benefits from, 128, 129

Taylor, Moses, 27

Telecommunicatons Act of 1996, 198

television. *See* media

Temporary National Economic Committee, 104

"10-K," 101

"10-Q," 101

Thompson, Robert, 197